des beaux Voyages qu'on a

*Coup d'Œil at Belœil*

Antoine Cardon, after Leclerq,
Portrait of Charles-Joseph de Ligne.
Engraving, 1784(?).

Courtesy Fondation Ligne, Belœil, Belgium.

# Coup d'Œil at Belœil

## and a Great Number of European Gardens

### Prince Charles-Joseph de Ligne

#### Translated and Edited by Basil Guy

University of California Press
Berkeley·Los Angeles·Oxford

University of California Press
Berkeley and Los Angeles, California

University of California Press, Ltd.
Oxford, England

© 1991 by The Regents of the University of California


LIBRARY OF CONGRESS CATALOGING-IN-PUBLICATION DATA

Ligne, Charles Joseph, prince de, 1735–1814.
[Coup d'œil sur Belœil et sur une grande partie
des jardins de l'Europe. English]
Coup d'œil at Belœil and a great number of European gardens /
Prince Charles-Joseph de Ligne;
translated and edited by Basil Guy.     p.   cm.
"A Centennial book"
Translation of: Coup d'œil sur Belœil
et sur une grande partie des jardins de l'Europe.
Bibliography: p.
Includes index.
ISBN 0-520-04668-4 (alk. paper)
1. Parc de Belœil (Belœil, Belgium) 2. Gardens—Europe.
3. Ligne, Charles Joseph, prince de, 1735–1814. Coup d'œil sur
Belœil et sur une grande partie des jardins de l'Europe.
I. Guy, Basil. II. Title.
SB466.B42P37513  1989
712'.094—dc19               89-30766

Printed in the United States of America

1  2  3  4  5  6  7  8  9

*For
my
mother*

# Contents

# Illustrations

# Preface

$S$OME YEARS AGO, in his article "Le prince de Ligne, amateur et écrivain des jardins," Ernest de Ganay called for a critical edition of the 1795 version of Ligne's *Coup d'Œil sur Belœil.* I hope that the following pages will in some measure answer that call, for readers still seem most familiar with the 1786 version of the work, while the 1795 version goes practically unnoticed. Ganay believes that the 1795 text deserves such attention because it is the last version of the *Coup d'Œil* that the prince revised, some fourteen years after he produced the first (in 1781); because it reveals the prince's constant preoccupation with the subject of gardens and their importance to him—their central position in his thought and work; and because it is a masterpiece in its own right. Today there are two additional reasons for a critical edition of the 1795 text, both of which reinforce the decision to prepare it in English.

One is the hope that it may prove useful to several scholars who are presently at work on Ligne and his masterpiece in Europe, without impeding their own contribution to a revitalized interest in both Ligne and his work. More generally, however, with the current interest in eighteenth-century garden art and literature among Anglo-Saxon critics, the *Coup d'Œil,* a title not often included in critical discussions, merits consideration—at least for the sake of completeness. Ligne's text covers many of the theoretical points that are at the heart of the current debate; moreover, many of the gardens he chooses to illustrate his argument still exist, so that his point of view, in contrast with that of some eighteenth-century theorists, can be corroborated at firsthand. The style and charm of Ligne's presentation may further increase the pleasure of such acquaintance and—who knows?—might even swell the numbers of "lignists" or "linéens."

A word about some of the conventions employed in this work is in order. In the notes to my introduction, citation is by short title only; full information is given in the bibliography. The primary sources listed there are those published or written during the years of Ligne's long life, 1735–1814; in the notes, reference to these works precedes citations of secondary materials whenever possible. In the citations of anthologies of Ligne's works, the publication dates and editors' names are given parenthetically.

I have numbered the four parts of Ligne's text consecutively by paragraph, omitting some paragraphs that seem marginal on the basis of comments made by Ernest de Ganay in his edition of the 1786 text. Reference is made in the notes each time an omission occurs. The paragraphs omitted here, however, are still considered to be part of the sequence, so that the text may jump from, say, paragraph 73 to paragraph 78. In Ligne's text all suspension points are integral and do not indicate ellipses. All measurements are approximate, as are dates for the formation of certain gardens whose development may have spanned several decades. The illustrations, with but few exceptions, are from works Ligne may have known, since they were available during his lifetime. Maps, plans, and garden layouts, whether eighteenth-century or modern, have been chosen for their clarity and appositeness to points made in the text; in certain instances a number of views have had to be sacrificed because of the wealth of documentation that would have made editorial comment on Sanssouci, for example, a guidebook in itself.

An undertaking like this, after an interval of some two hundred years that have seen both an enormous proliferation of interest in garden art and some changes in the gardens mentioned by the Prince de Ligne, would have been impossible without the extraordinary kindness of friends and acquaintances. Because of the political situation at the time of writing, it was difficult to view, much less to photograph or otherwise document, some of the gardens Ligne discusses. Several of the individuals listed below generously undertook to visit these gardens when feasible or to acquire on-the-spot documentation unavailable elsewhere. Others, by their solicitude or their knowledge, have contributed much, especially to the footnotes and illustrations, facilitating my task as editor and so, I hope, improving the quality of the final version.

It is again a pleasure to acknowledge the material aid and support that the following organizations have kindly furnished over the years: the Belgian-American Educational Foundation; the John Simon Guggenheim Memorial Foundation; and the Faculty Committee on Research, University of California, Berkeley. I gratefully acknowledge the permission granted me to reproduce copyright materials under the control of the Archives nationales, Paris; Biblioteca Estense, Modena; Bibliothèque royale Albert Ier, Brussels; Boston Athenaeum, Boston, Massachusetts; Cabinet des estampes, Bibliothèque nationale, Paris; Cooper-Hewitt Museum, New York; Fondation Ligne, Belœil, Belgium; Hauptstaatsarchiv, Stuttgart; Institut et Musée Voltaire, Geneva; Musée des Beaux-Arts, Besançon, France; Musée de Picardie, Amiens, France; Museen der Stadt, Vienna (including Graphische Sammlung Albertina; Historisches Museum der Stadt; Österreichische Nationalbibliothek); Niederösterreichische Landesbibliothek, Vienna; Houghton Library, Harvard University, Cambridge; San Francisco

Public Library; Trustees of the British Library, London; Trustees of the Chatsworth Settlement, Devonshire Collection, Chatsworth, Derby; University of California Libraries, Berkeley.

My debt to the following persons is very great and a pleasure to record: the late Professor Henri Peyre, for the initial inspiration more than thirty years ago; H. H. Prince Antoine de Ligne, for unfailing and generous encouragement in all matters regarding his illustrious ancestor and the family estates; Professors Jacques de Caso, Judith Colton, Simon Karlinsky, Peter Mailloux, Georges May, Gita May, Roland Mortier, Robert Niklaus, and George Rousseau, for counsel and advice, especially in reading successive versions of the introduction. I received information about specific localities from Dr. Robert Allen of the Library of Congress and Drs. Edward Kasinek and Jiři Svoboda of the University of California, Berkeley (Eastern Europe); Dr. Harald Marx of the Staatliche Kunstsammlungen, Dresden (East Germany); Professor Morris R. Brownell, University of Nevada-Reno (Great Britain); Dr. Christine van Ronnen of the Rijksarchief, Utrecht (the Netherlands); Professor Jeroom Vercruysse of the Free University of Brussels, along with Mademoiselle Lisette Danckaert of the Royal Library, Brussels (Belgium). Anthony Bliss, Elizabeth Byrne, Czeslaw Grycz, William McClung, Lori McCracken, Florence Meyer, Marilyn Schwartz, Jeanne Sugiyama, Susie Taylor, Arthur Waugh, and especially Stephanie Fay and Wolfgang Lederer have helped immeasurably with their kind attentions and expertise. Finally, heartfelt thanks are due to the person to whom this work is dedicated, for more than words can say.

# Introduction

## Ligne and Belœil

*C*HARLES-JOSEPH, seventh Prince de Ligne, Fieldmarshal, Grandee of Spain, Knight of the Golden Fleece, and author of the *Coup d'Œil sur Belœil*, was born a Hapsburg subject in Brussels on 25 May 1735. Descended, so he claimed, from both Charlemagne and Wedekind, linked to almost all the ruling families of his time, he was himself sovereign of the minuscule county of Fagnolles in the Ardennes. He pretended to be a native of "six or seven countries: the [Holy Roman] Empire, Flanders, France, Spain, Austria, Poland, Russia, and almost Hungary."[1] (This seems rather like seven or eight, but accuracy was not the strong suit of the great lords of his day, and Ligne was—if nothing else—a great lord.)

French by breeding, though not by nationality, this scion of one of the most illustrious houses of the Austrian Netherlands was educated from childhood in the arts of war and diplomacy, in which his forebears were most distinguished, as are his descendants. The dedication of his ancestors served to nurture in the young man a tradition in which "glory" was the greatest consideration, obsessing and unique. Ligne never really achieved the consecration of his life and labors, however, at least not in matters military. The roles of courtier and social lion preempted the Spartan ideal of the warrior.[2]

In Vienna, Ligne was among the intimates of Maria-Theresa and Joseph II, and at Versailles and Paris he was everbody's favorite, especially Marie-Antoinette's. He was feted in Russia, where he accompanied "Catherine le Grand" (his expression) on her triumphal progress to the Crimea in 1787 and was granted large tracts of land near Yalta. This prodigious traveler was acquainted with all the rulers, ministers, and authors and most of the interesting women of his day. He was one of the happy few who knew and enjoyed to the full the *douceur de vivre* that is said to have characterized life among the aristocracy at the end of the eighteenth century.

Ligne was ruined financially by the French Revolution. With his Belgian estates under sequestration, he was reduced to the straitened circumstances and pettiness of life as an exile in Vienna, where he became the object of Hapsburg ingratitude because of his alleged im-

---

1. The most recent biographical studies of Ligne are Carlo Bronne, *Belœil et la maison de Ligne*, 169–234, and Claude Pasteur, *Le Prince de Ligne;* but see also Louis Dumont-Wilden, *La Vie de Charles-Joseph de Ligne*. The prince refers to his ancestry in *Fragments* 1:2, and to his nationality in *Fragments* 1:48.
2. See Basil Guy, "The Prince de Ligne and the Exemplification of Heroic Virtue," 73–86.

plication in the Belgian revolt of 1789. He turned more and more to writing for consolation, trying to eke out his meager revenues by selling the products of his pen. Thirty-four volumes of his *Mélanges militaires, littéraires, et sentimentaires* came off the presses of Dresden and Vienna with some regularity between 1795 and 1811, even though the public largely ignored them. Not until 1809, when his fellow cosmopolitan Madame de Staël discovered in these volumes the materials for her collection *Lettres et réflexions du Maréchal-Prince de Ligne*, did he know at last the "glory" that had eluded him on the field of battle, to which the belated award of the title *Feldmarschall* was but an ironic counterpoint. His reputation as a prince of Frenchified Europe—refined and enlightened—was henceforth assured.

The prince was born in a country that was both borderland and crossroads. He felt at home wherever native sensibility and cosmopolitan wit found a welcome and easily slipped into his place among the foremost moralists of his time. Raised in the strictest discipline (when it was not merely haphazard),[3] he looked to his friends, and especially to women, for the cultivation of the naturalness that adds such charm to his character or to judgments like the following:

I have already said enough about the gracefulness, the delicacy, the attentions, and the style of women, so that I may analyze their peccadilloes as well as their great goodness. Whether in sickness or on business, in dreams or their realization, they are always wanting to give advice, and from the start. They disapprove, they find fault where there is none, they quarrel with their maids but prefer to believe them rather than sensible men. They do not possess the same eyes or ears as we; they partake only of man's childhoods [infancy and old age]. They are rife with talent. . . . Remember that I have explained why elsewhere. There are some who have been educated as men, but none of them have left anything to make them famous. By dint of constant exertion they possess more apparent sweetness and agreeableness than we, but their organs are different, inappropriate. . . . You can count on the fingers of one hand those who are truly good, without contradictions, envy, and so forth.[4]

For Ligne during the Seven Years' War (1756–63) and the fighting against the Turks (1787–90), the pleasures of the military equaled the pleasures of the boudoir. His bravura and his blundering were of a kind, and his sketch of Roger de Damas, a friend, that combines the two characteristics might represent himself as well:

I met a phenomenon . . . and a nice one at that, . . . who is the product of three eras. He wears his hair in the style of one with the grace of the second

---

3. See Félicien Leuridant, *Une Education de prince*, 18, and Ligne's *Fragments* 1:11–24.
4. Ligne, *Ecarts posthumes*, 21–22.

and the lightheartedness of the present. Francis the First [of France], Condé, and Marshal Saxe would have wished to have a son like him. He is heedless and harum-scarum in the midst of the liveliest cannonades, noisy, an irrepressible singer, yapping the finest operatic airs and breaking into the zaniest quotations in the midst of fusillades but nonetheless still keeps his wits in appraising every situation exactly. War does not go to his head, but he is keen with a pretty passion, such as is common at the end of a midnight supper.[5]

With his gift for improvisation and his freewheeling style, the Prince de Ligne has left us portraits of historic personages that are as apt as any. His pages on Voltaire, Frederick the Great, Rousseau, and Napoleon, for instance, are composed largely of personal asides that link them more to *la petite histoire* than to History. Yet thanks to his perspicacity, Ligne has caught just those details that might otherwise have been lost forever but contribute so much to our understanding of great personalities.

Nowhere are Ligne's qualities more evident than in a series of letters supposedly written in 1787 from the Crimea to a friend in Paris, the Marquise de Coigny. In them the prince is revealed as he undoubtedly was: the warrior trained to seek out danger and glory; the gallant sensitive to beauty; the moralist who is a born observer; the man of letters with a weakness for writing and puns and witty repartee. Here the philosopher, eager to shine for posterity, breaks out time and again, especially when he remarks, "I feel like a new person. Having escaped from grandeur, the tumult of feastings, the fatigue of pleasures and from their two Imperial Majesties of the Occident and the North whom I left on the other side of mountains linked—or almost—to the site made famous by the torment of Prometheus, I am able at last to enjoy my true self."[6] Then follows an explosion of sensibility not usually associated with the age of Voltaire. The man who has just considered the ravages of time turns to contemplating the state of his heart.

My heart! What a word! Is it the sorry state of my heart or that of nature which enraptures me, transporting me beyond myself? I burst into tears without knowing why. But how sweet they are! I feel a general emotion, an explosion of sensibility, without being able to determine its object. At this moment, whilst prey to the influx of so many ideas, so many feelings, and such contradictory ones at that, I weep without being sad.[7]

We do not know whether the prince really intended these letters for Madame de Coigny, or ever posted them to her, or merely wrote

---

5. Ligne, *Œuvres choisies* (1978, ed. Guy), 106.
6. Ligne, *Lettres à la Marquise de Coigny*, 47.
7. Ibid., 61.

them for his own solace. Whatever, he sounds an almost new note in French letters, one whose early whisper may be heard in the Rousseau of the *Rêveries* and whose cry would characterize the Romanticism of Chateaubriand (and of generations to come).

Ligne's work marks a discreet change in orientation for the eighteenth century. This writer who was always happy, whatever the circumstances, was yet sensitive to other conditions, other values than his own and so was able to appreciate every nice distinction attaching to the human condition.[8] As both a moralist and a man of his times, he discovers the individual in us all. Thus is he able to assert his objections to some of the Enlightenment's most cherished tenets. Reason, in particular, is suspect to him, as he makes patently clear in this fragment of a famous dialogue between a Freethinker and a Capuchin monk:

FREETHINKER. We seek the Truth.
CAPUCHIN. And have you found it? How proud and foolish not to rely on anyone, not even on God! Besides Him (whom a great lord of my acquaintance used to call "The Gentleman Upstairs," not in derision but as an aristocrat), I am quite content to have several leaders to direct me: my Church, my diocese, my convent, and my conscience. I don't worry about anything because I am philosophical.
FREETHINKER. Whilst I, I am into everything because I'm a *philosophe*. I am constantly writing, deepening my knowledge of things. I seize lightning from the Godhead, scepters from kings, peace from Europe, and posterity from ignorance.
CAPUCHIN. And you do all that without taking one single human life?
FREETHINKER. What does the present generation matter, so long as our children are happy?[9]

A practicing Christian, the subject of a Catholic monarch in a land notorious for bigotry, the Prince de Ligne was never a fanatic, any more than he was a charlatan. In his *Mémoire sur Paris,* he advocated the free practice of religion, demanding that the Revocation of the Edict of Nantes be rescinded and that the Church distribute part of her wealth to her needier members. He was aware, however, that religion has a social value and offers hope for the moral betterment of mankind. The commonplaces of "philosophical" intolerance offended him; Ligne noted, for example, that Frederick II "was too bent on seeking damnation" and found himself, after a visit to Ferney, more comfortable with the Jesuits than with Voltaire.[10]

Believing intuition to be as important as reason, the prince both follows and criticizes those moralists of the preceding age for whom the passions were evil. Even in his military treatises he could be

8. See Robert Mauzi's remarkable study *L'Idée du bonheur,* 42–43, 372–74.
9. Ligne, *Œuvres choisies* (1978, ed. Guy), 71.
10. For the "Mémoire sur Paris," see Ligne's *Mélanges* 10:256 (1796); for Frederick, *Mélanges* 6:117 (1796); for the Jesuits, *Fragments* 1:167.

*Fig. 1.* Emile Legros,
*The Prince de Ligne at 79.*
Watercolor, 1812.
Courtesy Fondation Ligne,
Belœil, Belgium
(photograph Guy Cussac).

This drawing by the son of
Ligne's secretary, Legros,
made when the prince was
seventy-seven (not seventy-
nine as the title suggests), is
more like a caricature than
several portrait paintings by
other artists from this same
period, but it is also probably
a more faithful depiction of
the subject.

swept away: "Let enthusiasm go to your heads, let honor (if this is
not too precious) electrify your heart, let the fire of victory shine in
your eyes. While proudly displaying the badges of glory, let your soul
be inspired—and pardon me if my own, which is perhaps a little too
much so at this moment, inclines me, despite myself, to a bit of
ranting."[11]

Whether in memoirs, poetry, plays, criticism, or any other genre,
topic, or theme, the writings of this man are a continual celebration.
But the only form that suited him, even when he was unaware of it,
was dialogue in the broadest sense. Because he needed an audience,
Ligne is frequently his own interlocutor. He does not feel the need to
seek elsewhere than in himself the good genie who often assisted him
by holding up the mirror of reality to his persona. We may be sure of
finding in his writings a retort to every statement he makes, a dialec-
tic by mimicry. Concentrating on the effect rather than on his message, Ligne did not hesitate to appear other than he really was. Behind the mask of paradox he pivoted around and around, and such
doubts as he may have had were dissipated in fashioning a work of
art.

At the end of his life, the Prince de Ligne pretended to be no
more than a man-of-letters-about-town (Fig. 1). Apparently recovered
from the slings and arrows to which he had fallen victim, but without
resources and in debt, he took to writing his memoirs in bed, reserv-
ing his ultimate judgments for a collection of maxims, adorned characteristically with a flighty title, *Mes Ecarts; ou, ma tête en liberté.* Nonetheless, these maxims display a good measure of common sense and
truth, and certain of his reflections remind us that it is difficult to
play "the happy man" everywhere, ever and always the same: "Life is
a rondeau; it ends just about as it began; witness our two childhoods."[12]

By closely identifying with his subject matter, Ligne frequently ar-
rives at a convincing presentation and tone, surprising in their affec-
tive, moral truth, if not in their detail or exactness. His own critical
faculties were ever alert to the possibilities inherent in refashioning antique ideals. As outmoded as his basic concepts may seem now, they
were not yet so old-fashioned that Chateaubriand could not adapt to
them, or Stendhal—among many others. Ligne himself recognized
the secret of this transformation when he wrote concerning novelists,
"I do not care for those writers who are in love with their hero: their
excess praise is fastidious; the picture demands *nuances,* shading."[13]

11. Ligne, *Fantaisies militaires,* 2; first edition dated 1780.
12. On Ligne's equanimity see Goethe's "Requiem dem frohesten Manne des Jahrhunderts" in Ligne's *Œuvres choisies* (1978, ed. Guy), 245–49, and Maren-Sophie
Røstvig, *The Happy Man;* on the passage "Life is a rondeau" see Ligne's *Fragments*
1:235 and his *Lettres à la Marquise de Coigny,* 65–66.
13. Ligne, *Mélanges* 3:89 (1795).

The shading that Ligne brought to some of his own works could not hide his training, caste, and prejudices, all of which have frequently led to negative assessments of him and his times as reactionary. On a more positive note, however, and judged according to his own terms, Ligne himself was probably more heroic than any of his creations. His ideal, based on moderation, may therefore seem vitiated or subverted not only by his addition of sensibility in its several manifestations but also by his insistence that such sensibility is to be found only in the context of traditional virtues. Yet were any other interpretation possible, it would surely be founded on the following unexceptional statement from the pen of this worldly-wise philosopher, alert and critical though never a cynic: "It is too bad that . . . there are also so few people who reflect upon themselves and others and still fewer who have been able to open the eyes of the world, which, nonetheless, still judges us amiss."[14] Because of his humanity, Ligne the writer occupies an even more prominent position than the mere rehearsal of his biography suggests.

The life and works of this great lord of the Old Regime offer both a witness and a lesson to the modern world. Even if he was neither a profound thinker nor the refined stylist he fancied himself, Ligne was endowed with imagination, sensitivity, and a rare expressiveness—important indicators of a transformation in Western attitudes between the Renaissance and our own time. Amid the jumble of his work appear pages that can charm by their sprightliness while providing the means for understanding a whole era. By surrendering to us the man such as he wished to appear (and as he may have been), they offer a portrait of the perfect cosmopolitan at a time when that ideal was about to disappear.

The moral of Ligne's life and writings is exemplified by his sanity, gaiety, and courage at the center of a world condemned. He chose grace of wit and warmth of the heart in preference to honors he might otherwise have sought (but without begging), advantages he would have renounced (without repudiating them), and pleasures he would have enjoyed (though not to the exclusion of all else). He was indeed "a phenomenon," as Madame de Staël proclaimed.[15] His several qualities enable us to understand why. Nowhere are they more in evidence than in the *Coup d'Œil sur Belœil.*

★

---

14. Ligne, *Nouveau Recueil* 2:139; written ca. 1810.
15. Ligne, *Lettres et réflexions* (1809, ed. de Staël), vi.

*Fig. 4.* Hubert Robert, *Temple of the Sibyl, Tivoli.* Drawing, 1760. Courtesy Musée des Beaux-Arts, Besançon, France (photograph Art Resource).

A world-famous ruin important to designers of eighteenth-century garden structures.

of the Sibyl's temple at Tivoli (Fig. 4), seemingly dilapidated, with a cascade beside it. Work continued on this section of the garden until 1791, carrying out the prince's plan to effect a contrast to the great regularity of the rest of the estate.[20]

Considering his many other activities, it is difficult to understand how Ligne managed to accomplish so much at Belœil in the years before the French Revolution. We know that around 1787 he created with clay, twigs, and branches on a sand table 25 by 10 feet an exact replica of his domain as he wished it to be developed (I.21). The results repaid his foresight and remain to this day, altered only by the addition of an obelisk to the memory of his son.[21] Although, he

20. *Coup d'Œil* (ed. Ganay), 22 n. a; see also this edition, I.17, 33. This project included the addition of islands and peninsulas, of which Ligne's favorite was l'Ile de Flore, so named in honor of his third daughter; it is now a peninsula. He liked to go there in the morning, he tells us, to seek seclusion from tuft hunters and the merely curious (I.18; see also II.58). Parenthetical references to this edition of the *Coup d'Œil* will include the part (roman numeral) and the number(s) (arabic) of the appropriate paragraph(s).

21. This obelisk, supposedly modeled on the Kagul column of Catherine II at Tsarskoye Selo, still stands at Belœil. It is dedicated to the memory of Ligne's favorite son, Charles (1759–92), cut down while fighting against the forces of the French Revolution in the Argonne. Although brave, he was perhaps a less adept military leader than his father imagined; he nonetheless possessed artistic talent and assembled a collection of prints that was famous in his time; see Bronne, *Belœil et la maison de Ligne,* 205–17. For further information on the monument, see *Coup d'Œil* I.22–23, II.41, IV.164. On the background of the obelisk, see *Coup d'Œil* (ed. Ganay), 32, and Aloys Kubiček, "L'Obélisque du Prince Charles de Ligne," 12–14.

planned additional structures (Fig. 5), only the obelisk, the Temple of Morpheus, and the temple "ruin" were actually built in the English garden. Magnificent copper beeches, larch, and one or two exotic species that still stand testify to Charles-Joseph's aptitude as a horticulturist, displaying in addition to his talent the scientific curiosity of a true child of the Enlightenment.[22] The prince devoted similar care and imagination to his nearby estate of Baudour, whose development he foretells in part II of the *Coup d'Œil*.[23] The original may still be seen, portrayed for the modern enthusiast in fascicles 7 and 8 of Lerouge's *Détail des nouveaux jardins* (see Figs. 50–56).

Toward the end of the eighteenth century, the prince's renown as a master of garden design spread far and wide as a result of all his undertakings at or near Belœil.[24] In France, for example, where he belonged to the select inner circle surrounding Marie-Antoinette, he was called upon for advice in planning the Queen's Garden at Petit Trianon. Indeed, the idea of the Temple of Love located there

22. An excellent résumé of Ligne's role as a horticulturist in the strictest sense is in H. Van der Linden, "Les Forêts du Hainaut," 199.

23. From 1774 to 1794 Ligne was assisted in the work at Baudour by F-L. de Staercke, according to *Coup d'Œil* (ed. Ganay), 27 n. c. Today only the outbuildings of Baudour remain; Ligne himself destroyed the rest around 1785, thinking to rebuild according to the plans outlined in the *Coup d'Œil*.

24. Mostly according to Ligne himself. See *Coup d'Œil* III.61 (Cobenzl's, near Vienna); IV.38 (Bishop of Vilna's at Verkhiai); IV.66 (Duke de Chartres's at Monceau); IV.68 (Racine de Monville's at Désert de Retz); IV.79 (Marie-Antoinette's at Petit Trianon); IV.124 (Chotek's, in Bohemia); IV.128–32 (Clary's, at Toeplitz); and IV.145 (Duke of Württemberg's, at Hohenheim). Louis Hautecoeur, *Histoire de l'architecture classique* 5:19, corroborates *Coup d'Œil* IV.68 (as does Roland Mortier, *La Poétique des ruines*, 117) and IV.79, while adding Count d'Artois's celebrated effort at Bagatelle (Paris) in 1778–80, although this last is normally attributed to Bélanger—among many others!—in collaboration with the Scot Thomas Blaikie; see the latter's *Diary of a Scotch Gardener*.
It is difficult to understand why Ligne failed to analyze in his text some of Europe's more famous gardens belonging either to his immediate family, like the Liechtensteins' Eisgrub in Moravia, or to close friends and associates, like the Duke of Croÿ's Hermitage near Valenciennes (Nord) and Count Laborde's Méréville (Essonne), not to mention such international favorites as the Elector Palatine's Schwetzingen (now in Baden, West Germany), or Isola Bella on Lake Maggiore, or even those others in which he may have had a hand, like Rambouillet (Yvelines) or Bagatelle, in Paris. (In this last case, however, as in England, his association with F-J. Bélanger deserves closer attention than it has received heretofore.) Ligne's curious choice of English gardens undoubtedly represents the political character of his friendships with men in the Opposition (Lord Tylney, Baron de Clifford, Lord Botetourt, Henry Seymour Conway) at the time of his visit, since he does not note the gardens belonging to men in the government in 1767, for instance, Lord Holderness's at Sion Hill (London), the Pelhams' at Claremont (Surrey), Sir Francis Dashwood's at West Wycombe (Buckinghamshire) or Lord Shelburne's at Bowood (Wiltshire), although their creations were not far from the almost-straight line Ligne seems to have traveled from London to Bristol and back. Such limitations also help to explain the omission of other gardens like the Cotterell-Dormers' at Rousham (Oxfordshire) or the Duke of Devonshire's at Chatsworth (Derbyshire). But see Ligne, *Fragments* 2:264.

*Fig. 5.* Charles de Wailly, *Project for Stables, Belœil.* Wash drawing, 1782. Courtesy Graphische Sammlung Albertina, Vienna.

An imaginary project for the "improvement" of Belœil.

(Fig. 6) has been credited to him by Pierre de Nolhac, the celebrated historian of the palace and gardens of Versailles.[25] Many others sought his advice, sensing that his competence reflected taste, innate ability, and experience gained from his travels, especially in England and the Crimea. To these travels (in 1767 and 1787, respectively) we owe the amusing presence in the *Coup d'Œil* of punning references to English gardenomania (III.46–47; IV.14–17) and the enthusiasm of the last paragraphs of part III, where we can sense Ligne's excitement of discovery amid the exotic attractions of Yalta's subtropical climate (III.93–97).

Possessed of a gregarious temperament, Ligne naturally drew up his garden plans with others in mind. His sociability contributed to his popularity in his own time and adds to the enjoyment still to be found in both his gardens and his literary remains. In the *Coup d'Œil,* for instance, he is careful to inform us that whenever he can create openings in hedges or copses for viewing others at work or play, he does so (see, for example, I.17; III.24, 39; IV.84, 166). The attention he lavished on his guests is likewise in evidence when he advocates shading visitors against too-strong sunlight whenever possi-

25. See Pierre de Nolhac, "Le Prince de Ligne à Trianon," 115–19. The Temple is more generally ascribed to Richard Mique (1728–94), Marie-Antoinette's favorite architect (see Hautecoeur, *Histoire de l'architecture classique* 5:30).

*Fig. 6 (above).* C-L. Châtelet,
*Temple of Love,*
*Petit Trianon, Versailles.*
Gouache, 1785. Courtesy
Biblioteca Estense, Modena,
Ms. Est. 119 = Alfa. &. 1. 2.

Though the design and siting of
this still-standing garden temple
are normally attributed to
Mique, Ligne claims them
for himself. See Figure 122
for another view.

*Fig. 7 (above, right). Colette et Lucas.*
Anonymous engraving, 1781,
from Ligne, *Colette et Lucas,*
title page of the original edition.
By permission of
the Houghton Library,
Harvard University.

ble (III.36). He wanted at once to minimize maintenance, enhance
neatness (I.15), and regulate the use of carriages and other vehicles on
estates like his (I, author's note; IV.62).

Ligne's concern for individuals and their happiness (see, for example, I.29 and author's note; IV.39–41) was also revealed by his
genuine desire to amuse or be amused by fashioning elegant garden
parties or bustling country fairs (I.27–31). Two such celebrations at
Belœil were among the most notable in the history of Europe before
the Revolution. The first marked the marriage of the prince's eldest
son, Charles, to the Polish heiress Hélène Massalska. At the wedding
in Paris, no less a personage than King Louis XVI witnessed the
marriage contract, and on 1 August 1779 the newlyweds entered
Belœil as they would have entered a fairyland. The party began that
very evening with a fireworks display of some four hundred pieces; it
lasted a fortnight, during which, among other pleasures, professional
actors performed the prince's own pastoral, *Colette et Lucas,* written
especially for the occasion (Fig. 7).[26]

The other celebration was held in July 1783 to honor Count
d'Artois (later Charles X of France), a boon companion from Versailles (Fig. 8). Neither guest nor host was present to enjoy the festivities, however. The royal scion fell ill upon arriving and soon left for
France, accompanied by the solicitous prince, who nonetheless insisted that "the show must go on," demonstrating that prodigality so
often associated with the Old Regime.[27]

26. Lucien Perey, *Histoire d'une grande dame* 1:249–71, and Ligne's *Colette et
Lucas.* The ceremonies and entertainment imitated to a surprising degree those
for the marriage of Louis XVI and Marie-Antoinette in 1770, described in Philippe Huisman and Marie Jallut, *Marie-Antoinette,* 61–70.
27. See Ligne, *Fragments* 1:119–20.

# Ligne and Eighteenth-Century Garden Theory

*L*igne's central theme of gardening was summarized by Saint-Lambert in the preface to his poem in imitation of Thomson, *Les Saisons:*

In times of discussion and reasonableness, when the pleasures of luxury are appreciated for what they are worth, the value of country life is better understood; our debt to agriculture is acknowledged, its object and activities are honored; its peacefulness and innocence are missed, when absent. Sybarites, bored with their vice and intrigue, like to observe the common man in themselves as he discovers a new way of feeling and thinking. They now admire country scenes even when their only merit lies in being revealed as new objects for their attention. (p. iv)

The ideas in this brief paragraph represent a complete program of renewal, especially in light of the far-reaching philosophical changes they suggest. There is, first of all, the almost smug appreciation of creature comforts that characterized the eighteenth century, with its pretension to right thinking. The time had come to consolidate and reflect both on the purported benefits for humanity in general of pursuing such comforts and on the advantages of progress. This position, combining reasonableness with morality, has been said by critics to constitute a new attitude toward the countryside and nature. Georges Gusdorf has aptly summed up this transformation of preexisting modes in *Naissance de la conscience romantique:* "One of the sources of romanticism is this renewal of the alliance of man with the countryside and its living rhythms. It is not merely a question of background or decoration; the countryside is more than the countryside, becoming for the garden amateur a passion, sometimes even a reason for living" (p. 121).

Behind this shift in values from the rigid principles of classicism (especially as it was known and practiced in France [Fig. 18]) lay the realization that the garden constitutes an enclosure containing, as in a microcosm, a meaning radically separated from an amorphous and limitless space beyond—in great measure a negative system fashioned not so much for protection against the content of the world outside as against its structure and orientation. The varied pattern and intimacy of gardens confirm the authenticity, depth, and independence of the self to be discovered therein.[68] The eighteenth century would con-

68. The reasons behind this shift have often been perceived only in terms of English Whiggism; see Nikolaus Pevsner, "The Genesis of the Picturesque," in *Studies in Art,* 1:78–101. But it is neither proven nor sure that so limited, or parochial, an enthusiasm exerted so broad an international influence. It might be wiser to assess the phenomenon rather in terms of a cultural or psychological transformation, using as a starting point such discussions as Paul Hazard, *La Crise de la conscience européenne,* 351–457.

*Fig. 18. Classical "French" Garden.*
Anonymous engraving, 1712,
from Dézallier d'Argenville, *The
Theory and Practice of Gardening.*

Straight lines, flower beds, and a
generally geometric layout were
said to characterize the typical
French garden developed in
imitation of Versailles.

tinue to reflect on the symbolism and ultimate satisfaction of gardens
and gardening (mirrored in a modern phenomenon as seemingly unre-
lated to gardens as the American love affair with the automobile) after
the appearance of Rousseau's best-selling novel *Julie; ou, la Nouvelle
Héloïse.* There the alert reader could discern a change in attitude that
augured well for the appreciation and approval of both a renewed self
and the means to that renewal, the garden.

"In contrast with the *topos* of the moralized landscape . . . in
which the subject read moral lessons into and out of nature with
equanimity, Rousseau hopes that Nature will engender a reading of
the self."[69] The plenitude and seemingly infinite fecundity of nature

69. Juliet F. McCannell, "A Re-Interpretation of Rousseau's *Passion Primitive,*"
892.

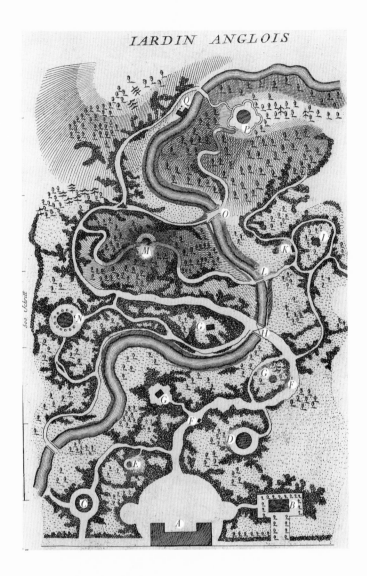

IARDIN ANGLOIS

A Dwelling
B Dining pavilion
C Game room
D Covered temple for concerts
E Small aviary
F Benches of crude woodwork
G Tiny cabins
H Covered wooden bridge
I Altar of grass and stone
K Covered bench
L Wooden bridge
M Temple of Apollo
N Pantheon
O Stone bridge
P Ancient Gothick belfry
Q Hermitage

*Fig. 19. "English" Garden.*
Anonymous engraving, 1802,
from Grohmann,
*Recueil de dessins.*

An almost-perfect example of the mechanical arrangement of garden space that at the end of the eighteenth century would lead to an abuse of picturesque elements as contrived as any in the so-called classical, or French, garden.

reinforced this newfound vision of mankind. For with each variation the garden could become an individual statement about general principles as well as about the owner. He alone could understand its every shade, inscribing in it, as on a tablet, his habits, his preferences, his enthusiasms. His domain would not reflect the preoccupations, the intelligence, the discipline of society, like gardens of old; it would reveal the intimacy of a soul to each individual who drew near, would be like a secret confided by the gardener to the world for mutual delectation. Moreover, although wit would be unlikely to find a place there, sentiment would speak out from every corner.[70]

The means to this end were legion, whether in France, England,

70. Adapted from Ernest de Ganay in *Jardins en France*, 121.

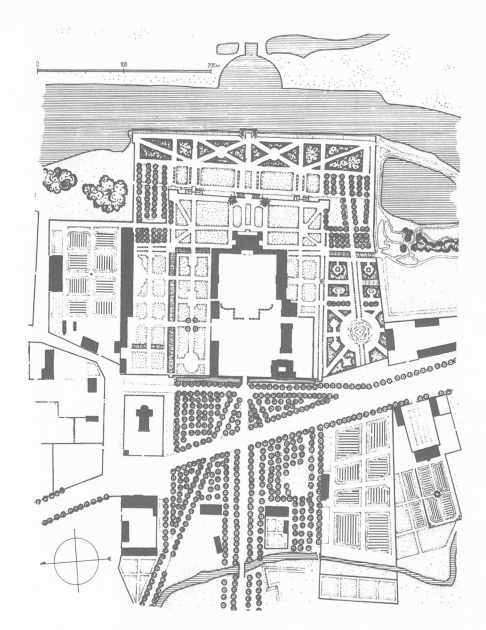

*Fig. 20. Plan of Wilanów, Poland, 1780.*
Anonymous drawing, from Ciołek,
*Gärten in Polen.*

A modern rendition of a garden plan dominated by the "French" style.

Germany, or elsewhere. But only two garden types ultimately emerged: the French and the English (Fig. 19). Although both were said to derive from nature, the former was seen as nature embellished (though some would say "constricted") by rules whereas the latter was touted for being untouched (untouched by whom? the question was never raised).

In the almost two hundred years since 1795, the English model has apparently predominated (Figs. 20, 21). Not that the French garden was completely abandoned; rather, because of their exaggerated claims and unbending adherence to pat formulas, proponents of the

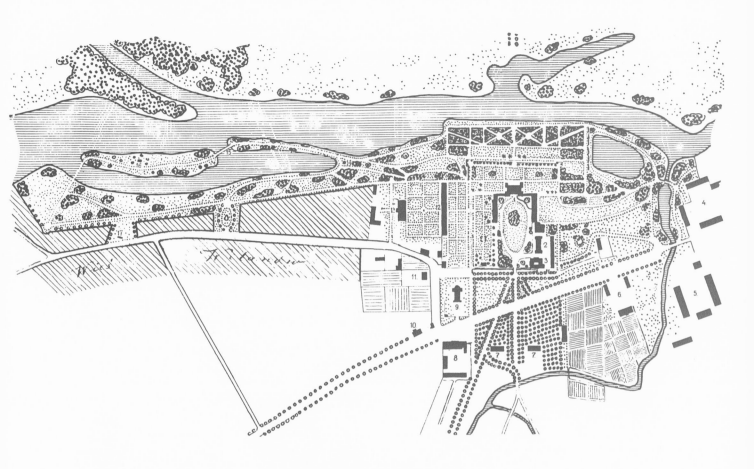

*Fig. 21. Plan of Wilanów, Poland, 1810.*
Anonymous drawing,
from Ciołek, *Gärten in Polen.*

The same garden as in Figure
20, but rearranged, after some
thirty years, to conform to the
"English" style.

model of Versailles were unequal to the challenge of a newer
weltanschauung. As one contemporary complained: this monument
erected by the best artists is a complete depravation of taste, mistak-
ing the natural for the supernatural.[71] Such a reaction to geometry
and pure abstraction corresponded to a deep-seated revolution in
thought. Freed from artifice, nature became revelation. This revitalized interest in what, until roughly mid-century, had been but a passing concern developed into a striving for naturalness. Yet nature was

71. Lord Kames, quoted in *Jardins en France*, 9.

to be subservient to other concepts, as Carmontelle attempted to explain in his guidebook *Le Jardin de Monceau:*

If we can create a country of illusions in a picturesque garden, why not? If we enjoy perfect liberty, we are never happy, except with illusions. Let these illusions be fashioned by art, and we shall never stray far from nature. Nature changes according to the climate. . . . Let us therefore vary ours by introducing different climates. Let us change the scenes in a garden as we change the scenery at the opera. Let us create another reality as painters do, presenting through decoration every age, everywhere. (p. 4)

This philosophical preoccupation with escape created the monstrosity of a Paradise Lost cluttered with mundane curios. As another contemporary, Watelet, phrased it in his *Essai sur les jardins,* "The monotony of beauty breeds a taste for oddity" (p. 113).

Coincidental with such theorizing, the Prince de Ligne's ideas on the importance of gardens are indeed a sign of the times. The *Coup d'Œil sur Belœil* underlines—albeit implicitly—much that had been written, noted, or merely bruited about the philosophical concepts attending the garden mania of the eighteenth century. In this respect, Ligne's contribution to a discussion of the return to nature has often been misunderstood, when not simply ignored. Placed at the conjuction of opposing traditions, he admirably sums up both while contributing to the development of yet a third. His qualities are exemplary and give a new dimension to some of the theories current in his time.[72] Rather than attacking French formalism in garden design or showing concern with "the Sublime," Ligne offers one more manifestation of the spirit of the *Encyclopédie* in attempting to encompass all knowledge for the enlightenment of mankind, touching on every human endeavor and concentrating on the creation of a world in a garden.

Ligne was assisted in this role by his predecessors who had set out in almost schematic fashion those elements they deemed essential to a rational approach to gardening. Their works were carefully arranged around certain commonplaces of inspiration or application, intended, as one writer claimed, "not only to excite or animate such

72. The importance of this position in regard to Continental theories can be gathered by comparing what the prince says with three important works from 1794 in England: Uvedale Price's *Essay on the Picturesque;* Richard Payne Knight's *The Landscape: A Didactic Poem;* and Humphry Repton's *Sketches and Hints on Landscape-Gardening.* See Nikolaus Pevsner, "Humphry Repton," in *Studies in Art,* 1:142. It is doubtful that Ligne knew these works, given the late date of their publication in relation to the 1795 edition of the *Coup d'Œil,* his quasi-isolation in Vienna from foreign influences, and his lack of knowledge of English. Yet the coincidence between his ideas and the Britons' is of signal importance. Perhaps more significant, because of the Duke of Nivernais's translation into French (1785), is Horace Walpole's *Essay;* see this text in Chase, *Horace Walpole, Gardenist,* 3–79.

as have fair estates and pleasant seats in the country, to adorn and beautify them; but to encourage the honest and plain countryman in the improvement of his villa by enlarging the bounds and limits of his gardens."[73] These theorists were eager to create gardens that would influence "the passions of the mind" and were concerned with the human dimension of the experiences they provided. Their instinct for florid and purely ornamental gardens, delightful to both sight and smell, not framed according to mystical considerations, reveals a bias that may be said to typify the Enlightenment in its mistrust of any religious argument and symbolism.[74]

The Prince de Ligne was quick to grasp the importance of these features. For instance, in adapting the garden to the site, with the dwelling properly integrated into the plan, Ligne preferred uneven terrain to low-lying flatlands—within reason. Too much and too great irregularity can be disturbing; it diminishes the invigorating enthusiasm provoked by a gently undulating champaign (IV.124–27). Furthermore, the work of previous owners must not be condemned out of hand (III.37–38).

Among the materials so amply furnished by nature, none was more important in his eyes than water, a prime necessity for any garden and the subject of more than thirty-five paragraphs of his work. Such extensive treatment was necessary in the eighteenth century, for water by its movement represented the soul of a landscape and the inspiration for happiness.[75] For the prince water implicitly symbolizes the life-giving substance, very much as it had for ancient and Renaissance theorists of garden design.[76] Water is to be dispersed in various ways throughout a garden, in deep, opaque—and noisy— cascading masses or in trickles winding to transparent fountains (III.4–6). No expense is to be spared in obtaining sufficient quantity and power (Fig. 22). Ligne's favorite forms for displaying water were the fountain, cascade, and pool, to which he later added brooks, waterfalls, and lakes. In his mind these forms were not interchangeable; many an otherwise interesting garden in Europe was spoiled for him by the inclusion of one form in a garden demanding another (III.54– 55). The delicate tuning of his ear required that the sonorous effects of the water conform not only to the site but also to the mood he would create (see, for example, II.23; IV.42, 149).

---

73. John Woolridge, quoted in *The Genius of the Place*, 88. On the notion of genius loci, see Geoffrey Hartmann, *Beyond Formalism*, 311–36.

74. At one point (III.44), Ligne mentions "Religious Gardens," but with no more than a suggestion, he moves on.

75. Monglond, *Le Préromantisme français* 1:118; see also Mauzi, *L'Idée du bonheur*, 369–72.

76. See Heinrich Wölfflin, *Renaissance and Baroque*, 144–60; see also Thacker, "Fountains," 19–26.

*Fig. 22.* Stanislas Trembecki, *Cascade, Sofiówka, Poland.* Lithograph, 1815, from Łojek, *Dzieje pięknej Bitynki.*

An illustration from Eastern Europe of the force of water necessary to create the right effect in a garden waterfall.

*Fig. 23.* Paul Sandby, *Flower Garden Belonging to the Poet William Mason, Nuneham Courtenay, Oxfordshire.* Engraving, 1770(?), from *Jardins et paysages.*

This garden was important for the banking and arrangement of flowers and shrubs according to their colors.

But the most challenging component was undoubtedly the vegetation itself, neatly subdivided into categories: flowers, shrubs, and trees (Fig. 23), which were further subdivided according to form and season, country of origin, and so forth.[77] All vegetation had its symbolic, even heuristic, value. Flowers had special importance because of their shapes and associations, in addition to their color.[78] Other elements of the garden—pebbles, stones, boulders, and rock outcroppings—likewise possessed special virtues. For the educated visitor a heap of stone or rubble could be imagined as a mountain, whatever its raison d'être. And such characteristically accidental features of nature as precipices, caverns, grottoes, cliffs, and hillocks were created by artifice to inspire the viewer, though the less sophisticated required some pointers, for example, inscriptions. Witness the

77. Nikolaus Pevsner, "Uvedale Price," in *Studies in Art*, 1:134, quotes Price, who echoed several predecessors, notably Antoine-Joseph Dézallier d'Argenville, *Theory and Practice of Gardening*, 266–67; [Thomas Whatley], *L'Art de former les jardins*, 63; and Jean Morel, *Théorie des jardins*, 122.

78. Sir William Chambers was among the first to advocate massing flowers according to their hue (Hugh Honour, *Chinoiserie*, 158). The wealth of classical allusion that Ligne associates with his enumeration of poppies, narcissi, hyacinths, anemones, and the like (for example, IV.8–13, 39–149) is but the formulation of an attitude that leads to the nineteenth-century abuse of "the language of the flowers."

*Fig. 24.* F. Gamble, after Bourgeois, *Boulder with Inscription from Abbé Delille*, Mor(te)fontaine (Oise), France. Engraving, 1808, from Laborde, *Description des nouveaux jardins.*

An example of the lengths to which garden enthusiasts would go to create an effect in their designs.

gigantic boulder in the forest at Mor(te)fontaine (Oise), presumably capable of action (no matter how massive or inarticulate, since being is its own excuse), with a quotation from Delille carved on the surface: "The indestructible mass has wearied Time" (Fig. 24).[79]

Rousseau had used inscriptions for a similar purpose in the *Nouvelle Héloïse*, where they provided the subject of a famous engraving, *Les Monuments des anciennes amours* (Memorials to Past Loves), that was much copied and praised (Fig. 25). Yet the story behind this illustration was but one incident in a lengthy text that amounted in parts to a polemic. One theme to which Rousseau returned again and again, modulating it in various ways and applying it to different sets of circumstances, was the superiority of nature and simplicity, in life as in gardens. Rousseau's view led to a direct attack on false naturalness, pretense, and cant in part 4, letter 11, where he criticized

79. The unintentional humor of such fatuousness cannot escape the modern reader, yet we must recognize that in the century of Voltaire and Rousseau—and Ligne—this mania for inscriptions had a more serious concomitant: garden visitors had to be able to read to appreciate the beauties of the site to the full. They had also to be intelligent enough to draw the proper conclusions from such literary associations, a signal manifestation of that universalized didacticism in which the age believed implicitly and whereby platitudes were said to make kin of all the world. This problem of inscriptions in gardens is convincingly and more fully treated—though from another point of view—by Geoffrey Hartmann, "Wordsworth, Inscriptions, and Nature Poetry," 389–413.

chinoiserie but not the English garden, one supposed intermediary of chinoiserie in France.[80]

Yet European culture in the eighteenth century had been dominated by a veritable passion for China and things Chinese. This was no longer the rococo phenomenon I have discussed in *The French Image of China* but a fascinating subject for ethnographers, for China was "better known than some parts of Europe," as Voltaire proclaimed, the object of overweening curiosity and study and imitation (Figs. 26, 27).[81] The floodgates were then opened to those eager for the latest information on Chinese economy, agriculture, writing, language, botany, or music, who found the ultimate satisfaction in publications sponsored by the French contrôleur général des finances, Henri-Léonard Bertin (1720–92), who was also a gardening enthusiast on his estate at Chatou, near Paris.[82] Without the example of this sinophile there would not exist such masterpieces as the Chinese belvedere at Cassan (Val d'Oise) or the Chinese house built by Racine de Monville at the Désert de Retz (Yvelines), which last, according to the Prince de Ligne, would have made the emperor of China proud.[83] Ligne shared Rousseau's view, despite the occasional interpretation by later readers of Rousseau's harsh words about Chinese gardens as condemning the English model as well (see, for example, I.24 and author's note; II.13, 33, 43).

The distinction to be made, according to the prince, is that too

*Fig. 25.* Hubert Gravelot, *Memorials to Past Loves*. Engraving, 1760, from Rousseau, *La Nouvelle Héloïse*.

Rousseau proposed the following legend to accompany this plate, which illustrates part 4, letter 17: "Julie's friend places a hand on one of two boulders blocking the esplanade [where he had once been exiled] while, with the other, he points out the characters [he had] engraved on the rocks a short distance away. At the same time he addresses her with passion. In Julie's eyes can be read the tenderness that his words and the objects he is showing awaken in her. But we may also infer that Virtue triumphs and has nothing to fear from these dangerous memorials."

80. "The two types [English and Chinese], whatever their origin, should not be confused, despite certain critics from the end of the eighteenth century. While it is true that both have in common a taste for follies, rock outcroppings, bridges, and streams, the English-style garden has a breadth and freshness that display a feeling for uncultivated nature not to be found in the Chinese model. This last is the creation of mandarins or connoisseurs of delicate curios, whereas the former was created by a hunt-loving, animal-loving, space-loving, country-loving gentry" (Hautecoeur, *Histoire de l'architecture classique* 5:15). See also Rousseau, *La Nouvelle Héloïse*, pt. 4, letter 11, and Ligne's *Nouveau Recueil* 2:61.

81. See Honour, *Chinoiserie*; Chase, *Horace Walpole, Gardenist*, 187–202; and Basil Guy, *The French Image of China*, 171–75; finally, Voltaire, "Relation du bannissement des Jésuites de la Chine," *Œuvres* 27:1. The *spirit* of Oriental gardens, both Chinese and Japanese, was to remain unappreciated for almost another hundred years. See the illuminating interpretation in Florence Ayscough, *A Chinese Mirror*, 213–56, and, more recently, Patrick Connor, "China and the Landscape Garden," 429–40; also Dora Wiebenson, "*L'Architecture terrible*," 136–39; and Madeleine Jarry, *Chinoiserie*.

82. See the important series of articles by Henri Cordier, "Les Correspondents de Bertin." On Bertin's role as a gardenist see Bourde, *Agronomie et agronomes*, 1079–89, and *Jardins en France*, illus. no. 79.

83. On the belvedere at Cassan (Val d'Oise) and on the Désert de Retz (Yvelines), see *Jardins en France*, no. 257 A–E and 101 (both with illustrations). Ligne speaks of the emperor of China's reaction in *Coup d'Œil* IV.68, where he could be smug with reason, for he is supposed to have participated in designing the Chinese house; see Hautecoeur, *Histoire de l'architecture classique* 5:19, and Mortier, *La Poétique des ruines*, 117.

But earlier painters had managed to evoke a mood or underline a message by a clever arrangement of natural forms, notably of trees and greenery. Among those who then returned to favor were the Italian Salvator Rosa (1615–73) and the Frenchmen Nicolas Poussin (1594–1665); Claude Gelée, called Le Lorrain (1600–1682); and Gaspard Dughet-Poussin (1615–75). When their names were quoted in treatises like Ligne's *Coup d'Œil,* they were almost always grouped together, so that mention of one name seemingly conjured up the others (for example, in II.19; III.64). Ligne, however, is not content merely to mimic his contemporaries; he adds to the list several seventeenth-century Dutch landscapists (II.8, 10) whose reputations were confirmed in Diderot's *Salons.* The most important among them were Philips Wouwerman (1619–68), Nicolaes Berghem (or Berchem) (1620–83), and Jacob van Ruisdael (1628/9–82), whose hour of glory would strike only with the advent of Romanticism.[91]

Because the picturesque results partly from a visual preoccupation, Ligne conceives of certain gardens, like Cobenzl's in the Wienerwald near Vienna (III.61), as paintings. As such, they must give pride of place to color and the effects of light and shade and, especially, of perspectives. Lawns, groves, and flower beds must be irregular in shape, and the ground on which they are planted must rise and fall, all as naturally as possible. Yet the picturesque garden, like the classical, is composed of conventions (III.48–53; IV.108, 127). Such a paradox leads the prince into a passage that is difficult to comprehend (unless his vaunted taste is at fault): his description of the Esterházy estate at Esterháza, Hungary, bordering the Lake of Neusiedl (IV.113–15).

Half the charm of Ligne's exaggeration lies exactly in his effort to improve an already interesting—not to say "arresting"—arrangement, since this particular Esterházy domain covered slightly more than ten square miles. He claims he would make of this territory a stage set,

91. The names Ligne frequently mentions—Claude, Poussin, and Salvator Rosa—are those given by nearly all his contemporaries, following Jonathan Richardson's *Theory of Painting,* so that in this respect he seems to be aping a fashion. See Claude-Henri Watelet, *Dictionnaire des arts* 2:248–53 and 4:8–21; *Jardins en France,* nos. 84–86; Elizabeth Manwaring, *Italian Landscape in Eighteenth-Century England;* Chase, *Horace Walpole, Gardenist,* 120.

In lumping these artists together, the theorists forgot that each of them may generally be distinguished by the *tone* of his creation: Poussin by the elegiac, Le Lorrain by passivity, and Salvator Rosa by torment or terror. Although all depended on nature for their effects, their treatments of it were often at variance with one another. In adding the names of the Dutch landscapists, Ligne is not only trying to show a new sensitivity and independence, but also suggesting changes in perspective that might broaden appreciation of the original trio. See Michael Cartwright, *Diderot, critique d'art,* 175–218; Marcel Brion, *Romantic Art,* 51; and John Dixon Hunt, *The Figure in the Landscape,* 259, under "Collins."

"with lighthouses, towers, pretended reefs, imaginary monsters and tales of corsairs, huts for fishermen, inscriptions about shipwrecks, a temple to the god of the sea, stone steps and balustrades of the finest stone for a landing place. . . ." If the enumeration of such a heteroclite collection has a purpose, it might be that the prince, well aware of the excesses to which ungoverned enthusiasms could lead, was as serious in making light of them as if preaching from the Gospel according to Saint Priapus.[92]

Further proof of this attitude is Ligne's advice that such structures as temples, grottoes, and baths be created only with the greatest circumspection (III.43) and that great discretion be used in creating ruins (III.47), since lack of control here produces nothing but "horrors that make us die laughing" (III.48). Again and again Ligne's taste seems to come to the rescue, frequently in pointed comments modulated by irony, sarcasm, or outright amusement. Modern readers can find relief from the tedium of even his detailed descriptions of the famous gardens he had visited throughout Europe before the French Revolution, in their knowledge that the faults and shortcomings he mentions are only too real if we insist on following passing fashions.

The prince's dependence on painters and the visual arts in general was not new. Since the early eighteenth century one of the most influential writers on art history and theory had been Roger de Piles (1635–1709), whose *Cours de peinture* (1708) had attracted the attention of connoisseurs and collectors almost as soon as it was published.[93] His appraisal of landscape painting as an independent genre also aroused the interest of gardenists; his recipes for the painter were easy to adapt and assimilate to the theories of garden art. His influence is therefore undeniable, although it may seem merely an offshoot of his contribution to the discussion then developing around the notion *ut pictura poesis*—the aesthetics of the sublime and the beautiful.[94] In this discussion of gardens, however, what matters is his insistence on the role of both the painter and the viewer and, especially, on variety in the landscape. Although his principles may seem too

92. In this passage Ligne is also imitating descriptions of imaginary theatrical gardens already parodied in existing garden literature, like P-M-G. de Chabanon's *Lettre sur la manie des jardins anglais*, and L.L.G.D.M.'s "Lettre sur les jardins anglais," 132–42; or Carmontelle's dramatic proverb "Le Jardin anglais," all from 1775.
93. See *The Genius of the Place*, 112.
94. See Edmund Burke, *An Enquiry into Our Ideas of the Sublime and the Beautiful;* Samuel H. Monk, *The Sublime;* and Rensselaer W. Lee, "*Ut pictura poesis,*" 197–269. More recently, Thacker claims that "admiration for the sublime was to prove both the climax and downfall of the landscape garden" (*The History of Gardens,* 179).

cut-and-dried or, again, a mere catalog, his overriding concerns may be discerned in much that eighteenth-century gardenists advocated, either in simple lists or diffused, as in the *Coup d'Œil,* where they provide the skeleton for much that Ligne advances.

The progress that eighteenth-century scientists and farmers made in botany, horticulture, and agriculture added to the colors on the palette of both painters and writers like Ligne and helped to make Ligne's theorizing more subtle and convincing.[95] Until the end of the reign of Louis XIV, the floral decoration of gardens had varied but little, the arboreal background of the classical park consisting of yew trees, clipped boxwood, and trees with silhouettes of regular shapes. When the irregular garden triumphed, exotic species appeared, largely the discoveries of recent voyagers. Louis XV created the famous nurseries of the Trianon, where several generations of the Richard family learned to acclimate various species. Missionaries, explorers, and diplomatic representatives had orders to collect and forward to France precious seed from the four corners of the earth—and even from the British Isles in 1764 seedlings of the black larch were brought to France, specimens from the cedars of Lebanon having arrived somewhat earlier. Following these efforts at collection, the systematic planting and exploitation of flowering shrubs began—lilacs, rhododendrons, wisteria, and laburnum—as well as the addition of less familiar conifers and evergreens to the established varieties of trees: copper beeches, birches, and Lombardy poplars. The taste for exotica spread and burgeoned amid general enthusiasm, particularly after the importation of the dahlia from Mexico, followed by camellias, chrysanthemums, hydrangeas, and mimosa from the Far East.[96] These new species had to be displayed as naturally as possible, adapted to scenic backgrounds where they would contribute to that modulation of nature so praised by the theorists. At one time the Prince de Ligne was as interested as others in importing and planting new species, believing they would improve the "painterly" effects he wanted to create at Belœil and Baudour.[97]

The many picturesque gardens developed on infertile sites required more than nature supplied to create a desired impression, a

95. See *The Genius of the Place,* 205, and *Jardins en France,* nos. 114–66.
96. See, for example, *Coup d'Œil* III.41, IV.22. Woburn Abbey (Bedfordshire) was one of the eighteenth-century estates used as horticultural laboratories; some of the first Chinese imports to Europe (ca. 1718) were grown successfully there (Honour, *Chinoiserie,* 159–60). For lists of selected plants, with dates of their entry into the British Isles, see Thacker, *The History of Gardens,* 127, 239, and Alice Coats, *Garden Shrubs.*
97. See Van der Linden, "Les Forêts du Hainaut," 199, and chap. 6 of Morel's *Théorie des Jardins.*

mood.[98] A garden had to do more than offer the spectator a picture; it had to frame that picture, move the soul of the man of feeling, and become a stage. The public, accustomed to theatricality even in everyday life, demanded that the gardens evoke dramatic effects by being composed of a succession of scenes.[99] Projects and models for the modernization of eighteenth-century Paris look like sketches for the theater or designs for a garden, with the same exaggeration of scale, the same clever use of perspective, the same symbolism. The garden and the stage set, which were conceived architecturally in the seventeenth century, were thought of as picturesque and sentimental in the eighteenth century, a change that led to a great demand in garden design for the equivalent of theatrical props, the mania for which, as John Summerson has pointed out, led to the confusion of the picturesque with "the cult of styles."[100]

Once again, the list of props is long. Although it is a typology, based on lists like those mentioned above, it was nonetheless conceived of in different terms and put to different uses. Such lists were necessary to the amateurs who flocked to this new fashion. Choosing the right prop for a special effect became for some the equivalent of modern shopping by catalog (see Figs. 30 and 62).

98. Regarding infertile sites, see André Parreaux's introduction to *Jardins et paysages* I.18. Unfortunately, one aspect of the design and planting of eighteenth-century gardens may escape twentieth-century visitors: prospects or views delightful to moderns may be far from what the first owners desired, since the normal course of growth and decay may have destroyed the intended effect while creating new ones. Although the eighteenth century might have appreciated the contrasts created by later growth, the scenery of certain gardens today conflicts with the original intentions. They may still inspire a sense of the picturesque, but "associations and overtones being transient, the *Zeitgeist* is probably beyond preservation," as Kenneth Woodbridge has noted ruefully in *The Stourhead Landscape*, 18.

99. The scenes were combined into circuits, allowing their sequence, approach, and so forth to be viewed most advantageously. See, for instance, Louis XIV's *Manière de montrer les jardins de Versailles* (Thacker, *The History of Gardens*, 149–52). Ligne cannot deny himself the pleasures of this mode as he devises a "Tableau of Human Life" (I.14–33). The next step was for the sequence or circuit to tell a story (or re-create one already familiar to visitors through literature), as is said to be the case at Stourhead (Thacker, *The History of Gardens*, 194), though the exact subject of this tour is still debated; see Woodbridge, *The Stourhead Landscape*, 9–13; Ronald Paulson, *Emblem and Expression*, 165–87; Dora Wiebenson, *The Picturesque Garden in France*, 108–21; and Max Schulz, "The Circuit Walk of the Eighteenth-Century Landscape Garden," 1–25.

On stage sets, see Hautecoeur, *Histoire de l'architecture classique* 5:1–50 and illustrations, as well as Peter V. Conroy, Jr., "French Classical Theater and Formal Garden Design," 666–82, and "Dramatic Theory and Eighteenth-Century Gardens," 252–65. For two extreme examples of theatricality in everyday life, see contemporary accounts of the torture and death of Damiens in 1757 and Abel Hermant, "Le 18ᵉ siècle vivant," 20–21.

100. John Summerson, *Architecture in Britain*, 276–88.

*Fig. 29. Diana's Grotto, Sofiówka.* Anonymous drawing, 1820, from Łojek, *Dzieje pięknej Bitynki.*

The search for origins gave rise to such creations as this one in an Eastern European garden.

Stones, boulders, and rock outcroppings—the primeval materials of which grottoes were a direct, potent, and mysterious expression— indicated our common origin as terrestrial inhabitants. They revealed in humanity a common yearning for a bond stronger than blood or kinship: a link with the unrecorded past about which little, if anything, was known (Fig. 29). Although grottoes had existed in gardens from classical antiquity at least, strictures in the canon of taste prevented the acknowledgment of their primitivism in the seventeenth century, when they were frequently preceded by porticoes or nymphaea. By the dawn of the eighteenth century, however, they were being revealed in all their baseness, in the gardens at Commercy (Meurthe-et-Moselle), for example, where Cerberus's Grotto was more like an animal's lair than a mere cavern.

Because each element demanded its own appropriate setting and decoration, follies were needed.[101] The search for exoticism in space

101. See René de Girardin's definition of follies: "In painting and architecture, follies are any building or construction whatever; a generic word" (*De la composition des paysages*, 69 n. a); Ernest de Ganay, "Fabriques aux jardins," 287–98.

*Fig. 30. Study of Temples.*
Anonymous engraving, 1780,
from Lerouge, *Détail des
nouveaux jardins à la mode,*
cahier 12.

As in modern sales catalogs,
some designers included a choice
of garden ornaments.

and/or time involved the many branches of knowledge about mankind
then burgeoning into an early ethnology. According to Edward Said:

In the eighteenth century the possibility of representing things in space—as
in a painting—derived from the acceptance of temporal succession which
thereby allowed the constitution of spatial simultaneity; the fact that objects
could exist together in the privileged space of a painting depended upon an
unquestioned belief in the continuing forward movement of time. Spatial
togetherness was conceived to be an emanation of temporal succession. Yet
in the modern era the profound sense of spatial distance between things
which separates like things from each other permits the modern mind to
contemplate time as only a dream of succession, as a promise of unity or of
a return to origins. Above all, Time is the most tenuous of spatial configura-
tions that attempt to bridge the gap between things. (p. 347)

Like his contemporaries, the Prince de Ligne was not slow to
seek, through garden design, the answers to philosophical questions
about such a concept—and perhaps to find those answers in the picturesque rearrangement of nature (for example, in III.25, 43, 48–49,
53).

Thus eighteenth-century gardeners borrowed for their follies the
shape of temples from ancient Greece and Rome. These follies (Fig.
30), according to the symbolism desired, could be round (like the
Sibyl's temple at Tivoli) or square (like the *cella* of the Maison Carrée
at Nîmes) or rectangular (like the Parthenon); they could be open or
half or completely enclosed by walls between columnar supports; and
the various orders of architecture could give an added interpretive
dimension to the supports themselves.[102] Ancient civilization had also

102. See Nikolaus Pevsner, "The Doric Revival," in *Studies in Art,* 1:197–211.

favored the creation of altars, commemorative columns, theaters, naumachiae, arches, and porticoes, whereas Egypt, newly appreciated after the abuses of Renaissance symbolists, was represented by fountains, pyramids, obelisks, and the like.[103] The novelty of the Orient particularly favored game rooms, tents, kiosks, gazebos, and of course pagodas (Fig. 31). The Orient could be subdivided between the Chinese and the Arabs (Japan had not yet come into its own), and the Arabs could be further divided among Moors, Turks, and Tartars, to which last group Ligne seems to have been unique in adding yet another, the Moldavians.[104]

If civilization with its suavity—and corruption—were too much, the gardenists could always find the opposite in rusticity, with its simplicity and virtue. This radical change in point of view encouraged the development of farms and villages where those eager to return to nature could follow their preference for milk over champagne. These notions of rusticity were carried even further when the owners, with ofttimes overheated imaginations, insisted that the follies were actually meant to be inhabited (Fig. 32). This insistence is not surprising when we consider that under the Old Regime many an estate was largely peopled by families whose condition was no better than that of serfs. And if for want of genuine Roman citizens or Chinese mandarins the owners' desires were found to be impractical, what more natural than to fall back on the farm scheme and use genuine laborers, who—given the size of many an estate where the villages were to be constructed—had to be housed in any case?[105]

*Fig. 31.* Johann Carl Krafft, *Bridge in the Chinese Taste.* Engraving, 1810, from Krafft, *Plans des plus beaux jardins.*

This temple was intended to be constructed as a bridge— one more example of the uses to which Sinomania could be put.

103. As in the illustrations to Francesco Colonna's *Hypnerotomachia Poliphili.* See Nikolaus Pevsner and Suzanne Lang, "The Egyptian Revival," in *Studies in Art,* 212–35; Anthony Blunt, "The *Hypnerotomachia Poliphili* in France," 117–37; and Richard G. Carrott, *The Egyptian Revival,* 1–46.

104. On the Chinese, see *Jardins en France,* nos. 247–63; Honour, *Chinoiserie,* 143–74; and Chase, *Horace Walpole, Gardenist,* 187–202. For the others, see the "Moorish" baths at Kew (Surrey) and Schwetzingen (West Germany), and *Coup d'Œil* III.30, 35. For Turks and Tartars, see *Jardins en France,* nos. 264–67, as well as *Coup d'Œil* III.9–10. Ligne's use of "the Moldavian style" in *Coup d'Œil* III.19–21 and 33 is undoubtedly a reminiscence of Potemkin's wonderful palace at Kremenchug on the Dnieper (near Cherkassy, Ukrainian SSR). The palace is now destroyed, but Ligne could have visited it in 1787 as Catherine II made her triumphal progress to the Crimea. It was characterized by wooden construction, with enormous tree trunks serving as columnar supports, both inside and out, and by extensive loggias; see Lady Craven, *Journey through the Crimea,* 207.

Ligne's touting of the "Moldavian" style was also perhaps a reaction to the number and inanity of "Moorish" kiosks and other structures that he decries in III.35.

105. See *Coup d'Œil* I.10, 31, for example. Though the prince does not mention them here, we know from other texts, notably *Fragments* 1:187, that there were dashes of exotic color at Belœil in the persons and costumes of one Tartar, two Turks, and four Russians whom he had brought back from the Crimea and Belgrade (not including his manservant Norokos, or Ismaël).

*Fig. 32 (right).* C. G. Nestler,
*Pheasantry at
the Moritzburg, Dresden.*
Engraving, 1734(?),
from Friedrich Löffler,
*Das alte Dresden.*

One example of a garden
structure intended to be both
decorative and practical, since it
was to house the keeper of the
pheasant run and his family.

*Fig. 33 (above).* Carl P. Schallhas,
*Laudhon's Tomb.*
Tinted engraving, 1790(?).
Courtesy Akademie
der bildenden Künste,
Vienna.

A real tomb in the garden
of Hadersdorf Castle,
near Vienna.

From the countries of the intellect it was but a short step to the
realms of fancy. Literary follies soon made their appearance. There
were statues erected to great authors (as at Stowe or even as described
in the *Coup d'Œil,* I.15, 17); there were tombs to commemorate both
authors (J-J. Rousseau at Ermenonville and in the *Coup d'Œil,* I,
author's note) and literary characters (Young's daughter at Franconville, Val d'Oise), with funereal emblems and monuments to historical personages, frequently family members (as at Méréville [Essonne]
and in the *Coup d'Œil,* IV.164) (Fig. 33). The Prince de Ligne does
not hesitate to follow this trend by planning for a corner at Belœil
that would have included his own tomb (I.15). Some of these *memento mori* that still stand can be extremely touching in their evocation of a mood. But at Betz around 1780 a nostalgia for vanished
civilizations arose (Fig. 34), and with it an inclination to allow the
garden to keep pace with historical writing in the manner of Gibbon
or Volney. From there only one step remained to bring this sentimental ideography full circle: ruins.

Realizing that some gardens—Gémenos in France (III.69–88) or
Studley Royal in England (Fig. 35)—contained genuine ruins, we can
appreciate the confusion of both motif and expression to which this
last expansion of the picturesque would lead. Whatever its origins
(whether they lay in the losses France incurred at the Treaty of Paris
in 1763 or in the interest in the Gothic arising from Horace Walpole's
works in England), the use of the ruin has been admirably summarized by Roland Mortier in *La Poétique des ruines en France:*

from being a systematic thinker, Ligne reflected contemporary concerns in ways that are nonetheless informative. But if his thinking represents only the end result of what others had proposed, is he only a mirror? The answer is no. For the *Coup d'Œil* goes beyond commonplace horticultural considerations to become a work of the imagination, a travel guide, and the treatise of a moralist that reflects, more than the importance of one man's concerns, the quality of a whole culture.

# *The Achievement of the* Coup d'Œil

*A*t a time when the imagination was more highly prized than ever before, it was only natural for a writer like the Prince de Ligne to participate in the general movement and to lay his own small offering on the altar of a newfound sensibility. Like some contemporaries caught "between tears and laughter,"[113] he believed ever more firmly that the pleasures of the imagination and the delights of the senses are no less than those of the intelligence (IV.149). And if the ideological novelty of his choice of genre—neither a tragedy nor a treatise—were not sufficient indication of his leanings in this respect, certain instances in the *Coup d'Œil* reveal the pleasure he took in the imagination.

The most specific of these occur in the paragraphs treating Belœil and Baudour (parts I and II) and in part IV, where the prince deals with European gardens needing "improvement" to embody his ideal. It is easy enough to separate Ligne's fancy from fact when with regard to his own property he begins to enumerate the changes he would effect and his plans for some vague time in the future (I.9–21; II.9–22). The effect of his presentation is more than intellectual or even stylistic. Especially in the case of Belœil and Baudour he enables us to envision certain parts of these estates now irretrievably lost (I.5–8, author's note; II.15–16). Thanks to such an inspired intermediary as the prince, we can delight in those pleasures that are indispensable to a fuller understanding of the garden and his world.

If, as Coleridge would have it,[114] the imagination is no less than that shaping and modifying power that unifies disparate materials through idealization, it is easy to understand how the world of the *Coup d'Œil* is more than a garden: in Ligne's imagination it becomes

---

113. My interpretation follows Hazard's general analysis in *La Crise de la conscience européenne*, 373–74.

114. The *locus classicus* of this idea is Coleridge, *Biographia Litteraria*, chap. 14. More recently, see Ernest Tuveson, *The Imagination as a Means of Grace*, and George S. Rousseau, "Science and the Discovery of the Imagination," 108–35.

the perfect *locus amoenus* where good may be not only observed but put to use as an influence on morals and morality (for example, I.22–24, 28–33; II.23–27). Ligne is at one with his time, notably with Hume, when he proclaims that even in horticulture aesthetic and moral judgments are akin.[115] And so, from the application of his imagination to the topics of his discourse, Ligne advances to an explanation of his attitudes concerning people—including the inhabitants of his text, real or imaginary (Fig. 38). He gives so freely of himself in genuine concern that he goes beyond the cold morality of those ancients whose lessons he frequently invokes. As in the following statement, his good sense, balanced with feeling, imagination, and humor, adds another dimension to the notion of civilized decency: "I am neither moral enough, nor moralist enough, nor moralizing enough, to preach. And I don't give a fig for those who do not believe in my morality, which consists in making everyone around me happy."[116]

Out of this particular approach to happiness, Ligne's sensibility expands to encompass the ever-popular attractions of travel literature. It is doubtful whether European interest in the natural garden would have developed without the impetus afforded by these extraliterary, though nonetheless cultural, expressions. Deriving from changed social conditions in Europe, especially at the end of the seventeenth century, they were indicative of the combination of uneasiness and sensitivity, analyzed by Paul Hazard in *La Crise de la conscience européenne* (pp. 3–12 and 26–29), that gave rise to the publication of innumerable guidebooks, the tours of Defoe (1724) and Boswell (1773) perhaps being the high points of this literature in English. A parallel development is to be seen in France, where by the end of the eighteenth century the need for more than factual guides resulted in just such interpretations as Ligne offers in the *Coup d'Œil*.

On both sides of the Channel after roughly 1715 touring became *de rigueur,* and virtuosos discovered the wilderness of the North while dilettantes went into esctasies over the ruins of the South. Once home, all these travelers wanted to preserve the memory of what they had seen,[117] whether in the texts, engravings, and paintings they had purchased or, ultimately, in the scenes they re-created in gardens. In several passages Ligne seems to have been so earnest a follower of this fashion that he included in his text almost verbatim descriptions from

---

115. David Hume, "On the Standard of Taste," 231–55.
116. *Fragments* 2:38. See Goethe in the same edition, 245–49; also Røstvig, *The Happy Man,* and Mauzi, *L'Idée du bonheur,* 373–74. Ligne largely ignores the dark, wild, primitive, and frightening "terrible garden," though the idea was popular in his own time and beyond; see Sir William Chambers, *Designs of Chinese Buildings,* 179, and Thacker, *The History of Gardens,* 216.
117. See Christopher Hibbert, *The Grand Tour;* the stimulating discussion of Alan McKillop in "Local Attachment and Cosmopolitanism," 191–218; and Malcolm Andrews, *The Search for the Picturesque.*

*Fig. 38. Entrance
to the Désert
de Retz by Night.*
Anonymous engraving,
1780(?), from Lerouge,
*Détail des nouveaux
jardins à la mode,*
cahier 13.

This fanciful
representation of satyrs
with torches lighting the
way of nighttime visitors
exemplifies Sir William
Chambers's idea of a
"jardin terrible" but
seems to leave the guests
strangely impassive.

authentic guidebooks (IV.73, 150–62). His enthusiastic effort to paint pictures with words follows a trend well documented and analyzed by Christopher Hussey.[118] When he described properties and regions that were decided novelties, he encouraged his readers to visit, say, Ermenonville (a paradigm of picturesqueness) or to dream of otherwise inaccessible spots like those in the Crimea (recently conquered by Catherine II). But because the taste for travel during the last quarter of the eighteenth century was nurtured by a wider interest in the aesthetics of the picturesque fostered in England by William Gilpin's and Uvedale Price's essays (1782 and 1794, respectively), the *Coup d'Œil* reflects—and how well!—that preoccupation too.[119]

Changing circumstances—intellectual, political, and economic—made tours of country houses in the last half of the eighteenth century in France a popular pastime—a fashionable way to spend the summer months. This custom finds a direct echo in Ligne's remarks about the country houses he visited when in England in 1767 (IV.14–23). Ligne

118. Christopher Hussey, *The Picturesque*, chap. 4. See also Edward Malins, *English Landscaping and Literature, 1660–1840;* Kenneth Woodbridge, *Landscape and Antiquity;* and Charles Batten, *Pleasurable Instruction*.
119. Selections in *The Genius of the Place:* Gilpin, 337–41; Price, 351–57. See also Wiebenson, *The Picturesque Garden in France*, 105–6.

obviously intended the *Coup d'Œil* to provide information, like the guidebooks then proliferating.[120]

The shaping of this interest in visiting estates can be traced in numerous chronicles and diaries from the period, like that of Madame Roland. Though such tours were probably not taken for purely educational reasons, as had been the case earlier in England, nontheless, by the time of the Revolution some tourists traveled as much for artistic or even archaeological reasons as for curiosity or tuft hunting (see I.18). When modernized family seats or newer country houses arose as if by magic, largely in the vicinity of Paris or near the provincial *parlements,* local lords established terms and conditions for visits to their estates that reflect the subservience previously shown to king and court. In that they differed from their English counterparts.[121]

Visitors were required to observe opening times and conditions for admission; they paid a fee, and their names were recorded in a logbook.[122] The curious could then circulate freely if the owners themselves were not present. Although unarmed men were not required to rent a sword or uncovered women a mobcap, as propriety demanded at royal residences, a guidebook became the sine qua non for those with enough instruction to read. These volumes were frequently of small format, usually poorly printed, and sometimes poorly written; but as in England, they indicated an owner's conviction of the merits of his creation (or his pride), his belief in the powers of education (or his own open-mindedness), and his commitment to spreading enlightenment (or charity), even in the landscape garden.

When techniques of reproduction improved, these guidebooks began to be illustrated. By the time of the French Revolution the luxurious gift book had appeared, beautifully illustrated and bound; the owner of the property would present it to close friends.[123] When the

---

120. Lists of these guides have been established for Great Britain by John Harris, "English Country-House Guides," and Esther Moir, *The Discovery of Britain.* See also Robert A. Aubin, *Topographical Poetry in Eighteenth-Century England;* John Barrell, *The Idea of Landscape and the Sense of Place;* Paul Fussell, *Abroad;* Dean McCannell, *The Tourist;* and Ann Ridehalgh, "Pre-Romantic Attitudes." To the best of my knowledge, nothing comparable to these studies exists for France, but see Mornet, *Le Sentiment de la nature en France,* pt. 2, chap. 2.

121. Compare Luc-Vincent Thiéry, *Guide des amateurs* 1:64, 140, with the regulations dated 1845 and still posted at Bicton Gardens (Devonshire), or Horace Walpole's ticket and rules for visiting Strawberry Hill in Wilmarth S. Lewis, *Horace Walpole,* plate 50.

122. See Ligne's *Mélanges* 21:196 (1801).

123. See Christian Hirschfeld, *Théorie de l'art des jardins* 5:420 n., 424. For examples of the various types of guidebook, see Jean Benjamin de Laborde, *Description générale et particulière de la France;* C-M. Saugrain, *Curiosités de Paris;* Luc-Vincent Thiéry's two guides; Nicolas Le Camus de Mézières, *Description des eaux de Chantilly;* Stanislas de Girardin, *Promenade; ou, intinéraire des jardins d'Ermenonville;* Carmontelle, *Le Jardin de Monceau;* and Alexandre de Laborde, *Description des nouveaux jardins.*

novelty of this custom wore off, editors and even authors attempted to continue the trend by publishing magnificent folios or oversize volumes (now the treasures of great library collections), underwriting the enormous cost by subscription, as in the case of Alexandre de Laborde's various publications. Because of political and social change—not so much under the Revolution and Empire as under the Restoration—this curious cultural manifestation ended around 1830, when great landowners, because of their prodigious wealth and possibly their snobbishness, retreated from the ideals of the Enlightenment.

Indeed, by 1795 picturesque travelers (for whom the word *tourist* was coined around 1773 in English, 1796 in French) had become recognized figures, seeking to find in nature scenes that realized their ideal of landscape.[124] Although their chances of finding their ideal were slight, hope constantly urged them forward. This sentimental element of travel, requiring, in addition to delicacy of feeling, a stout heart and sometimes an even stouter pair of legs, encouraged the development of tourism. Walking for pleasure was a novelty, especially after the publication of Rousseau's *Emile* (1762), with the famous digression of part 5, beginning, "I can conceive of but one way to travel . . . walking."[125]

But the seekers after picturesque beauty were soon a subject of ridicule. Incapable of appreciating the gardens they inspected, they turned their visits into picnics,[126] or they hurried from house to house, never staying long enough at any one to relish the scene they had traveled so far to see. Journeys through the more remote parts of Europe were subject to the same criticism. Enthusiastic rapture over the irregularity of mountains was to prove so long-lasting a fad that a later era could satirize it as pointedly as the earlier part of the century had satirized the mania for chinoiserie.

This criticism, though far removed from the Prince de Ligne and his *Coup d'Œil,* was similarly concerned with human beings and their values. Impersonal nature provided the initial impulse and the background for garden treatises like Ligne's, but the ultimate development

124. See B. Sprague Allen, *Tides in English Taste, 1619–1800* 2:200–207, 224–30.
125. See, for England, the important contribution of Harris, "English Country-House Guides," 58–74, and Moir, *The Discovery of Britain;* and for France, pt. 2, chap. 2 of Mornet, *Le Sentiment de la nature en France,* as well as Michèle Duchet, "La Littérature de voyages," 1–14; Pierre Laubriet, "Les Guides de voyage au début du 18ᵉ siècle," 296–325; Denis Pageaux, "Voyages romanesques au siècle des lumières," 205–14; René Pomeau, "Voyage et lumières," 1269–89; and Robert Shackleton, "Travel and the Enlightenment," 281–91, though these last are of only limited use and interest in our context. More to the point is Marcel Dumolin, *Notes sur les vieux guides de Paris.*
126. *Coup d'Œil* III.46. See Ligne, *Nouveau Recueil* 1:216 n. 2.

of gardens related to human activities. Little by little, Ligne peoples the garden with individuals as well as with types. In admitting them to his treatise, he redirects our attention from the primary focus of the gardenist to that of the moralist (for example, III.45; IV.49, 166–67). In this he seems unique.

The people in his gardens are to be visitors, but they will make few demands (see I.18) since so much of the garden was to be prepared with them in mind—wagons and rides for sightseeing, sufficient protection from the sun, no stairways, and so forth (I.24, 27–31; III.39, 77; IV.69, 129–30). Undoubtedly, tourists are more present to the prince's mind than houseguests, though even these are not excluded from his thoughts (III.51, author's note); tradesmen, however, are strictly to be refused admission (IV.12).

By far the largest group to whom Ligne gives his attention are his villagers, farmers, servants, retired soldiers, and their families (I.9; III.45; IV.36). His thoughts return again and again to these people, whom he considered his responsibility—for material help as well as spiritual reassurance. Yet Ligne was no democrat. Like some of his contemporaries, he fleetingly envisions lads and lasses gaily bedecked as for some perpetual house party or dressed as the demigods and demigoddesses of mythology, engaging in sexual escapades (IV.11).[127] But behind such visions, especially those resting on motifs from Greco-Roman antiquity, are the moral concerns that legend is supposed to symbolize or metaphor to teach.

It was on you [nouveaux riches, living in the country] that Fortune should have rained her benefits. You might not then have been so proud or hard-hearted. You would have extended your hand to the unfortunate, assisting the poor, doing good to your brethren. They might not have made you blush. You would have raised your children properly. And that priest of Plutus, who has not even the merit of having any, makes his entry into his village with the luxurious trappings of an Oriental satrap. People bow before this idol. Happily, as I have said, there is no taste. (IV.82)

---

127. *Coup d'Œil* I.10. In this context, Marie-Antoinette "playing" at the Petit Trianon was not so exceptional; see Huisman and Jallut, *Marie-Antoinette*, 132–35, 150, as well as the famous portrait of the Queen *en bergère* by Mme Vigée-Lebrun (ca. 1785) at Versailles. On "playfulness," see Jean Duvignaud, *Sociologie du théâtre*:

> These incidents were supposed to reveal their meaning, shape, and content by themselves. But since dramatic imitation is inherent in humanity, it cannot be developed secondhand, at a distance from "subjects" enlarged by separation in time and space, but must derive from some form of active participation assimilated to popular consciousness. "La volonté générale" [of J.-J. Rousseau's *Contrat social*] welds together different groups of society; man becomes both agent and patient, and spectacle is born of the body politic, which itself becomes another stage in the unfolding of the subconscious. (349)

*Fig. 39.* Tony Johannot, *Act of Charity.* Lithograph, 1845, from Goethe, *Die Leiden des jungen Werthers.*

A late rendering of a famous scene from Goethe's *Werther* (1774) that may have inspired some of Ligne's moralizing about life in the garden.

Ligne becomes more and more involved throughout parts III and IV in ensuring that his charges are genuinely employed. He sees in the small scale of his estates a model for humanity in general. Certain paragraphs of part IV (166–68) set forth a Fourier-like vision of his own society that indicates, albeit indirectly, how some of the nineteenth century's concerns for harmony, progress, and brotherhood were indeed derived from earlier modes of thought and action. And when, at the very end, we arrive at the scene of seignorial beneficence (Fig. 39), there is much to be said beyond a mere recounting of the literary model and its influence.[128] Whatever our repugnance at the facility and possible insincerity of almsgiving, we must take seriously its moral overtones, the example of Christian purposiveness that Ligne pretends the garden affords.[129]

Openness and variety characterize Ligne's moral perspective as much as they do his attitude toward the picturesque garden. Only a paragraph before the almsgiving incident the prince makes it clear that his religious beliefs are as free from dogma as were his designs for Belœil (IV.168). He readily acknowledges the need for charity without doctrine, proclaiming thereby that his outlook, though perhaps traditional, is hardly sectarian or bigoted. In this respect Hélène Wahlbröhl, one of the better among more recent critics of Ligne, properly sees in the prince a spiritual affinity with Montaigne,[130] one that is easily supported by pithy sayings from Ligne's treatise, among which he wanted his readers to stroll as through his gardens. In this respect, the *Coup d'Œil* is like a palimpsest of a book of ethics, especially when he proclaims:

let us help one another all we can. Let us render to Humanity the tribute that is her due; later on, I shall return to Poverty that which is hers by right. Let us relieve Misery, but also let us refrain from representing her in oils—it would make her blush too much. But let happiness and comfort preside here. This is the Vale of Tempe. (IV.82)

The Prince's code seems sunny and gracious because his attitude is psychologically correct. And his remarks, though his expression is light and leisurely, are frequently profound.

Ligne is true to himself and to his calling as a moralist when at the head of part III he writes: "I shall preface, or mix, my descrip-

128. So far as I am aware, the literary origin for scenes of benevolence and philanthropy (ridiculed by Laclos in *Les Liaisons dangereuses*) is to be found in Rousseau's *Nouvelle Héloïse,* pt. 5, letter 2. See Fargher, *Life and Letters in France,* 16–27; *Coup d'Œil* IV.169; and *Jardins en France,* nos. 202–3.
129. On Ligne as moralist, see the essays by Paul Champagne and Daniel Acke, both entitled "Le Prince de Ligne, moraliste."
130. Wahlbröhl, *Der Fürst von Ligne,* 97–101. I highly recommend her section on Ligne's *Coup d'Œil,* 51–69, though her perspective differs from my own.

tions with a few principles, doubts, and reflections" (III.1); or again at the beginning of part IV: "Inspire *gardenomania* in your children! They will only be the better for it. Let the other arts be cultivated only to embellish the one I preach" (IV.2). Other critics have amply commented on Ligne's virtues in this rather difficult pose. For he cannot refrain from considering war, art, religion, and of course gardens—no matter what subject—*sub specie morum*. Many of his apothegms are merely home truths with probably little originality. Yet the bias common to one of Ligne's caste and standing helps him not only to defend himself and the best of what he represented but to advance commonsense positions that later generations can only appreciate the more. And everything, even his "disjointed, disparate style" (III.1), tends to reinforce that creation—all in nuances and novelty, because of a format ostensibly emphasizing horticultural concerns.

In the 1795 edition of the *Coup d'Œil*, for example, the garden may be conceived of as a vehicle for political expression, if not as a political structure itself. Several times the prince reverts to the paradoxes, disappointments, and disadvantages occasioned by the French Revolution. But his tone never rises to a perfervid pitch. Rather, for instance, in the remarks about Marie-Antoinette (I.10; IV.78, author's note) or the Jesuit renegade Cerutti (IV.62, author's note) a sadness covers his attitude with the myrtles of an elegy.

Thus, through the means afforded him by a treatise on gardens, the Prince de Ligne broadens the range of his work, creating a dimension that many of his contemporaries, like d'Harcourt and Girardin, might have wished to adapt to their own discourse but were prevented from developing by their lack of perspective. The prince's bemused toleration allowed him to make a significant contribution to the intellectual history of his time.

That the effort went largely unnoticed was in great measure the fault of the times, not of Ligne. Writing at the end of a long development that he summarizes brilliantly, he could not foresee that the gardening movement had peaked just before the end of the century. Because of Ligne's own isolation in Vienna, his telling commentary was refused recognition until a later time, when it was only a curiosity, not a factor in the subsequent history of gardenomania.[131]

Toward the end of his preface to the 1795 edition, Ligne avers that his work is intended to give counsel and example to others. His claim is amply supported by the wealth of illustration and the lessons that adorn the *Coup d'Œil*. And his conclusion, "These are not the tales of a traveler but rather the precepts of a gardener," reinforces his belief that it is possible for human beings, however fallible, to

---

131. As proof of the argument I am advancing, see the anonymous pastiche *Description des principaux parcs et jardins de l'Europe*, from 1812.

build more than a garden—an ordered, harmonious society. These and similar considerations make the *Coup d'Œil sur Belœil* a masterpiece, as Casanova was aware in *Quelques Remarques:*

> The conclusion to this little book is a fine Horatian sermon in prose. It is a lesson pointing the way to happiness, all the more sure as the author of this pastoral is already so. No one in the world is either more happy or less happy than he feels. Horace has said that *sapiens . . . nisi cum pituita molesta est* ["Man is ever wise, except when his stomach is upset" (*Epistolae* I.1)]. The Prince de Ligne could say as much, if the profession he entered at eighteen had not subjected him to the cruel effects of a father's tenderness. . . . The man weeps; then, a hero, takes his courage in hand and silences his sadness, studies nature, war, politics, hunting, the fine arts, indoctrinating his contemporaries through his writing; and because she amuses him, amuses society. . . . this work is bright and good. *Populatrix misit Hymetti / Pallidis et sylvis nobile nectar, apis* ["The people sent the noble nectar of the bee from the green forests to Hymettus" (Martial, *Epigrammata* 13.104)]. (p. 12)

By an odd paradox, however, Ligne's work has often been read in our own time as an apology for the English garden, just as Belœil is known today as the Belgian Versailles. More careful attention, however, would easily reveal that Belœil combines some features of both the seventeenth and the eighteenth centuries. And the oft-quoted line "No rules or compasses" (IV.53) is clearly gainsaid by the quotation from Delille at the very beginning of the text: "I do not choose between Kent and Le Nôtre" (meaning, "I cannot make up my mind in favor of either the English or the French"—with all the attitudes these words imply). And this statement provides as nice a metaphor as could be desired to characterize the prince's achievement in the *Coup d'Œil sur Belœil* of 1795.

# Remarks on the Translation

*I*n my translation I have kept in the title the words *Coup d'Œil,* not merely because of the paronomasia with the name *Belœil* that follows but because, as befitted a man born for soldiering and the martial arts, Ligne was very much oriented toward the military. From the military vocabulary of the late seventeenth century, English derived the term *coup d'œil,* denoting "the action or faculty of rapidly taking a general view of a position and estimating its advantages" (*OED*). Only later in Ligne's time did the expression revert to an approximation of the original French, that is, "a comprehensive glance; a view as it strikes the eye at a glance" (Littré). In both respects, therefore, this word seemed more suitable than Leigh Ashton's term *prospect,* more elegant and familiar, at least to English ears.[132]

132. See Leigh Ashton's translation of Ligne's *Letters and Memoirs,* 89–107.

I have preferred the awkward (but genuine) translation "goosefoot" for *patte-d'oie* but have varied the translation of *charmille* because English offers choices that are both more precise and more colorful: "bower," "arbor," and "pergola." In the same way *pièce d'eau* is variously "sheet of water" and "ornamental lake" and *le bosquet,* "grove," "clump," and "coppice." And though the etymology of *fabrique* ("that which has been created") would more than amply justify using an anglicized version of the word, the eighteenth-century British use—or abuse—of it as "folly" seemed preferable to any other and so has been retained throughout (see III.25). A similar choice had to be made regarding "(hunting) box" for *pavillon,* rather than "lodge," particularly in part II on Baudour, the site of Ligne's own hunt, and in parts III and IV, notably the passage on the Borély estate near Marseille, where "lodges" would suggest something too large, spoiling the effect the prince undoubtedly wished to create (III.88).

Other difficulties attend the prince's inordinate use of diminutives to achieve the right shade of meaning, an end that in his eyes transcends the need to maintain the straightforward beauty of classical norms. He shared with many of his contemporaries from the end of the eighteenth century a delight in the minute, or miniature, for its own sake.[133] Although through repetition this pleasure may sometimes become annoying or seem exaggerated to modern readers, it does allow us to situate him more precisely, especially in relation to other aspects of the eighteenth-century garden that attracted him as they did his age. So we happen on difficult situations, where to maintain the flavor of the original we must accommodate words representing "plashes" or "rivulets" or diminutives of every kind, which today seem affected, or untoward, or merely cute. Ligne's spelling of proper names was often phonetic, erratic, or merely fanciful; I have tacitly corrected his errors according to a standard—though not necessarily a "modern"—spelling (the Russian town, for instance, is Tsarskoye Selo, not Pushkin, in part IV, paragraph 36). The translation of technical terms relating to garden art has been corroborated with John James's famous English translation of A-J. Dézallier d'Argenville's *Théorie et pratique du jardinage* (1728 edition). All translations of quotations, both in the text and in the notes, are my own; those of the classics have been reviewed for conformity with the best available versions.

Some difficulties in Ligne's descriptions—for instance, his enumeration of improvements to be made in the arrangement of the stream northwest of the castle at Belœil (I.27) or his imagined layout for a Moldavian building (IV.19)—are difficult to visualize and, so,

133. See note 64 above.

interpret. My solution to such problems has sometimes been to recast Ligne's phrases and to strive for clarity, even though in the process some of Ligne's vaunted charm and fancy have had to be sacrificed to a better understanding of the man and his message.

The prince, following correct French usage, almost always hides behind the impersonal third-person singular pronoun *on;* but too much "one-ness" in English is awkward and can lead to serious stylistic problems. I have therefore tried to vary the traditional "one" with other possible translations, such as "we" and the impersonal "you." The prince himself uses *nous* and *vous,* though only occasionally. When he does use *je,* the effect can be startling, and for good reason: he wants to draw attention to himself, his ideas, his creation.

Despite what Ligne says at the beginning of part III about his own style (III.1–2), the learned researches of Antonio Mor and Roland Mortier have proved beyond a doubt that very few of his writings were composed under the immediate inspiration of the Muse and never retouched.[134] Indeed, the contrary would seem to be true here, where Ligne's style—light and airy if not superficial—is the outward manifestation of something deeper, more truly philosophic and sincere, as I have just attempted to demonstrate. In this respect, one passage (IV.164) that might lead to some confusion has been rearranged for a more telling effect than the prince was able to realize; it is hoped that the present version has nonetheless remained true to the original inspiration, to the mood in which it was composed, and therefore to the author's intent. Such considerations have also prompted me to capture as much as possible of the playfulness of Ligne's puns (outrageous though they may be today), the confusion resulting from his abuse of zeugma and other figures from the repertory of classical rhetoric, and the tartness of some of his peeves and dislikes.

Additionally, the prince is notorious for his use of neologisms (see, for instance, his play upon the word "philosophomaniac" in II.24, note 22). This was but another fashion of the time that he embraced wholeheartedly. But we can be grateful for the lessons such a passing fancy can teach no matter how he may abuse paronomasia (as in the adjectival endings in the title of his collected works: *Mélanges militaires, littéraires, et sentimentaires*)—witness such neologisms in French as *picnic* (not the modern *pique-nique,* derived from Diderot)[135] in III.46; *gardenomania* (IV.2); and *Gothie et Grécie*

---

134. Antonio Mor, "Le Prince de Ligne, prosateur," 15–37, and Mortier, "Le Prince de Ligne," 221–32.
135. Note also that by 1795 the *sense* of *pique-nique* had changed from that recognized by the *Dictionnaire de l'Académie* (1762)—a meal for which everyone pays his share—to the modern meaning, a meal taken at an outdoor pleasure party.

(III.48). (In my translation I have assiduously adhered to the form *Gothick* as retaining at least some of the flavor of Ligne's—and the century's—meaning.)

In these examples the prince shows another facet of his rich personality. He can indeed annoy moderns by a seeming lack of high seriousness, but such a lapse becomes a telling indication of his talent and cast of mind. For in his personal statements of belief or attitude we find that ultimate validation of this undertaking, where text and author are one, even to flaws of expression or character, whether intended, pretended, or merely "natural."

And in the mingling of sentiment with traditional vocabulary, where the latter is incapable of rendering feeling exactly without wrenching the sense or stretching the reader's imagination, we discern at last the charm of this work. Ligne's genius for linguistic approximation lends itself so readily to his newfound perceptions that we can easily appreciate the uniqueness of his creation. Despite the superficial attractions of his subject, the Prince de Ligne would have been among the first to acknowledge that "the glory of the garden lies in more than meets the eye."[136]

136. Kipling, quoted in Peter Coats, *Great Gardens of Britain*, 13.

*Coup d'Œil at Belœil*

# Coup d'Œil at Belœil and a Great Number of European Gardens

## Preface
### [1795]

*Sit meae sedes utinam senectae,*
*Sit modus lasso maris et viarum militiaeque.*

Horace

[O let the abode of my old age be this,
The guerdon for the soldier tired of
the sea and travel.][1]

THIS WORK, which has gone through two editions, has lost and, at the same time, gained in merit. I do not know whether the gardens I saw twenty years ago in England, eight years ago in France, seven years ago in the North are still what they used to be. Neither do I know whether my own gardens are as I left them a year ago. I have described them as they were when our forces abandoned my estates, my government, my regiment.[2] These pages were composed in happy days, when the world was not sullied with crime and when our blood and tears had not been shed. I wrote names then that I no longer have the strength to utter. Now everything is altered. But that does not change the intent of my work, which was simply to give counsel and example to others. These are not the tales of a traveler but rather the precepts of a gardener.

1. *Odes* 2.4. In his edition of the *Coup d'Œil*, Ernest de Ganay states that the epigraph is omitted from the the 1795 edition in the *Mélanges;* it is not. See Casanova, *Quelques Remarques*, 8:

> The epigraph . . . tells us that the noble author, master of Belœil, does not speak of Belœil, but of [his dwelling outside Vienna] *Mon Refuge!* In all of Horace you cannot find two other verses more suited to this subject, for Horace himself says, in the same ode, that if he should lose his country estate, he will go and seek rest in his old age on the banks of the Galesus where Phalantus, the Spartan, used to reign. This estate [that he has lost] is Belœil; the other, *Mon Refuge.* Horace calls his [refuge] *angulus* [a retreat], and so it is in comparison with Belœil.

2. The armies of the French Revolution invaded the Low Countries after the battle of Fleurus in 1794.

*O Vous que je vois peu, mais que je lis souvent,*
*De l'art touchant des vers le plus bel ornement,*
*Apôtre de Cérès, Archidiâcre de Flore,*
*Favori de Pomone et d'autres Dieux encore,*
*Archevêque du Pinde, Abbé de l'Hélicon,*
*Grand-Prêtre, Chapelain, Confesseur d'Apollon:*
*O Poète charmant que sans cesse j'admire!*
*A mon petit ouvrage, à moi daignez sourire.*
*Sur vous, dès qu'il fut fait, je jetai mon coup d'œil.*
*Je voudrais vous montrer moi-même mon Belœil,*
*Où nos amis communs vous mèneront, j'espère.*
*Et de même qu'à Homère on vit jadis la terre*
*S'empresser de produire aux héros laboureurs,*
*Votre présence seule embellira mes fleurs.*
*Ainsi que le soleil, par votre Poésie,*
*Au sol le plus ingrat, vous donneriez la vie;*
*    La nature s'anime à vos coups de pinceau,*
*L'exemple et le précepte, aidés par l'harmonie,*
*    Etendront la lumière et le vrai goût du beau.*
*Nouveau Dieu des jardins! sans effrayer ces Dames,*
*Vous savez, comme l'autre, en énchauffer les âmes.*
*Vous qui l'êtes bien plus que celui des payens,*
*Acceptez-en le nom, pour l'honneur des Chrétiens.*
*L'autre faisait grand' peur aux bergers, aux bergères;*
*Elles vous aimeraient, et ne vous craindraient guères.*
*Vos moyens sont plus doux. Cependant de l'ancien*
*    N'allez pas attirer sur vous la jalousie.*
*Laissez là votre esprit: il se sert peu du sien,*
*    Sachant que d'en avoir nuit souvent dans la vie:*
*Et s'il ne vous fait pas son premier Jardinier,*
*Faites en sorte, au moins, d'être son Aumônier.*

# To
# Abbé Delille

O you whom I seldom see but often read,
The finest ornament of the touching art of verse,
The apostle of Ceres, the archdeacon of Flora,
Favorite of Pomona's and still other gods,
Archbishop of Pindus, abbot of Helicon,
High priest, chaplain, and confessor to Apollo,
O charming poet whom I admire without ceasing,
Deign to smile on me and my little book.
I looked to you as soon as I put pen to paper
And should like myself to show you my Belœil,
Where mutual friends will guide you, I trust.
And just as for Homer of yore Earth
Hastened to transform farmers into heroes,
Your presence alone will brighten my flowers,
Like the sun, and you will give life
In verse to the most unproductive soil.
    Nature revives with your brush strokes;
Your example and precept, helped by your harmonies,
    Will spread enlightenment and a true taste for beauty.
New God of gardens! without alarming the ladies,
You know, like that other,[3] how to warm their hearts.
You who are more than the pagan god,[4]
Accept his name for the honor of Christians.
He caused great dread among shepherd boys and girls;
The ladies would love but scarcely fear you;
Your tactics are more gentle. But do not provoke
    The jealousy of that quondam deity;
Abandon all wit: he uses his sparingly,
    Knowing that it is frequently detrimental to living.
And if he does not make you his head gardener,
At least arrange to be his almoner.

3. An allusion to Priapus, the god of fertility and tutelary deity of gardens.
4. Perhaps an allusion to the god Terminus.

*Fig. 40.* Gossard, after Bourgeois,
*View of Belœil, with Obelisk.*
Engraving, 1808, from Laborde,
*Description des nouveaux jardins.*

This view is from the garden side
of the castle.
See Figure 49 for a
nearer view of the obelisk.

# · I ·

## Coup d'Œil
## at Belœil

1   Belœil [Fig. 40]. In the first place, nobody knows exactly what this name means. Belœil is old, an old village, so called by my forefathers.[1] And as this book is of a sort that resembles nothing in particular, and as I am writing it solely for the sake of Belœil, which daily I love more and more, this title will do as well as any. Sometimes I give a description of my gardens, my country houses, and my hunting boxes; sometimes mere jottings on the gardens of other nations. Occasionally my remarks are precise, at other times imaginative, whimsical, or even quaint. (I used to prefer pastorals in books to those in nature.) Then there is some fancy too, for I am often carried away by my subject: fables enthrall me, and the gardener forgets himself. Along with all this foolishness there may also be some philosophy and reason. In short (as Martial says of himself), both good and bad are here: *bona et mala. . .*[2]

2   There is only one standard for good or bad taste, just as there is only one kind of music. For a long time, I used to think it improper for people to say: This is French, that is Italian. I would have liked them to say merely: It's good. I might make the same remark about gardens, but I realize there is a certain convention to be observed. Simplicity, nature, and disorder are the specialty of the English, whereas perspectives with straight lines and set pieces are the specialty of the French. Without deciding which music is best or which gardens the handsomest, I think we should make the most of what we have, that Jupiter ought not to trouble himself for long with vowels, or Versailles strive to be Covent Garden.

When I began this little work, I did not know how it would turn out. I was like Fr. Buffier, who used to say: There's something I don't know; I must write a book about it.[3]

3   The glory of Belœil is due to my father.[4] He won thereby as much honor as if he had written an epic poem. Credit for all that is grand, dignified, noble, majestic belongs to him [Fig. 41]. After his

---

1. The name Belœil derives from VL *baliolum* ("small enclosure") < *bajulus* < Gk βαιοῦλος ("porter," or "tutor"); cf. OF *baillie* and the place names Bailleul (Nord), Beaulieu (Côtes-du-Nord) [*sic*], Baliol College (Oxford). See Leuridant, *Le Vieux Château*. Belœil is some eleven miles northwest of Mons in modern Belgium.

2. Martial, *Epigrammata* I.45, incorrectly quoted.

3. Fr. Claude Buffier, S.J. (1661–1737), a popularizer of Locke's philosophy who attracted the admiration of Voltaire; see the latter's *Lettres philosophiques*, no. 13.

4. Claude-Lamoral II de Ligne (1685–1766); see *Coup d'Œil* (ed. Ganay), 13–18.

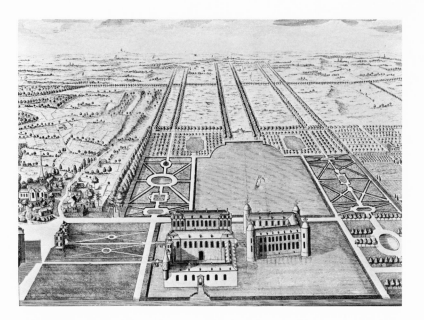

*Fig. 41.* Lamarcade, *Belœil from the North.* Engraving, undated, from *Annales Prince de Ligne* 1 (1920). Courtesy Fondation Ligne, Belœil, Belgium.

The artist known as Lamarcade who drew early views of Belœil had a reasonable eye for perspective but not necessarily for proportion, as evidenced in this and in Figures 42–44.

great ideas, there were none left for me, save what are pleasing and interesting. After all, grandeur and greatness usually grow wearisome. I prefer a song by Anacreon to the *Iliad;* the Chevalier de Boufflers to the *Encyclopédie.*[5] I am easily consoled for not knowing how to write an *Aeneïd;* a little couplet or a coppice pleases me more.

4  A sojourn in the country is never more agreeable than when we see the woods, the meadows, the streams assuming new forms under our hand. Satisfied with the harmony of the majestic proportions that I found in my garden, I have been careful to maintain them, and I have sought to be creative in a different way. I began by pulling down a portion of the main building that did not please me and making a second courtyard; I narrowed the wide moat and, with new plantations, made vistas through the old ones filled with diverse subtle shapes that studiously avoided distortion—a new approach that hundreds of workmen carried out in a manner proving I was right [Fig. 42].

5. Anacreon, Greek lyric poet of the fifth century B.C.. His graceful works, though said to be characterized by a facile style, are probably not authentic; they are contrasted here with Homer's epic masterpiece the *Iliad,* just as those of Stanislas-Jean, Chevalier de Boufflers (1738–1815), a friend of the prince's and the author of light verse and stories (he edited an anthology of the prince's work in 1809), are contrasted with the great eighteenth-century enterprise the *Encyclopédie,* 35 vols. (1751–80). See Casanova, *Quelques Remarques,* 9: "When the author admits his unpretentiousness in this little work, he overcomes the resistance of his readers. Thus we must not hold it against him when he says on page 15 that he prefers Anacreon to the *Iliad,* for he is not lying; he believes what he says."

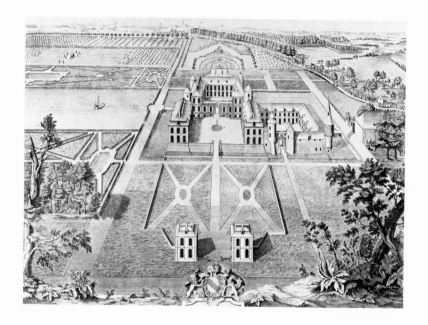

*Fig. 42.* Lamarcade, *Belœil from the East.* Engraving, undated. Courtesy Fondation Ligne, Belœil, Belgium (photograph Guy Cussac).

The modern visitor approaching the castle from the east still sees a view much like this.

5   Everywhere there are ornamental lakes: one is surrounded by a marble balustrade, another by slender bars of iron, partly gilded. I have left tall arbors of elms—fresh and stately but not monotonous or closely trimmed—as frames with which to enclose, in some secluded gardens, Italian, or magic, bowers, with still others of grand and noble proportions. There are saloons of verdure, a charming cloister around a pool, round flower beds, and a little forest of roses in quincunx [Fig. 43]. On all sides flow the loveliest streams in the world, pure, limpid, sparkling, each connecting with the others. All my paths are green and lead into the forest beyond.[6] This French garden extends for two hundred acres. A lake of twenty acres divides it into equal parts [Fig. 44], each part flanked by canals that, viewed from the forest and surrounding enclosures, are disguised as rivers. These parks are the preserve of stags, wild boar, and deer, the overplus of which are turned out into woods fifteen leagues long and six wide. At the end of the large ornamental lake, beyond the drawbridge and over one of the peripheral canals, there is a large goosefoot from which the main road runs 120 feet wide, setting the layout of this forest. I need not speak of the glades, the openings, the broad spaces, the groups of noble oaks and beeches to be met with here and there, all designed to give a view of stag and hounds.

6. "I have dared to seed turf on all sides. My sheep are my gardeners; they make my lawn, or rather my green velvet carpet" (Ligne's note). Unlike some critics, Ligne is careful to distinguish between the garden and the parkland beyond.

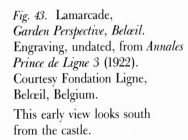

*Fig. 43.* Lamarcade, *Garden Perspective, Belœil.* Engraving, undated, from *Annales Prince de Ligne 3* (1922). Courtesy Fondation Ligne, Belœil, Belgium.

This early view looks south from the castle.

6 I return to my garden. There are twenty acres of kitchen garden surrounded by a wall covered with the finest espaliers. Within are four fountains, and at the center the Temple of Pomona, where we go to eat fruit.[7] The hothouses, a garden of melons, and another of figs deserve, so I am told, much praise.[8] That much has been completed as I write. Here is what I am to do this coming year:[9] in a greenhouse of charming construction, between five little boxes raised to break the monotony (the building is seven hundred feet long), there will be marble basins and a fountain to refresh the eye; and here will grow the earliest and most abundant fruits.

7 A winter garden at the end of the hothouses will benefit by its location. Because of its situation the gallery will serve for promenading in cold weather. Two huge mirrors will repeat the vista as far as the eye can reach [Fig. 45]. An antechamber and a greening room will be asylums for the most valuable hothouse plants until the sun and springtime come to fetch them out and present them to all nature. Inside, the southern exposure of the vault will be covered with glass, with mirrors to the north along each side. Standing at a right angle to one end of this building, and in the shape of a hammerhead, is the gardener's house, decorated in the Dutch manner. There I

7. This temple, a brick pavilion with stone quoins, still stands in the kitchen garden at Belœil. In Roman mythology, Pomona was the goddess of fruit trees.
8. See *Coup d'Œil* (ed. Ganay), 30 and note.
9. That is, in 1782; this paragraph is simply transposed from the 1781 edition.

*13* But more seriously: at one end of my Tartar village and farm a hill will rise by imperceptible degrees, very natural, very real, commanding my international gardens, and on it will stand the Column of Marathon. But instead of the names of the Ten Thousand,[19] it will bear those of Hannibal, Alexander, Epaminondas, Xenophon, Caesar, Scipio, Maurice and Frederick Henry of Nassau, "le Grand Diable" de Ligne,[20] Lamoral de Ligne, Farnese, Condé, Turenne, Luxembourg, Catinat, Gustav Adolph, Charles XII, Montecucculi, Louis of Baden, Eugene, Lascy,[21] Frederick the Great, Laudhon.

*14* At this point begins that Tableau of Human Life that has been finished for some time. Come and walk here, proud philosophers who know everything—except yourselves. I despise your ostentatious march; mine is meeker, truer and will bring me to my end more pleasantly. Come misers, grasping, ambitious beings, foolish preceptors of the human race, stern guardians of others' morals, presumptuous men of letters and false legislators, courtiers and men of fashion, come into my groves.[22]

*15* First, there is the Arbor of Childhood. A little barrier separates it from Adolescence, where there begins a pathway bordered with roses and lilies, carpeted with moss, charming in its freshness, that leads to a confessional around the statue of Love in white marble. Here is the altar, the sacrifice, the oblation—all in one, whenever you will. Grapevines bordering a little walk bring us to old Silenus,[23] crowned with tendrils and holding a cup, which he gaily proffers. We may linger here for a moment, I should think, without coming to any harm. Thence, the same path, rejoining that of Love, leads to a dusky thicket in which are statues of Laughter and Games, likewise in white marble. There is also one in black marble, more serious, pointing to the only trace that pierces deeper into the thicket and leads to a semicircular ruin: twelve marble columns, three stories high, give an idea of the prettiest baths of antiquity without seeming to overwhelm

19. There seems to be some confusion in Ligne's mind between the battle of Marathon (490 B.C.) and the escapade of Xenophon's ten thousand men (401 B.C.), recounted in the *Anabasis*.

20. For more information about this curious ancestor (1483–1531), see II.26 and Ligne's *Fragments* 1:4.

21. "I have included him here, even though he lives on, to the honor of this age" (Ligne's note). Marshal Count Maurice Lascy (1725–1801) was one of Austria's great military leaders in the eighteenth century, highly regarded by Frederick II and adored by Ligne, who served under him.

22. "Thus, the present reader may gather that there were no Monsters when this was written and that criticism, when offered in days of yore, concerned merely attitudes and a few abuses" (Ligne's note).

23. Silenus was a forest god of Greek mythology, depicted as an old man with horse's ears, usually drunk and uncommonly wise.

*Fig. 46.* Sauveur Legros,
*Temple Ruins*, Belœil.
Drawing, 1792,
courtesy Fondation Ligne,
Belœil, Belgium.

One of the follies Ligne
intended to erect in his
"English" garden north of the
castle at Belœil, as imagined
by his secretary, Legros.

this small plot [Fig. 46]. Other statues of games, more pleasing still, point the way to the Cabinet of Philosophy. This is a verdant saloon where a rivulet finds its way through the champlevé of flower gardens or over golden sands and silvery pebbles. Across it are one or two tiny marble bridges, which may also be used as seats. Here stands the statue of Voltaire in a bower of winter roses.[24]

Farther on, at the end of an alley without a shadow, good La Fontaine listens to the various animals of my numerous family and catches their beastliness in the act. I invoke his own to brighten mine and say to him: "Make me speak like your menagerie, your dovecote,

24. "Yes, here, divine Voltaire, I make this offering to you. Though you love only your own sheep, mine come and browse upon the flowers I have planted at your feet. My vassals and I bless him who gave wit to some and bread to others. Here I sacrifice to the author of *Epistles* from Lake Geneva on agriculture, to the apostle of toleration and beneficence, to the lord of the village, to the pioneer of Ferney. If it were only to the author of the *Henriade* and other masterpieces, my wealth would not suffice to raise to him a temple, which ought to be of gold and azure. I would outstrip the pagan gods in ostentation. They would then be put in their place as true gods, and every 21 November I would ruin myself in solemn games worthy of the glory that was Greece" (Ligne's note).

This paean to Voltaire (1694–1778) is in keeping with Ligne's admiration for the glory of his time, summing up what Voltaire means to him with allusions to Voltaire's works (the reference to the sheep comes from his *Epître à Mme Denis sur l'agriculture*) and to some of the practical accomplishments on his estate at Ferney after 1759. November 21 was Voltaire's birthday; for his name day, see Voltaire's letter to Mme de La Tour-Du Pin, 5 October 1775. For further information on Ligne's relations with Voltaire, see *Œuvres choisies du Prince de Ligne* (1978, ed. Guy), 10–28, 228–30.

*Fig. 47.* Sauveur Legros, *Grove Dedicated to Jean-Jacques Rousseau at Belœil.* Drawing, 1805, courtesy Fondation Ligne, Belœil, Belgium.

One of several groves Ligne attempted to create at Belœil in honor of the great men of his time, rendered by his secretary, Legros.

your aviary. Console me, inspire me, protect me, sublime and simple La Fontaine." Molière, in a corner, is laughing at all this and makes me laugh. I think of that great line: "Vous êtes orfèvre, Monsieur Josse?" [You're a goldsmith, M. Josse?].[25] That is what won him the small distinction of being placed here. But before entering the dwelling of the three greatest of all philosophers, we pass on the left the statue of one who was none at all—the unhappy, the eloquent, the stupendous Jean-Jacques [Rousseau; Fig. 47]. He is in bronze because of the blackness of his spirit; there are thorns and some stones on the path that leads to him through a rather wild wood. It is because of his paradoxes and his bad temper that I have put him there for punishment, at the entrance to the Cabinet of Philosophy. From this saloon we go by flowery paths to a funeral chamber surrounded by cypress, myrtle, and laurel. In it is a sepulcher of white marble for which, before building, I took my measure so that I might lie at ease in case, perchance, I end my days at Belœil. For since I shall undoubtedly be as lazy after death as I have been in life, I shall wish to be left wherever I last shut my eyes. Meantime, this last retreat is a long parallelogram filled summer and winter with roses, heartsease, and immortelles.

*16*   At the Crossroads of Sport where I have already described two paths there is a third on the left that, as it rises, becomes steeper until at last it is quite difficult and very dangerous to negotiate (but

25. Molière *L'Amour médecin,* act 1, scene 1, where the line is merely declarative.

only to the eye). There we find a gilded statue of Plutus,[26] in bad taste like that of any financier. Farther on, atop a very tall arch, is the statue of Fortuna.[27] This project is incomplete, however, since on the right, before we reach the arch, the workmen have not yet finished the Cave of Envy, which should be like the one described in Ovid.[28] Trust in the deceitful favors of the first two idols makes people undertake this trip, with small boulders, rocks, and landslip forming so many obstacles. From the arch you go quickly down to that same funeral chamber to which I led you by flowery paths. But instead of coming at once upon the urn and tomb that await Philosophy, you find only a void, represented by a small cliff. He who has preferred high adventure to the charm and easy ways of a calm and peaceful existence will fall. This part is now finished. The following should be complete in six months.

*17*    We shall have to pretend that this small abyss, whose revetment in black rock has by now been installed on the side toward the philosophical garden, is the imaginary moat of an imaginary garden for the imaginary governor of an imaginary fort. From another angle, this group forms a little tableau, which I have tried to arrange according to the verse of Abbé Delille representing a child at play or struggling with its parents.[29] In order to vary the picturesque—but not rustic—style of the bridges in the vale and meadow, [I have decided that] the one passing over the canal toward the philosophic scenes will be half bridge, half gateway. At the angle where the western and northern canals intersect like two bastions, there will be a sentry box; and in this box will be a chamber created by raising half the bridge for defense, not against one's enemies, but against one's friends. Thus shall I be able to hide from any importunate visitor and protect myself. I have extended this tableau by including one of the three buildings that form the orangery. Decorated appropriately in the Gothick fashion on the side that overlooks the main garden, this wing will be in a somber, antique—but not low—style, on the side toward the sentry box. The second building, offering a vantage point over the middle trace, will be in the Egyptian fashion while the third, containing the theater and dedicated to Flora, will dominate her island and baths by emphasizing the background decoration. Painted roses, garlands, allegories, and inscriptions will identify its nature and purpose.

26. Plutus was the personification of wealth in Greek mythology.
27. In Roman religion, Fortuna was the goddess of good luck.
28. Ovid describes the Cave of Envy in *Metamorphoses* 2.775–82.
29. Delille, *Les Jardins*, canto 2, verses 750–72.

*18*    The true Temple of Flora is on an island of turf and flowers whose blooms are all rounded with grace.[30] There is a marble pool set off by a colonnade made from stone to be found on my land. A balustrade closes it on one side. The fountain jet is forty feet high, and as the water falls between the columns, it strikes tin plates shaped like Turkish tents with such force that it sounds like a sudden downpour of rain. It serves to water the myraid flowers and even to freshen the air on sultry afternoons. Truth to tell, I turn it on only for these reasons, for there is another fountain, less furious and noisy, that is always flowing. Otherwise, the noise would prevent me from sitting down peacefully on one of the four marble benches when I go, undressed, to read and hide from the horticulturists or even from people who have business with me. The pool I mentioned is shaped in the Russian manner, that is, with several steps down so one may bathe in comfort, whereas around it there are curtains that, gracefully spread and draped, should protect young Susannas from the curiosity of indiscreet swains.[31]

*19*    The canal forming the large ornamental lake where this island is located extends in due course to another canal by way of a high, broad, and abundant cascade. The water forms in turn a peninsula for the Temple of Diana, a lodging for my huntsmen and dogs, and for the Temple of Mars, a sort of arch-Ostrogothick tower with triangular gables that houses my collection of ancient weapons and a few rare military pieces, the sad reminders of our Time of Troubles. Then honor and feats of arms were in vogue, while we awaited the days of philosophy, good taste, and gardens. Alas! No temples were erected then, for valor and loyalty had their own rewards. . . But let us forget such ideas and enjoy ourselves. Water from the cascade flows from great rocks above that can be used as stepping-stones to a place where we can watch the villagers at play. They are preceded at either end by benches and groves of timber trees where fathers and mothers may observe in comfort their boys' daring, their children's pranks, and the coquetry of their daughters' awakening to the quest for lovers or husbands.

*20*    Near two great trees as old as the land an upper canal, which surrounds my riding stable, is always cooled by a little waterfall leading into it and all the other canals. It issues from a spring that by way of the first watercourse supplies the whole castle—bathrooms,

---

30. The island dedicated to Ligne's third daughter, Flore, Baroness Spiegel (1775–1849); it is now a peninsula.

31. The story of Susanna, renowned for her chastity, drawn from a book of the Apocrypha by the same name, was a favorite subject of Renaissance artists.

kitchens, and barns. Stone balustrades with iron railings enclose and separate these watercourses, whereas bridges everywhere assist us in going from one island to another. On one of these [islands] rise the main buildings of the castle, which has forty-six suites of rooms, twelve of them magnificent and made extremely cheerful by twelve salons in the four towers of the castle.

21 From the windows of the three chief salons, I had under my eyes the most formal and unappealing part of the grounds: a sheet of water without effects, a patch of flowers without grass, hedges like the frame of a mirror defining the limits of the whole. Here is what I did: just before leaving to fight in the Crimea,[32] I made a model with my own hands from clay and little branches on a table twenty-five feet long. After spending five years without seeing Belœil, I came back to find that melancholy part of my garden to the west metamorphosed into the loveliest of meadows cut by banks of flowers here and there, with a river flowing through a smiling vale. I had created a varied landscape for my eye, but not for my legs. I am fond neither of tiring myself nor of tiring others. But in order to get this very considerable flow of water, I was, perforce, obliged to narrow the ground; and in this I succeeded perfectly, thanks to a hidden draw, which, before the water falls to the level of the river below, is outlined by a wealth of the rarest shrubs to one side and to the other by a small forest of orange trees planted in their tubs. Above the waterfall I built a temple to I don't know what god—dedicate it to whom you will—a superb ruin [Fig. 48] all in marble, the columns of which, though well preserved, instead of presenting the repellent aspect of the ruins I know, suggest the most luxurious ideas.[33] In the apse are four pilasters of the finest Genoa marble carved with arabesques; the seats are pieces that I imagine to have fallen from the pediment. This hall, rather vast and paved with marble, is crossed by a small conduit that forcefully carries water from the river over three cascades, each about twenty feet long, between the columns of the portico, or supposed peristyle, into the river below.

22 There is scarcely one statue that I have not changed a dozen times from year to year to be sure that each would have its due effect; and people say I have succeeded. Following the river, which in flowing onward makes an isle of roses, we find on the left bank an obelisk, dedicated to [my son] Charles [Fig. 49]. It is not my fault if Charles distinguished himself in war; nor is it my fault if I gave life to a being so perfect. The father is nought, the son remains, and the

---

32. That is, in 1787.
33. One of the two follies still standing at Belœil.

*Fig. 48.* Sauveur Legros, *Ruin in the English Garden*, Belœil. Drawing, undated. Courtesy Fondation Ligne, Belœil, Belgium.

Another view of the "English" garden at Belœil, sometimes identified as Ligne's own tomb, imagined by his secretary.

hero is everything. Accuse me not, therefore, of partiality. Of pride, if you will, and I can imagine how that may be.[34]

23 This obelisk, also in marble, which we approach through a sacred wood by a path strewn with marble chips that crosses a beautiful lawn, is forty feet high. On one side is written in gold letters "A mon cher Charles, pour Sabacz et Ismaïl" [To my dear Charles, for

34. "Great Gods! How I have been punished for this conceit! But I have not strength enough to change it. What I have added may be seen elsewhere" (Ligne's note). Ligne's favorite son, Charles, was destined for a military career but was cut down in the prime of life, and his father never recovered from that loss. Ligne is alluding here to IV.65, where the inscriptions for the monument are considerably different from those given in the next paragraph. See Leuridant, *Guide*, 60–61.

*Fig. 49.* Sauveur Legros.
*Obelisk at Belœil.* Drawing, 1793(?),
from Leuridant, *Guide . . . de Belœil.*

Before Ligne was forced to abandon Belœil in 1794, his
secretary, Legros, was able to sketch the obelisk to the
memory of the prince's son Charles that had been
erected in 1792, but with a much simpler inscription
than Ligne had originally envisioned.

Sabacz and Ismaïl]; on the second side, from Virgil, "Nec te, Juvenis
memorande silebo" [I shall be comforted, remembering thee, O
Youth (*Aeneid* 10.793)]; and on the third, "Sein Ruhm macht meinen
Stolz, seine Freundschaft mein Glück" [His fame is my pride, his
friendship my joy].[35] I have carried the lawn to the moat close by the
castle towers. I have grassed over two peninsulas, an island of swans,
another of ducks, a third of geese—which latter have a little throne
of four tiny marble columns on a mound of turf—as well as a floating island, a Chinese island, and another island still, on which there
is a very strange building, the lower floor belonging to bees, the next
to birds, the third to pigeons, and the fourth to storks. I thus break
up a mass of water that was too extensive, and I bring my natural
garden, my meadow as I modestly call it, beneath the windows of my
three grand salons. Lest the façade seem too bare, I have had built in

35. This obelisk still stands. The following inscription is engraved on one side:

| | |
|---|---|
| *A mon fils, Charles,* | (To my son, Charles, |
| *Pour l'assaut de Sabatz et Ismaïl.* | For the attack at Sabacz and Ismaïl. |
| *L'an MDCCLXXXXI.* | A.D.1791. |
| *D'un prince valeureux, monument de la* | "O Monument to the glory of a val- |
| *gloire* | iant prince |
| *A la postérité fais passer la mémoire.* | Transmit the memory of him to pos- |
| | terity" [Delille].) |

Sabacz was one of the outlying defenses of Belgrade (Yugoslavia) and Ismaïl a Turkish fortress at the mouth of the Danube where Ligne's son distinguished himself in
1791. The source of the quotation from Virgil is *Aeneid* 10.793. Note how even in
German Ligne tries to make his verse conform to French standards for the alexan-
drine. On the background of this monument, see *Coup d'Œil* (ed. Ganay), 32, and
Kubiček, "L'Obélisque du Prince Charles de Ligne," 12–14.

the middle a wide balcony supported by two large columns in each of which there is a double staircase that leads down to my Chinese island. There a mandarin grotesque holds a large parasol over porcelain vases used for seats. Chinaware paving the contours of this island, a few poles flying pink and yellow pennants, a lantern, and some lampposts help to create an excellent and rich effect. I illuminate everything, even the vale, every night with four firepots placed around the obelisk to Charles, two lamps near the temple, and another at the foot of the bust of Marshal Lascy which is, as it should be, in white marble surrounded by laurels and pomegranate trees planted in their tubs.[36] It shows off to advantage, thanks to a little grove of orange trees rising like an amphitheater around it. Criticism, that resort of the witless, a little subaltern deity worshiped only by those who have the misfortune of never feeling happiness or the very errors of enthusiasm, can sometimes alert and inspire us. On occasion I have been reproached for the names and promenades of my allegory. But strollers who do not like to think have only to consider them quite simply as groves and paths amid shrubs and flowers. I have attempted sometimes to make a narrow place seem wide and to reveal a pyramid in the countryside, creating the impression that the philosophical garden extends thus far. One cutting made to the left, toward the Temple of Venus, and another toward the Mausoleum of Adonis form ensembles remarkable in this mysterious garden, which may be observed without entering.

24    The spirit of detraction is, as I have said elsewhere, the sign of mediocrity. Many of these details will be thought perhaps too petty: playing the genius demands that we call some things trivial. It is this point of view alone that can apply to creative works of gardening and, if appropriate, indicate those objects most interesting to the soul. It would have been easy for me to find a more considerable scale, instead of this debauchery of wit in the little gardens of metaphor, mythology, and morals, and to give up my Tartar park. But instead of abandoning a curiosity seeker there for a whole day, I have only wished to amuse him in a more restricted space where, however, he will be able to see everything within a few hours at most. Then people will no doubt say to me: Why have you presented so many things pell-mell? And I shall reply that I never wished to have so close to home what I might find in the fields on leaving my village. Must we be poor and insignificant in order to have the pleasure of being natural? Since there is neither horror, nor mountains, nor precipice there, I shall not call these gardens English. I desire only that

36. Ligne makes a punning allusion here to the military career of Lascy: the French for "pomegranate trees" also translates "grenadiers." See also IV.47.

they be set out and furnished like a saloon. I do not like one gazebo atop another.[37] Mine are separate, and in the intervening space bridges, busts, pretty intentions (and attentions), neither too confused nor obvious, are treated in a rich and precious manner.

25    In these surroundings, and toward the Tartar park, before you enter the Tableau of Human Life, there is yet one more philosophical scene. In a little clearing surrounded by trees on the river bank the portico of the Temple of Truth may be seen, austere in style, made of great building blocks without an ornament from the five orders but noble and simple,[38] with a little cabin in the rear. Opposite, there is another cabin, through whose door we reach the Temple of Illusion. This construction is made of a new metal that imitates silver,[39] and the exterior is encrusted with pieces of mirror. Between these dwellings, representative of a profound moral sense, is the Philosopher's Lodge, proving that the golden mean must be maintained between the desiccation of too-harsh truth and the misleading brilliance of illusion. To be happy, one must know how to mix the one with the other. The two little cabins may be furnished as you desire. But the philosopher's dwelling will contain an excellent bed, two chairs with rush seats, a table, a desk, and a single book—the *Fables* of La Fontaine.[40] As a crowning delight, this lodge is located opposite the mourza's house and on the bank of the stream that enters my ruin farther on and flows into the Dendre at Ath.[41] By harnessing all the springs to be found in my forest for more than a league around the castle, I endowed it with this considerable volume of water navigable in every part by my pretty gondolas.

26    As you turn around the ruined temple, the thicket on the left (the one on the right lies near the Garden of Philosophy) encloses the Mausoleum of Adonis, standing amid an island of anemone, the choice of which conveys the idea that these flowers are still stained with his blood. Thence we pass to another scene, the Temple of Venus in white marble beside the river Cephissus,[42] which, as we know, compels the nymph to bestow the kiss she has promised. Then

37. See, however, the two Chinese belvederes in II.13 as well as *Jardins en France*, nos. 63B–C, 255A.
38. Ligne refers to the five "orders of Architecture": Doric, Ionic, Corinthian, Composite, and Tuscan.
39. A discreet allusion to the new—and rare—metal, aluminum?
40. In this passage Ligne offers a brief reminder of another treatise with which he was familiar, Rousseau's *Emile*, that recommends but a single book (*Robinson Crusoe*) and contains an attack on La Fontaine.
41. Today the stream is called La Hunelle.
42. Cephissus was the sacred river of Delphi beside which Deucalion and Pyrrha (or Venus) learned how to procreate after the Flood.

side is flat, without water or other notable features, you have to be handsome in, of, and for yourself—as bedecked and bedizened as possible.

Aside from the walls of the kitchen garden in my Tartar village, with openings through which you can see the sheep—and the shepherdesses—go by, I have no others. I have laid out canals for the garden and hedgerows, planted diamond-like, for my four or five parks, and that is all. There is no false mount, no rocky crag.[48] I shrug [at such features] while visiting others' gardens. In order not to weary foreign strollers who would be critical of French gardens that they might not encompass at a glance, I have made available two dromedaries and a cab for six, plus a four-horse *wurst,* to take people over my property as well as into the kitchen garden, my melon and fig gardens, my hothouses, and my model farm. The wheels are broad and do not spoil the grass of the roadways. The conveyances may be had near the bridge separating the regular garden from the irregular. Both are public.[49] But to maintain my privacy, I have two sections of the regular garden under lock and key, with three in the irregular. Their mystery arouses curiosity. Nowadays, since some pettiness is to be expected in people, they still come [to Belœil] seeking admittance; because of my desire for solitude, whether for meditating or for relaxation, the padlock has been clicked shut. There would be still one more [condition for admittance], placed in what I call the Cloister, if we may follow the Turks in their practices.

In one of the two greening rooms in this part of the garden I shall have a little canal built from the pool to a marble fountain surrounded by divans in a Turkish gazebo like the one I painted in my description of the gardens at Bakhchisarai.[50] In the other greening room, as a pendant, there will be still another little canal, a duplicate of the one I have just described, so that around the pool I shall have built, there will be pretty alcoves—likewise in the Turkish manner— for all my exotic and valuable aquatic birds with the most brilliantly colored plumage.

48. See, for example, I.17, II.19.
49. See d'Harcourt, *Traité,* 162, where he too would regulate the use of vehicles in his park. A *wurst* was an uncovered one-horse caisson, capable of carrying up to eight persons, sometimes used for sightseeing in the eighteenth century. The dromedaries mentioned, gifts from Catherine II, were confiscated by the French in 1794 and taken to the Jardin des Plantes in Paris, where they could still be seen in 1810 (Leuridant, *Guide,* 39).
50. See III.93–96.

It is permissible for me, more perhaps than for any other man, to say: Je ne décide point entre Kent et Le Nôtre [I do not choose between Kent and Le Nôtre].[51] And to prove that my mind is of neither persuasion (though my heart is for the irregular), I will admit that visitors to Belœil are struck with the French manner and do not willingly turn from admiring the superb development of my father's work to come and dream in mine. One cannot force men to think; and the greater number prefer looking to feeling.

51.  Quoted from Delille's *Les Jardins*, canto 1, verse 247. See also canto 1, verse 544, and Delille's *L'Homme des champs*, canto I, verse 158. William Kent (1685–1748), famous English landscape designer and decorator; André Le Nôtre (1613–1700), landscape gardener to Louis XIV, especially at Versailles.

26   A sort of tyrant from among my ancestors will also share a nook. He was known as "le Grand Diable."[24] His armor suggests his great physical strength; his numerous progeny convince me of it. Their offspring may still be seen among the superb oaks trimmed as timber trees, which supplied me with the materials for a pyramid I had built. There are a few ancient trophies to his glory and pleasures, but none to his gallantry, since he was apparently ill suited to seduction, preferring merely to abduct the wives and daughters of his vassals. A rock inscribed with some of his mighty deeds and his traits of character, even his rebelliousness, will transmit them to posterity. Once he went so far as to found an Order of the Wolf because, he said, he wanted to eat lamb—alluding thereby to the Order of the Golden Fleece that the emperor had conferred on his brother, apparently more delicate than he, while refusing it to him.

27   Modern advances in geography (which seems more and more like *plain* geometry) are not worth much. Forgive me, Dear Reader, for those digressions that allow me to ignore them. I am unable to resist what inspires or consoles me. There are such things as sweet sorrows in which we need consolation. The slight agitation of brooks, preferable to an overquiet calm, draws me to this capital of my thoughts. Baudour! 'Tis there I return to find myself. Close to my dwelling, beyond my groves and the flowers that grow there without care, perfuming all the garden, all the waters from the upper reaches of my domain come together in a drinking trough for which the wild animals vie with my pets.

28   Nearby there is a small shell grotto [Fig. 56] where the seepage that supplies the pool hastens over pebbles that obstruct its passage only to make its course more interesting. The flow is interrupted by eight or ten little cascades. There are four bridges, each treated in a different way, and at the end, groves that mark the edge of my forest toward the west and north. There are several waterfalls below a bench used as a bridge; and then in the middle of a rock outcropping covered with wild roses, there is a small drinking trough, where the village herds come at even to tell me that it is time for them, like the sun, to go to bed since Tityrus and Meliboeus have seen the shadows lengthening over their cottage.[25]

24. See I.13 and *Fragments* I.4. Since Antoine de Ligne, "le Grande Diable" (ca. 1475–1532), was an only son, Ligne undoubtedly refers later in this paragraph to Antoine's brother-in-law, Jean II de Luxembourg-Saint-Pol (1467–1520), who sided with the emperor Charles V against the Tudor king Henry VIII, liege lord of "le Grand Diable," to whom he (and his descendants) owed the title Prince of Mortagne (1519). See Bronne, *Belœil et la maison de Ligne*, 52–61.
25. Tityrus and Meliboeus are characters in Virgil's *Eclogues*, or *Bucolics*.

29   The brook winds slowly away from this site, creating a tiny island with flowers, woods, and fields before breaking away completely. Little paths bordered with natural flower beds console me for the loss [of more tiny islands] and lead me to a green where benches of grass give on to a superb amphitheater to the south, revealing a fine view over the abbey of Saint-Ghislain as well as over the ruined castle of Boussu.[26]

30   Somewhat farther along, on a slight rise at the intersection of lines drawn from this abbey and the castle at Mons to the east and from two other points in the forest, there is a marble table surrounded by natural arbors that are not, thank heavens! closed off by an artfulness that distorts Nature. Thence you can rejoin the avenue of fir trees that goes from the center of the near façade of my castle and leads to an ancient gateway. This gives on to an enclosure where little paths drawn at random form a sort of maze, as rudimentary as the labyrinth, in an area that is excellent cover for small game, right at the doorstep of my dwelling.

31   On the side toward the fields, the hedge around this enclosure continues my plantings and is one with them until you reach the quincunxes. There is a superb arrangement of firs at the entrance to the forest along the road to Belœil. Near them on the right are stone benches and on the left a shady platform next to little covered lanes leading back to the castle through cropped trees that unite all my walks in harmony. Grapevines at the foot of this platform and in the hollows adjoining the house sort agreeably with the red Turkey wheat that also grows there and a small field or enclosure of fruits and vegetables. Thus have I tried to draw upon all the resources of Nature for utility, taste, variety, and pleasure. A mind open to every enjoyment does not disdain any and, not jealous of what it does not possess, can here give itself over to love, friendship, the contemplation of duty, the beautiful spectacle of creation, or humanity, and the charms of poetry.

## Author's Note

The lesson to be derived from this account of my possessions concerns what it is better to strive after—and find—than to do. The author of a book on gardens, a painter, an architect, an Anglophile, would have disturbed all of Belœil in order to create great effects with mountains, valleys, vistas, lakes, and greenswards that I already have in my natural surroundings. And again there is a lesson to be

26. Today Saint-Ghislain and Boussu are important industrial centers, some seven and eight miles, respectively, south-southeast of Belœil.

*Fig. 56. Rockery, Baudour.*
Anonymous engraving, 1780(?),
from Lerouge, *Détail des nouveaux
jardins à la mode*, cahier 8.

An artist's rendering of the
rockery or grotto described by
Ligne in the *Coup d'Œil* II.28.

learned, namely, that instead of feebly imitating these beauties, which
would have cost me more than one million [livres], you must use
what you have to advantage, either in precious and elegant details, if
a part of the garden is devoted to those, or in picturesque details, if
you have much land. Indeed, the two types should be combined. For
this, I found grace in the eyes of Abbé Delille who gave me immortal-
ity with the verse "Belœil tout à la fois magnifique et champêtre"
[Belœil, at once rustic and grand (*Les Jardins,* canto 1, verse 79)].

I do not like hermitages. They are trivial and facile and always

*Fig. 57.* Athanase Massard, after Bourgeois, *Château de Tracy,* Nièvre (detail). Engraving, 1808, from Laborde, *Description des nouveaux jardins.*

The workmen represent but one aspect of eighteenth-century estate maintenance, which, as Ligne says, demanded sufficient financing. See *Coup d'Œil* III. 39–41.

look alike. Some people possessing barely two rods of enclosed space build a hermitage for show, as they would some mysterious retreat for a master who rests from the magnificence that is not his. The hermitage at Baudour is genuine and would still be in use if the hermit who succeeded the saint I mentioned had not been a lost soul, damned for hanging himself in the chapel (no longer one thereafter), which has now become an excellent shelter for strollers since it is located in a wild part of the forest, half a league from the castle. The other features I have just described are also about the same distance away.

You will note that the garden, not including three hunting boxes, stretches from Belœil to Baudour as far as the cabin that, as I mentioned, is furnished with antiques, mirrors, and old bas-reliefs—that is to say, for three leagues.[27] The roundabouts and considerable arrangements in the forest seem to be but an extension of the park, just as the great ponds, the hillocks, and the moors with irregular plantings seem to belong to a more natural type of garden. Thus, for example, after floating for two hours on my streams, from the ruin of a waterfall under the natural arbors of the pheasant run and past the park, you see on the right, a site more than one hundred rods long where all the village cattle take care of the greenest, trimmest lawn [Fig. 57]. In the middle of this parish, not far from one of the ponds, I hope to build a hangar sixty feet in diameter, with eighteen rustic columns supporting a thatched roof; it can be used as a refuge from storms by the herds and by those, male and female, who are responsible for them.

27. See II.18.

# · III ·

## Coup d'Œil at the Handsomest Sites and Natural Gardens

1 My disjointed, disparate style impels me, of necessity, to prefer the natural, irregular garden. Let those authors who like a straightforward style celebrate the French garden. I shall preface, or mix, my descriptions with a few principles, doubts, and reflections.

2 I do not want people to plant but rather to uproot. Axe in hand, a ladder on the shoulder, let them go into a forest. Let them stop where they find the most ancient oaks and flowing springs of limpid water, now swift, now still, now broad as a river, now contained and bubbling as a brook, majestic if dammed, threatening if merely thwarted. Let these people on their ladder try to discern mountains (if there be any nearby), cliffs, or smiling vales where the eye comes to rest on the verdure of the fields. Then let them open a clearing on to vistas with a mill, a bell tower, a torrent, a turret, and superb coppices amid a handsome greensward. Let the axe continue to clear a place for a dwelling in appropriate style. And to be more certain of the pretty contours of the paths, of grassy saloons, of the location of flower beds, bridges, follies, and sad or happy scenes, let your pencil correct all simple, uncomplicated forms on the plan.

3 Now this is what you must ask the owner of the estate. What is your humor, Sir? How old are you? What is your profession, and how much income do you enjoy?[1]

After these four questions, I would say to the sovereign for whom I would be working, Beware of those who want to create something *pretty* for you. Be magnificent! Taste is oftentimes the child of poverty and grace the resort of those who lack nobility in their thinking.

This sovereign needs a residence; a very wealthy great lord, a palace; he who is not, a castle; the financier, a villa; the wealthy gentleman, a manor; he who is not, a hunting box; and all, a country house, a vineyard hut, a cabin, and a cottage in some corner or other of their domain if they truly wish to enjoy the charms of the countryside.

4 The size of these seats (as they are sometimes called in garden parlance) must dictate the extent of the lawns where they are located.

---

1. "Apropos of this: if ever I find workmen clever enough to carry out my ideas, I want them to prepare miniature models in relief, representing every estate with six thousand to sixty thousand francs income" (Ligne's note). This idea was undoubtedly inspired by Ligne's own experience with a model of Belœil in 1786; see I.21.

5   The residence will have rows of columns and a lead terrace covered with gardens instead of a roof.

6   The palace will have columns only in the middle [of the façade], with two wings and an Italianate roof.

7   The kitchens, stables, and carriage sheds for these two types of building will be hidden in the wood, where roofless structures will vie for air with the trees, the grass, and the pond.

8   For these two types of building I would have only a ground floor with an attic above. Thus, there is more pleasure, more show, greater desire and ease in strolling about.

9   The residence and the palace, built of large, well-chosen blocks of masonry, have no need of a coat of paint. Time will confer on them a patina that will seem ever more appropriate.

10   The castle will have four towers and will be linked, to seem more like a castle, with all the other necessary buildings, separated, if desired, only by a few drawbridges. There shall be two stories and a slate roof. Since it will be constructed of large rough-cut stones or of brick, it will have to have a darker tint, the sign of factitious aging, especially if the site is wild; or, if treated in a somewhat more precious way, it shall be painted with a wash that imitates blocks of masonry, including chalk lines and bluestone frames for the doors and windows. And, as at Belœil, the courtyards, projecting stable pavilions, carriage sheds, and so forth shall be done in the same style too.

11   The villa may have one or two stories, with the roof hidden by a balustrade. All it really needs is an air of cleanliness, but not of magnificence. No columns, but oblong bas-reliefs, with niches for busts. The doors and windows must be treated in the manner of the Ancients, with broken pediments above. The color should be a uniform off-yellow, or else light lead gray.

12   The manor house could be painted in a soft brick color with white interstices, whereas the framework of the quoins, doors, and windows might be the color of gray stone. These two shades go so well together that there is no need for decoration. If you wish [the manor house might have] a garret covered in slate; a balcony above the door; little gilded knobs above the garret windows; or a small tower in the middle, just peering over the roof, with a handsome weathervane and clock.

*Fig. 59.* Jean-Baptiste Huet, *Crowning a Rosière.* Textile, 1780(?). Courtesy Cooper-Hewitt Museum, The Smithsonian Institution's National Museum of Design (photograph by Scott Hyde; Art Resource).

A representation of a village entertainment, popular before the French Revolution, at which ordinary village girls were honored for their virtue. See *Coup d'Œil* III.24.

more ill chosen as the word would be more likely to people a park, thanks to a veritable folly, if some five hundred attractive young people of both sexes would gather at their leisure to see and be seen, to play, or to bed upon the lawns.

26 Residences demand rooms with mirrors, even below the wainscoting and between half columns or pilasters superbly carved and gilded; halls of marble, stucco columns, an antique patina overall, with paintings by the greatest masters, the most lovely tapestries, Etruscan baths, private rooms completely gilded and set with pleasing and voluptuous precious stones; other rooms treated in the Moorish fashion, with indoor and outdoor furniture, velvets, watered silks, taffetas, and so forth for decoration.

27 Palaces will have all that, but without so much gilding, and they can substitute elegance for magnificence. Nonetheless, it will be an expensive elegance, with Lyons or Vienna embroidery, tapestries representing baskets of flowers, vestibules made of cut stone, with columns and superbly sculpted bas-reliefs—details of the greatest refinement, along with private rooms filled with mirrors.

28 Castles may be allowed to have bedrooms with balustrades and all sorts of old-fashioned things like that, the residue of the splendor

of our forebears, as well as paneled rooms with carvings, paintings, and varnish. If the gardens are extensive, some gilding is permissible, and a private room or two may be more elaborate still without seeming to be unduly mannered.

29 Villas must follow the taste of the times, with nice frescoes and columned reception rooms, wainscoting, or painted panels of roses, or the finest Indian hangings, and all that sort of thing. There should also be mahogany or rosewood furniture, provided it is handsome, simple, modern, and graceful.

30 Country houses should have a few paneled rooms, a few hangings, and, for the private rooms or apartments, wallpaper properly decorated with cutouts, rose garlands, frames that imitate Etruscan or Moorish panels, or baskets of flowers.

31 Hunting boxes, cabins, and so forth may have simple and pleasing wall paintings in the public rooms, [while] the private rooms are hung with wallpaper of a single color.

32 Huts and cottages should have much red or black lacquer, with mirrors, paintings on glass, little gilded pilasters, and so forth—in a word, magnificence—because of the contrast and the surprise. This need not be terribly expensive, since neither of these two types of folly is very large.[6]

33 Chinese, Gothick, or Moldavian houses (if there are any) will be treated inside according to the taste of the country they represent, so that the visitor can imagine he is in that country. This style should be carried throughout consistently, even to the clearing where they will be located.

34 Thus you can see that I like only simple shapes, no matter how precious, or rich, or elegant, or round, or square, for I have long detested wood paneling with shell-form designs that are uneven or curved, with the affectation of garlands and ridiculous vases—since before the time when Englishmen brought back from their tours of Greece handsome antique forms. You may also gauge my disdain for

6. At this point, Ganay remarks in his edition of the *Coup d'Œil:* "Two famous examples of the startling contrast between a rustic exterior and a luxurious interior in eighteenth-century gardens are the saloon in 'the Hamlet' at Chantilly (still standing, but greatly altered [see Fig. 113]) and 'the cottage' of Marshal de Noailles on his estate at Saint-Germain (now destroyed)" (277 n. a). See Le Camus de Mézières, *Description des eaux de Chantilly,* and Wiebenson, *The Picturesque Garden in France,* 115–30, passim.

so-called fine flowered wallpaper with patterns and branches, which people want to use for beautifying a salon. I relegate them to wardrobe closets with framed engravings, which I do not care for either. But the wallpaper I have recommended imitates the Stanze at the Vatican, the Farnese Palace, Herculaneum, Pompeii, and so forth under glass the size of the paneling where it is hung in boudoirs and private apartments.

35   The time has come to forgo the Etruscan and the Moorish styles; neither must be used to excess. The Arab or Turkish style, however, can be charming. In order not to expatiate on precepts when I have examples at hand, [let me say that] the houses of those lands are to be seen (at least from the outside) in those descriptions I have composed for the mourza's cottage in my Tartar colony at Belœil and, for the inside, the Turkish room of my "Refuge" on the Leopoldberg.[7]

36   If I may return for a moment to all the different types of dwelling for garden parks, I would advise avoiding stairways. It would be best to locate stairs on a greensward, with either a peristyle for the noble structures, or a vault for the castles, or a stoop or shade of canvas for the others, so that people might climb up under cover while taking the air protected from the sun.

37   To prove that progress has been made in the art of gardening, I think it would be well to trace the history of those who have owned gardens over at least three generations.

The grandfather, whose father had perhaps importuned him to travel before entering the tomb of his ancestors in the middle of his castle, near a well where large stones could be dropped to plumb the depths, was only too eager to dismantle the turrets, keeping but a single one for his pigeons and weathervane. He planted the remains of one bastion with salad greens and another with birds and pyramids of clipped box as ordained by his chaplain, who had the reputation in the neighborhood of being a man of taste. He thought he was in the country because he had spoiled the respectable Gothick appearance of his ancestral home, just as he had renounced a respected order of knighthood to become a country gentleman.

His son, who, thanks to him, is unable for want of funds to become a great lord, turns out to have bourgeois tastes. He builds a regular but vulgar house; levels his property; creates a goosefoot, proving how short he is; hides in his arbors; and cuts up his flower beds to make one dry lake and another that, for only half an hour, has a fountain jet three feet high, the cynosure of all his workmen as they

7. See I.9–11 and III.59.

come from evening Benediction. It's easy to see, they say, that our master has been to Versailles; he works things out in the French way. This man is buried in a modern and mediocre church, a pitiful substitute for the dark and noble chapel where the remains of his own good-natured father were laid to rest.

*His* son runs off to London. He returns. Our young master, say the peasants, is going to work things out in the English way. But he has not the courage to remove the trees from straight avenues, so he traces a drunkard's path through the midst of his bowers and creates—instead of the flower beds that though in admittedly bad taste did nonetheless decorate the front of the house—an ill-kept meadow that he calls a lawn and tries, at the expense of his own father's fountain jet, to make a twisting trickle two feet wide into what he calls a brook as it makes three turns across his so-called English garden.

Blessed be the grandfather! A large walnut tree (or perhaps his wine cellar) was probably all that gave him shade in this spot. Yet he was able to observe for at least six leagues around all those—friend and foe—who approached his fortified dwelling.

38   If you wish to know more about this family and garden genealogy, let me say that a son of the last-named man who did such "good" work made a very fortunate marriage. But he found his quarters too cramped. He abandoned the heights because of his wife, who found the air there too brisk. He built in the village at the feet of his forebears and his fortress, half in the French style, half in the English. He piled error on error at great cost.

39   If you really want to accomplish something along this line, you must have the courage to forget what has been done. Just as it is futile to fortify a poorly chosen city to make a stronghold, so it is better to build where you wish and to fortify afterward.

I would not at all like having to import shadows and water; I would rather abandon the site and seek them elsewhere. If you are not rich, you will still have all that is necessary if you own a neat house with but one story, a hidden roof, a colorful wash, a few plaster bas-reliefs, or a rustic frame; a wide and flowing brook, issuing from genuine rock; a swaying bridge like Aline's;[8] a few benches; perhaps a stone table; a shepherd's hut; a mobile salon on four wheels; a few proud but not arrogant pines alongside tall and simple poplars, slim and supple; a weeping willow; a Judas tree; an acacia; a plane tree; three beds of flowers, sown at random, with daisies on a section of your lawn; a small field of poppies and cornflowers; a few

8. Heroine of *Aline, la Reine de Golconde* by Ligne's friend Stanislas-Jean de Boufflers (1738–1815). The bridge was in fact a plank.

hieroglyphics on a small monument with a couple of inscriptions, for I do not want to abuse this fashion. [There should be] no common-places, no vague or petty ideas, which are often wrong. Do not put a label on each tree. Do not force the visitor to reflect, but assist the lazy. Let thinking be increased, expanded, and inspired. Let the philosopher find consolation in it, the lover sensitivity, and the poet novelty and liveliness. You must always give prime consideration to those three types especially. With all that and an unsuspected ha-ha as a boundary to allow you full enjoyment of the hillsides, the plains, the wood, the meadows, the villages, and the old castles of the surroundings, I would surpass Kent and Le Nôtre.[9] With twenty thousand francs for the work and two hundred for maintenance, I would attract every traveler from at least ten leagues around. Must we be Croesus to dwell in the woods or fields? From a certain distance a house that cost five hundred ducats yet looks odd seems merely to have an air of petty magnificence. A reed colonnade can have the appearance of marble. You must think almost exclusively of pleasing only the eyes. You may even fool them; but let it not be with some sort of theatrical decoration, painted planks, wooden pyramids, and so forth. Such tricks are unworthy, vulgar, and mean.

40    If the owner's wealth allows him to spend a million, he need only develop what I have just said on a larger scale. But let there be no half measures to conspicuous consumption.

He must not say, I have not done this or cut down that in order to save money. As soon as you decide in favor of magnificence, you must avoid all such questions as, Why is this here? Why not somewhere else? and so forth. A gardenist is well rewarded when, sitting unobserved beneath a great oak, he overhears visitors walking past say that his garden leaves nothing to be desired, that the soul is satisfied. Let me repeat: I am laboring only for this. After having been busied but uninspired in town, the soul must be able to take wing in the country.

41    If you are wealthy, I would want you to have an obelisk sixty feet high; three valuable statues each in the depths of its own grove; four handsome, beautifully carved vases; an antique bath; a few ancient bas-reliefs; a balustrade for a bridge thrown across one of your many streams—all in white marble. Leave no stone unturned in Paros or Carrara, and have one of your ships, on returning from the isles of Greece, bring back to you a few of the famous remains of learned antiquity, while another, sailing full speed for America, should there seek out the rarest birds and plants for you. Have a yacht transport

9. Ligne's choice of "Kent and Le Nôtre" is a possible indication that he is following Delille's *Les Jardins*, canto 1, verse 544.

*Fig. 60. Glorietta,*
Veltrusy, Czechoslovakia.
Anonymous lithograph,
1820(?), from Dokoupil,
*Historické zahrady.*

Example of a "detested
engraving" (see *Coup d'Œil
III.43*), representative of some
contemporary gardens where
a monopteral temple
surrounded by a few
plantings was considered
sufficient for the creation of a
"fashionable" space. Compare
with Uvedale Price's
condemnation of "vile prints
of places" in *The Picturesque
Garden*, p. 65, note 6.

whole fields of tulips from Delft and Haarlem. Vary the color of your
lawn with gold and silver grass.

I would also want you to have magnificent galleys, flying bridges,
sluices made from cut stone, bronze busts, a closed saloon surrounded by a gallery of eight columns that support a dome of gilded
copper or a lead terrace. And I would like all that to be spaced over
great distances in your garden, where there should be an interplay
between the water, the greensward, and the finest oaks.

*42* Vary the scenery, O fortunate inhabitants of your own countryside, you who are excused from serving at court or in the army for a
time in order to see to your business! Enjoy your gardens, and then
lift up your heart in your forests! Go there with an inquisitive eye.
Seek out peace and quiet. And if you find them, raise a monument to
the gods. That is another way of developing your garden.

*43* But I find no merit in having the engraving of a famous monument reproduced for one hundred thousand crowns. I appreciate
more the man who, disdaining Vitruvius and the five orders of architecture, is confident of his own talent. Perhaps his strange constructions will give rather more pleasure than twelve Doric columns imitated by rote. Bizarre buildings, without being fancy (which I detest)
or childish (which I disdain), sometimes come off best when set out
on a lawn. The bark encampments of savages, the huts of Peruvian
natives, the retreats of Laplanders, and the tiny palaces of the
Caucasus are more vibrant than eternal parodies of the gods of the
sun, of war, of wine, or of the heroes of antiquity who are not so
deserving as those under whom I served.

Today everything is so predictable that we need new approaches,
new attitudes. English monotony, by driving out the French, has become so popular that we must make "modern" gardens still more
modern by imitating no one. Look at those engravings of the London

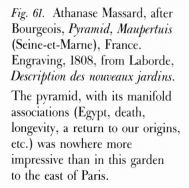

*Fig. 61.* Athanase Massard, after Bourgeois, *Pyramid, Maupertuis* (Seine-et-Marne), France. Engraving, 1808, from Laborde, *Description des nouveaux jardins.*

The pyramid, with its manifold associations (Egypt, death, longevity, a return to our origins, etc.) was nowhere more impressive than in this garden to the east of Paris.

suburbs or of Yorkshire in toilets or in corridors. It is always and ever the same: an open temple between a few trees atop some hill or other. I am truly annoyed by them [Fig. 60].

44    If you must absolutely have a temple, do not be the tutelary deity yourself. Do not let people find you sitting on a wooden chair of the type called, I believe, *une pelle à cul* [shovel seat]. If, however, you have chosen a site for its emplacement so inviting that you must go and hide there, hang it with draperies made of oilcloth on the outside and some rich material inside, so that you can open or close them according to the hour and the time of day. Your colonnade will be more readily approved if you have a beautiful statue in the middle. And the great oaks round about will elicit praise because they represent religious feeling for a favorite deity whom you are attempting to appease. If Christian follies were in better taste, I would recommend them as fervently, for gardens are accessible even to superstition. Whatever your inspiration, you must surrender your soul to it as fancy dictates. And if some devout person were to offer me one hundred thousand crowns, I wager I could create for him a charming garden that would inspire devotion and do some good for the cause of religion.

45    If, since we are surfeited with mythologizing, I should allow a closed temple, do not pay it the same attention in decoration as is usually indicated; house your gardener, your porter, your sheepherder in the sanctuary of the gods. People will be surprised to see there, between two Corinthian columns, the wife of one of the resident deities in street dress, working with truly maternal care at examining and grooming the hair of one of her children. But it would probably be better to let these people lodge with a peasant of the district in a house hidden by some coppice if its location too close to a noble section of the garden is displeasing to the eye.

46    In the same way, people have overreacted to tombs [Fig. 61].
There are kitchens, wine cellars, pantries, and other rooms of a still
lower order that have assumed the shape of tombs. Monuments ex-
pressive of genuine sadness are not included here; I can easily imagine that a somber and melancholy spot should be destined to receive
the ashes of the most beloved persons; but that does not happen so
easily, or so often. For every sensitive soul who has heard of such a
monument and finds it after much difficulty in order to weep over it,
there are several groups of picnickers who on arriving at this precious
repository set out the makings of the lunch they have brought from
town, using the black marble pedestal of the urn containing the remains of the adored creature, now reduced to powder. If there is
nothing in this handsome monument with bas-reliefs, which resembles a sepulcher or a rock cave or grotto, before which there is a
lighted lamp, 'tis but a paltry joke: a few vipers are the high priests of
this Temple to Death, and the frogs are its musicians.

47    Ruin yourselves in creating ruins. Why are there so many remains of temples and amphitheaters that, you note at first glance,
never did exist? The image of destruction is always terrible, and all
these airs of earthquakes are dreadful airs. All these columns, half of
them standing, half of them on the ground, look more like a game of
bowls. These pieces of wall, the remains of an ordinary building, are
still more ridiculous. We are tempted to ask why all the debris has
not been swept away.

48    What are these modern Alps and Apennines? And these mountains that can be carried off in a hod? As an ill-humored man once
asked in complaining about the tiny modern gardens of Paris, what
are these rivers that can as easily be found in a bottle? And what are
these horrors that make us die laughing?

49    If there were enough faith to move mountains, as the Gospel
would have it,[10] I would approve. But I blame fakery and the mania
for rock outcroppings. Do people not know that sham rocks are but
the skeleton of mountains and that however many are brought into
the garden and wherever they may be placed, the same layering of
earth cannot be reproduced as in Nature [Fig. 62]? Do people not
realize that, whatever the character of rocks to left or right, it can be
spoiled by any one rock? I congratulate you if, by dint of cleverness,
you can naturalize a rock enough to dispense the water you wish to
bring from afar at great expense through its clefts. But it will cost you
less to purchase an estate with uneven terrain where you can lay out
your garden, building your castle two hundred feet to one side. Seek
and ye shall find!

10. See Matthew 17:20.

*Fig. 62. Studies of Rocks.*
Anonymous engraving, 1780(?),
from Lerouge, *Détail des nouveaux
jardins à la mode*, cahier 12.

This plate from Lerouge's
celebrated collection displays the
care with which Nature was to
be re-created by eighteenth-
century garden enthusiasts.

*50*   If niggardly Nature has hidden her treasures from you, you need only hire a woodsman for the work I recommend. Let it be neither limited, nor sad, nor gloomy—as it frequently is in gardens in the modern style when the end of a lawn is marked off by plantings. From the house I should like to be able to see halfway up a very gentle slope at least beyond the framework of the trees, for all these lake-shaped grassy vales filled with large and small clumps of trees, with a white roadway across or around them, resemble one another, and though they may be agreeable to behold, are annoying to inhabit.

*51*   I would not be disappointed were it possible to catch a glimpse of some great capital from the house.[11] "There," I'd say, sitting at the foot of some old oak, "is the concert of foibles and vices. There on a parade ground you may notice the minatory air of peacetime heroes nervous, perhaps, about their performance in plays that every day they will have to rehearse." Or again, I'd say, "Those foolish people there are hastening to waste their time at shows that they must know by heart. And others, more dangerous, are running after ambition

11. "Proximity to towns is a disadvantage for vistas and dinners. You should be some reasonable distance away in order to force your guests to spend the night. Only the initiated profit by this, but there are few enough of them" (Ligne's note).

and ready to intrigue against someone in high places. There you see lovers going to profess to several women what they do not believe, perhaps incapable of proving what they claim. And there you see spiteful people, husbands on the alert, wives in arms, out to make amorous conquests." The more I recognize such agitation, the more I enjoy my peace and quiet.

52    If it is impossible to see over the top of the woods or to procure intermittently an opening in some interesting and distant object, I would almost prefer to have a goosefoot formed by three long straight lines starting at any façade of the castle. And so as to be in the shade immediately on leaving the building, I insist on having the forest behind the house. Without the goosefoot, we are once more cooped up in the mistakes of a French garden; and without the forest, we are no less tanned by the sun in going across a lawn than at Versailles.

53    If you are so favored by Heaven as not to have to plant or to uproot or to fell trees—if your tutelary deity has provided you with a prearranged site—raise an altar to him in gratitude in the deepest part of your forest and locate your manor accordingly. Such a place was Eichwald,[12] which I discovered while hunting at the foot of the heights that separate Bohemia from Saxony. The only improvement necessary is the construction, in place of the mill, of a vault beneath the house that could pipe so considerable a volume of water as to make a rushing noise heard for more than a league around. To left and right are the most beautiful green lawns. Behind the backdrop between the two last wings of the stage set, as it were, is a narrow, funnel-shaped vale ending in the superb yet frightening forest. This forest also hides a road that skirts a torrent needing only to be channeled while rising to the source of this wild white water. The fourth side, which is to say, the front of the house, is the handsomest composition in all nature. You would think that the mountains had opened on purpose to reveal, over two short leagues through a large fan-shaped aperture, a pretty spa, famous for its baths and the number of strangers they attract, a sugarloaf mountain with an ancient stronghold dominating the richest of valleys, and then the highest mountains and scenes of cataclysmic destruction covered with woods for a crowning glory.

54    Now consider for a moment the difference between a nature garden where there is not the slightest expense incurred and a natural

12. Eichwald is modern Dubí (near Toeplitz, Czechoslovakia), some forty miles northwest of Prague, once the site of a hunting lodge of the Clary family.

artistic garden. Compare Eichwald with the Duke of Aumont's Guiscard,[13] which I know thanks to M. Morel, who laid it out in an even, elegant, and eloquent style expressing at length what we hear either too much or too little. I think that by dint of attentiveness he has transformed a great garden into a mean, ordinary forest with clearings and, as was to be expected, weeping willows where there is a brook, alders where there is boggy ground, reeds where there is a marsh, and hedges where there are enclosures of arable land.

55　Since I have come upon no detail, no interesting setting, and no mysterious object, I am forced to conclude that all the beauty of Guiscard is the great mass of water in its lake and the great mass of greenery on its lawns. The brick castle does not create a good impression, and its wings, too obvious, destroy the perspectives. I am limited to seeking rest at Guiscard, for this site seems more appropriate to repose than to movement. On all sides the view is arrested by coppices and clumps of trees, and the viewer is hemmed in, as I have said. I might have preferred a few visible openings (or at least the suggestion of openings) indicating how I might leave this place, a sadder example of the English fashion than of the French, where, without absolutely destroying everything, at least a disagreeable two-thirds of this genre might have been undone.

Guiscard in the French manner would have cost perhaps eight hundred thousand francs, Guiscard in the English manner only four hundred. I would thus have saved the lords of Guiscard some million two hundred thousand francs, and I would have left Guiscard as it had been before that enemy of Nature, Le Nôtre, ruined Louis XIV and all the kingdom.[14]

But examine now the side effects of the other style. Look at the works of the authors of modern gardens—part men of letters, part painters, part architects—who have no private residences to build and so outline a project over an intimate supper with ladies of the night, who become their agents. Note how on their scraps of paper a whole estate is turned upside down to represent all Rome, Athens, or Peking by a cliff left hanging, a river shooting through the air, a prison with chains, a sepulchral vault, or a lamp.

13. Guiscard (about twelve miles northwest of Compiègne, Oise) was originally conceived with an enormous garden in the French manner. Under the direction of Jean Morel in 1774, it was transformed by Louis d'Aumont (1732–94) at great expense. It is now destroyed, except for part of the castle. See Morel, *Théorie des jardins*, 263–306, and Hirschfeld, *Théorie de l'art des jardins* 2:225–40.

14. "It is easy enough to hold this against him. Versailles is at the root of those financial difficulties, one of the pretexts of the Revolution, although they would have been easy enough to correct" (Ligne's note).

56  I return to my ladder and my clearing.

After pruning, cutting, and felling trees have made, perhaps, a river, a rock outcropping, or a hamlet worth framing appear before your eyes, you will have the oldest of gardens in the newest, instead of those stillborn affairs whose effects are to be judged only in fifty years.

The massing of color by a great painter, in plantings placed around the manor house as I have already indicated, will bring together by imperceptible gradations in perspective all the interesting features of your garden. Now it is up to the poet and the miniaturist to do their part if you wish to partake of garden wit. But just as you would not wish to own a gallery of paintings all by the same hand, my advice is to seek variety. Suddenly change from simplicity to ornate styles; abandon a wild effect for a more cultivated one. And I would quit one type of work in order to return to it with more pleasure, developing, for example, a French-style grove after a wide meadow, then an arbor after a natural saloon with narrow, winding paths, next a noble and ornamental lake after a great crossroads, and finally a regular-shaped plot in the garden after an odd-shaped pond.

57  I was unaware that in making these prescriptions I was also describing Neuwaldegg, near Dornbach, the seat of Marshal Lascy.[15] There, one league from Vienna, with the silhouette of the city appearing at one end of a valley treated in the manner I have mentioned, are a pheasant run, a Chinese pavilion, a ruin, two high waterfalls, bridges, a grand setting for the gladiator, the temple, airy and open birdcages, vineyards planted in beds, flowers and fruits in patterns, a hamlet with two little houses, a saloon furnished to perfection—in sum, a mixture of greatness, prettiness, rusticity, and ornamentation. Marvelous contrasts are there—a vale surrounded by mountains, a Scotch bath by terraces or gentle inclines, green and charming— severe and sad from time to time but never boring.

58  The owner, while galloping over mountains he denuded as he went, chose prime points as he did in war for cutting and replanting whenever he had the opportunity [see endpapers]. His belvederes are located where he would have sited his cannon. That is what the most fecund imagination of a great man laid out in the midst of woods and wastelands; that is what genius, which is of all sorts, was able to embellish. I once observed him plotting his gardens as he did his victories, and he took possession of his terrain as he did Hochkirch

15. Marshal Count Maurice Lascy (see part I, note 21) had an estate on the edge of the Wienerwald, about five miles west-northwest of Vienna, now within the city limits and much reduced in size.

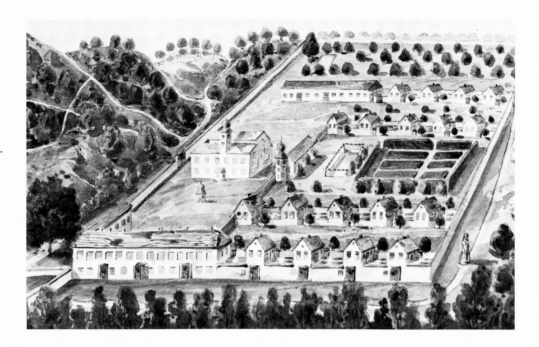

*Fig. 63. Cloister on the Kahlenberg,* Vienna. Anonymous watercolor, 1780. Courtesy Östereichische Nationalbibliothek, Vienna.

This cloister is the site of Ligne's creation "Little Belœil," with the view emphasizing many of the paradoxes of this misnomer mentioned in the Introduction to this book.

and Maxen.[16] This beautiful site is neither English nor French. It is his alone. And because of this fact, it is better than any other. Nowhere else have I seen so extensive a property so well maintained—both that adjoining the marshal's home and the rest of his domain for one league around. From his hamlet, through the handsomest of forests, the road leads to the Kahlenberg,[17] three-quarters of a league away.

On this mountain not far from Vienna the disused dwellings of some Carthusian monks [Fig. 63] have been purchased by a corporation—six of us make up this group. We each have one or more of the several cells that are all the same size but decorated individually, separated by small gardens and surrounded by a wall that serves only to retain the earth toward the escarpment. In one angle I erected a little temple of twelve slender columns with windows between; it has a tin roof with a gilded ball at the peak on which all perspectives converge. I call it Little Belœil. There I have a

16. Hochkirch (1758) and Maxen (1759): famous battles fought in Bohemia during the Seven Years' War, won by the Austrians under Marshal Daun (1705–66). At the first, Ligne received his commission as colonel; after the second, he was sent as messenger to Versailles.

17. The Kahlenberg (1,685 ft.) is a wooded eminence, the last spur of the Alps rising sharply above the Danube plain some four miles north of Vienna. There the Turks were ultimately defeated in 1683, and there Ligne had a residence such as the one he describes here. The Kahlenberg is also the site of his tomb. The Leopoldberg (1,390 ft.) is a ramification of the Kahlenberg. See Ligne's *Nouveau Recueil* 1:67, and Mahler, "Le Kahlenberg au cours des âges," 5–11.

*Fig. 64.* L. Janscha, *The Kahlenberg,* Vienna. Watercolor, 1795(?). Courtesy Graphische Sammlung Albertina, Vienna.

A "picturesque" view of the eminence north of Vienna where the Turkish attack on the capital was finally repulsed in 1683 and where Ligne had a retreat after 1794, the site of his last resting place.

theater in the orangery that formed part of the refectory of those poor Carthusians whom we replaced. My friends and I have extra cells for our servants. The Danube pays us homage, kissing our feet, and offers us, beyond a number of closely packed isles, the panorama of a forest extending over five or six leagues. Vienna is to our right, the Leopoldberg to our left. Two hundred villages and the great Hungarian and Moravian plains, with the fortress of Pressburg [Bratislava] twenty leagues distant, close the horizon in that direction; toward the south it is the mountains of Styria and at our back the forest, which after fifteen minutes' walk under a dense vault of inviting branches leads to the Leopoldberg itself [Fig. 64].

59  There Nature, like the fostering mother she is (unnatural only toward unworthy children), has given up even more of her treasures, adding to the benefits she scattered so liberally on the Kahlenberg the refreshing and necessary vista to the north of the beautiful valley and rich monastery of Klosterneuburg[18] with the islands in the Danube. On the steepest part of the mountain, I have built a dwelling called Mon Refuge in an old ruin, once the stronghold of the Margraves of Austria, cutting windows in walls eight feet thick. If this half circle of beauty and wealth distracts my eye or astonishes it and my wandering imagination, I may rest them by glancing quickly at the hollows of wooded valleys that roll steeply toward the northwest and unfold to

18. Klosterneuburg was once an important monastery town on the Danube, about six miles north of Vienna, where the Lignes were lords of the manor and had a small estate, Dürnhof (Albrechtsgasse 93–95), sold by Ligne in 1767; it is now almost within the limits of Vienna.

the skies. Here I have thought only of myself; here I am alone. It is truly my refuge.

I have a Gothick hall, an Egyptian bedroom, and a Turkish salon. In them are platforms, steps, prettily painted balustrades, precious divans, cushions in the most lavish materials from the East, luxurious ceilings with gilded moldings painted in the manner of the country, quotations from the Koran in gilded lettering and gaudy pyramidlike mantelpieces. I have assembled and outdone the finest things I saw in those small parts of Turkey and the Crimea that I visited.[19] The name Mon Refuge was not chosen by chance. This place is the only thing left to me in this world, and the following inscription on the wall of one of my little gardens merely proves too well what I foresaw:

*Fortunatus et ille, Deos qui novit agrestes!*
*Panaque, Sylvanumque senem, Nymphasque sorores!*
*Illum non populi fasces, non purpura regum*
*Felix, et infidos agitans discordia fratres,*
*Aut conjurato descendens; Dacus ab Histro*
*Non res Romanae perituraque regna.*

[Happy is the man who revives rustic gods,
Pan, and old Sylvanus, and his sister-nymphs;
Who seeks neither the people's government nor the purple of kings,
Nor the arguments vexing unfaithful brothers (promoting civil strife),
Nor (help from) the Dacian invaders descending the conspiring
                                                        Danube—
No, not the great Roman state and the death throes of (subject)
                                                        kingdoms.]
[Virgil, *Georgics*, II:493–98]

Aside from a path, picked out among the rocks with difficulty for descending to a spring I have embellished, I could not have impoved on what I found there. I would defy even the cleverest artists to know more about decorating this site than Nature, my gardener, who cut the road through the woods between my two mountains with two meadows. One is immense, shaped like an amphitheater, and has wings of the most ancient trees; the other has the softest outlines, with a grove in the middle. The only thing I had to do was to add benches and a table. First you meditate only by yourself there; then you see the Danube, seeming only as wide as a room; then a part of the capital; and then an islet, after which there is nothing at all.

19. In 1787–89.

*Fig. 65.* Carl P. Schallhas, *Cobenzl's Estate on the Reisenberg,* from below. Watercolor, 1791(?), courtesy Historisches Museum der Stadt, Vienna.

A view illustrating Ligne's description of the hills and woods surrounding the Kahlenberg (*Coup d'Œil* III.61).

*60* You may consider my refuge to be either the first or the last Alp, as you would. It is neither the head nor the tail of that uninterrupted range that starts from the Danube and goes across Austria, the Tyrol, Italy, and Switzerland.

*61* The first time you might wish to take the air beyond the forest, so helpful in preserving walkers from the heat of the sun or the chill of the wind, there is, sheltered from both, the country seat of Count Philipp Cobenzl, one-quarter league from the Kahlenberg, halfway up a slope facing East [Fig. 65].[20]

A natural vault of the biggest trees, bent to afford protective shelter, leads first to a pond where the water seems to be floating between orchards and banks of shrubs and flowers. Next there is a veritable suspension bridge, anchored to the huge trees on the edge of a prodigiously deep ravine. You have to cross the bridge in order to arrive at a valley, which you enter by following the eddies of a stream. [The valley is] closed at one end by a grotto, a masterpiece of ingenuity—large, simple, high, and majestic. Night and day the water from the upper reaches of the valley falls into this cave, where you can distinguish things clearly only after a few minutes' adjustment.

20. Count Jean-Philipp Cobenzl (1741–1810), a politician and diplomat and a friend of Ligne's; his estate, about four miles north-northwest of Vienna, is now much changed; only a folly remains, which is used as a café in summertime. See Hirschfeld, *Théorie de l'art des jardins* 5:425–27.

*Fig. 66.* L. Janscha, *Cobenzl's Estate on the Reisenberg*, Vienna, looking toward the Danube. Watercolor, 1795(?). Courtesy Historisches Museum der Stadt, Vienna.

A view from the hills surrounding Vienna, with their vast panorama, illustrative of the difficulties Ligne mentions in III.61 that the alert gardenist must overcome.

The short, easy exercise of going up and down another ravine leads to Narcissus's Spring, whence through narrow natural openings there is a panorama of Vienna, the Danube, and so forth that disarms many a gardenist [Fig. 66]. In these hilly reserves I have just reviewed there is not one proud Herr Inspektor who, with the help of two hundred workmen, is going to try to make the terrain more undulating than it is.

62 Sometimes people ask, What is a fine view? You get used to it; it is a joy forever. If you are continually going to the window, I must say that is because you never tire of the wonderful spectacle of Nature. It helps to expand the mind, which is limited, because of the sense of sight—or so it seems to me. The ocean on which our eyes can never come to rest, whether because of its uniform flatness or because of the agitation of the waves, does not give the same impression as a fine decorative skyline. A view over the earth is forever varied by effects of light. Storms and the rising or setting of the sun change, or restlessly renew, the same tableaux. What would you rather do: build so that you can enjoy perspectives over beautiful surroundings or create a garden? If the latter, it is much better that it be hidden, so that contemplation becomes a substitute for that other pleasure.[21] Let this garden be only for meditation. Let it be small and enclosed by a low, lightweight grille. You need only one large tree in

21. The "other pleasure" is probably activity, or busyness.

*Fig. 67.* J. Ziegler, *In the Prater,* Vienna. Tinted engraving, 1783. Courtesy Historisches Museum der Stadt, Vienna.

A view displaying some of the varied perspectives to be found in the still-popular garden park in Vienna.

the middle and, beside it, a small but broad waterfall, two feet high with a bench over it. There should be an open greening room and a closed one, somewhat farther along, likewise hidden, containing a parrot or perhaps a monkey with a large perch near a round bed of flowers, amid which there should be a round basin with a six-foot fountain jet at the center. In all this garden should take up no more than an acre, since all the surroundings are gardens, thanks to my clearing—or to fate—which has set me as an example on two mountains that together gratify me to the full.

63  We own nothing to Art, either. Just beyond the city limits in Vienna is the premier garden of all on an immense island where twelve thousand people, two thousand carriages, and five hundred head of deer go about together amid trees that have seen two centuries happier than the end of the present one.[22] Everything there is arranged in perspectives: river, mountains, cabaret, dance halls, gaming rooms, towers, does, boar, greensward, and forest (whether isolated or busy, dark or open). This Prater [Fig. 67], for such is the name of this garden, is continued (though on the other side of the Danube) by the garden of Count Cyril Razumowsky, the Russian

22. Another indication of the later date at which Ligne composed this section. For the development of the Prater, see IV.119.

*Fig. 68.* Eduard Gurk, *Razumowsky Palace*, Vienna. Tinted engraving, 1810. Courtesy Historisches Museum der Stadt, Vienna.

A famous landmark with garden in Vienna, mentioned by Ligne in III.63.

ambassador,[23] which is made more attractive with the inexpressible charm of an imperceptible slope toward the river [Fig. 68]. Here the awkward Art that disfigures Nature has merely been refashioned, so that the visitor is unaware of the work that has been done. The garden has again assumed a natural air, which only goes to reinforce my precept: seek Nature out, but do not imitate her.

64    I do not have to beg forgiveness from the living for the few exaggerations I have perhaps allowed myself in the course of this work, which is not a work of art. It may be that sympathy with some owner of gardens or with someone related to them has urged me on from time to time. But here, August Truth, I call upon you to bear witness, or rather, that I may be more sure of you, to speak.

I once landed not far from the banks of a river that separated Christians from infidels [Fig. 69], where the heavenly creature I now wish to discuss, who is capable of recognizing these sects in name only, first saw the light of day.[24] In the midst of Barbary are to be encountered rustic promenades that alone would make you love their

23. Count (later Prince) André-Cyrilovitch Razumowsky (1752–1836), Russian ambassador to Vienna, patron of Beethoven, known to Ligne; his estate adjoining the Prater, described in this paragraph, was devastated by fire in 1814. See Lagarde, *Fêtes et souvenirs* 2:59–70.
24. In this paragraph Ligne gives an account of Sophie de Witte (1766–1822), "la belle Fanariote," famous for her beauty and courage. She married first Joseph de Witte, a Russian general and the governor of Kamenets-Podolskiy (Ukrainian SSR), and then (1798) Stanislas-Félix Potocki (1751–1805). The gardens at Kamenets-Podolskiy, overlooking the Dniester, have been utterly destroyed since Ligne recorded this description. See Ligne, *Nouvenau Recueil* 2:125 and *Fragments* 2:44; Lagarde, *Fêtes et souvenirs* 2:317–34; and Jerzy Łojek, *Dzieje pięknej Bitynki* (Works of the beautiful Bythinian).

creator. This person is the most beautiful woman in the world, admired equally by Europe and Asia: C'est Vénus en personne de son trône descendue ['Tis Venus in person come down from her throne].[25] So sang the poet in a hymn to Beauty, and I was the poet. She embellishes Nature who beautified her. You would think that she pays homage to Nature out of gratitude. In her gardens, however, she cannot put the grace of her body, the refinement and details of her features, the charming shape of her limbs, her movements, the pleasures of her silhouette, the suppleness of her wit, the beauty of her soul. And just as in her flower beds you find only roses and lilies, there are only roses and lilies on her cheeks. She has built Turkish kiosks, grottoes, and belvederes; laid out pathways; planted flowers; formed plantations of trees alongside a stream; and created the Vale of Tempe from an awful ravine.[26] She conceived of a delightful bath of extraordinary shape at the foot of a fifty-foot waterfall that descends from rock to rock to the basin where this Greek goddess plunges into the water with her myriad—but unknown—charms. One-half league thence she has created a small colony combined with a sharecropper's farm. There you will find another kiosk from which you have a charming view. From this prospect she formed five different pictures according to the way the mirrors of the kiosk were placed in their frames. Half a league farther on she has conceived of three pictures in yet another, different, style: one is a Claude, the second a Berghem, and the third a Salvator Rosa,[27] which is to say that she discovered various vistas in a fine wood with tall timber trees whose immense trunks hid the tops from everyone's eyes. But Nature—not to mention our hearts—cannot escape her beautiful glance. She built a cabin at one point from which she could observe a Turkish fortress, Hotin. The siege of this stronghold animated her composition when she took me in a cabriolet to the trenches under cannon fire from our own fortress, where her husband was in command.[28] She constructed a brook that seems to follow her everywhere; her rock outcroppings are almost masked by branches and grass. To her composition she added a mill and a singularly pretty hamlet bearing one of her beautiful

25. Although Ligne identifies the verse as his own, it nonetheless owes a great deal to Racine's *Phèdre* 1.306: "C'est Vénus tout entière à sa proie attachée" ('Tis Venus inseparably joined to her prey); moreover, it is but one more indication of Ligne's culture.

26. Tempe, in Greece, was supposed to be the site of the earthly paradise in ancient mythology.

27. For information on these artists whose names are always evoked together by Ligne, see part II, note 17; see also Chase, *Horace Walpole, Gardenist*, 94–99, 120–21.

28. A reminiscence of Ligne's participation (1787–88) on the Russian side in Catherine II's Turkish War (1787–92) when, after occupying Bessarabia, he was present at the third siege of Hotin on the Dniester (modern Khotin, Ukrainian SSR).

Amphitrite.[42] They would not be handsome enough to deserve the statues, groups, busts, marbles, bas-reliefs, and paintings of M. Borély. From every room in his house you can see the ocean in all its different moods, varied with effects of light glancing off the rocks that frame it to the south and even more off those to the north. To cap it all, there are four thousand shooting boxes, a surprise after so cursory a glance at the scene, since in the absence of natural or even artificial greenery, like trelliswork, they are not normally to be recommended.[43] At the background of this superb amphitheater is the superb city of Marseille.

89   If the natives of Provence, less interested in gain, would only sacrifice the silver from their olives to the gold of Ceres's sheaves in diversifying the plantations that would separate these shooting boxes, they would give relief to the view.[44] And if they would rely on the eternal dusty green color of their olive trees less often, mixing it more artfully with their pomegranates, their figs, their poppies, their lemons, their bergamots, their oranges, and their vines, or if God would that I were a new Adam in a new earthly paradise, where without being the first man in the world, I would be happiest with some Eve I could choose or replace at will, then would I prefer this domicile.

Occasional Verses Inspired by a Visit to Provence

*Dans ce pays de la franchise*
*Je ne craindrais point de serpents.*
*C'est de celui qui trompa nos parents,*
*Quand de se rendre Eve fit la sottise,*
*Que les fourbes qu'on voit, sont, je crois, des enfants.*
*Avec bien moins de friandise,*
*La mienne, contente de moi,*
*Cultiverait l'arbre de la vie:*
*Et sans en rien manger, si c'était une loi,*
*Se priverait fort bien de cette fantaisie.*
*Les exemples, d'ailleurs, en pommes sont frappants.*
*C'est à l'une qu'on doit de durs accouchements,*
*Une autre d'Ilion fit un monceau de cendres.*
*S'il est encor quelques cœurs tendres,*

42. In ancient Greek mythology, Amphitrite was a personification of the sea, governing its inhabitants and the waves.
43. This startling detail of "four thousand shooting boxes" is probably not to be taken seriously (no more so, in any case, than some others in the *Coup d'Œil*), as Ligne's playfulness is called forth by a feeling of futility, or tedium, in his description of the Borély estate.
44. In ancient mythology, Ceres is the goddess of grain and the harvest.

Soyez mon Eve, et que la volupté
Qu'inspire le climat d'un éternel été
    Fasse nos soins, et notre unique étude:
    De nous plaire et d'aimer faisons-nous l'habitude,
De peur de quelque tort, sans cesse entre mes bras,
    Bien couverts par notre innocence,
    Vêtement de climat, symbole de décence,
La curiosité ne vous séduira pas;
L'esprit naturel en Provence
Du bien, du mal, tient lieu de la science.
    La meilleure est de vivre entier à son plaisir,
    On en sait bien assez lorsque l'on sait jouir,
Et sans vouloir de Dieu partager l'existence,
    Plus gais, mais paresseux, nous ne mettrons la main
    Qu'à faire beaucoup mieux, un autre genre humain.

[In this land of candor
    I am not afraid of snakes.
    The one who deceived our ancestors
When Eve was foolish enough to yield
    Sired the rascals we see today, I do believe.
My own good nature, though less delicate,
    Would much prefer to be happy,
To cultivate the tree of life
    And not bite (the apple) if there were a law against it,
Since I can do quite well without such a conceit.
Moreover, there are striking lessons from apples:
To one alone do we owe difficult births,
    While another reduced Troy to a heap of ashes.
    If there are still a few tender hearts,
Be my Eve, and let (sensual) delights
Inspired by the climate of eternal summer
    Suffice and be our only concern.
    Let us get used to pleasing and loving one another,
Lest, being always in my arms
    That are covered by our innocence—
    A garment for the climate, a symbol of decency—
Curiosity about some fault beguile you.
In Provence a natural feeling
For good and evil takes the place of knowledge.
    The best thing is to live completely for a pleasure
    That we know enough about when we enjoy it,
And, without wishing to share God's own existence,
    More gay, but indolent, we need only apply ourselves
    To doing better than He in creating another race of men.]

90   When my enthusiasm for Nature raises me to the skies, I fly over all the earth and in a trice go from west to east and from south to north, where my gaze is suddenly fixed. There I have found the most

den is lawn for stud farms or aromatic carpet with wildflowers that charm the eye with color as perfume charms the nose. I have seen the old fortress of Stariy Krim surrounded, as I discovered, by the Black Sea, by the Zivach, or Sea of Azov, and by that august mountain famous for the punishment of Prometheus.[53]

*94*  At last I have found the mythological land that H.M. the Empress of All the Russias gave me, made famous by the Temple of Diana, where Iphigenia was a priestess, and by the cruelty of Thoas.[54] The cliff from which he cast down strangers to his domain is mine. Only the stump of a column remains from the temple. Cape Parthenion, or Virgin Cape, is so called because of Iphigenia. Nowadays the little

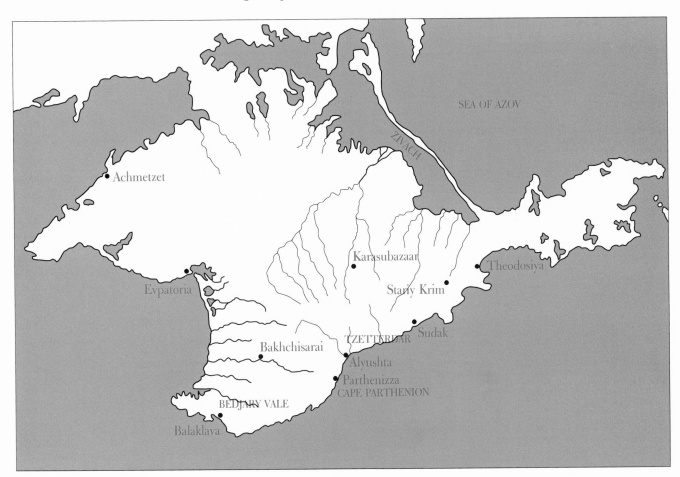

*Fig. 73. Map of the Crimea,* showing places mentioned by Ligne in the *Coup d'Œil.* Based on an anonymous engraving, 1783, from Lady Craven, *A Journey through the Crimea.*

53. According to tradition, Prometheus was chained to Mt. Elbrus (18,481 ft., the highest peak in the Caucasus—and Europe) for having taken the part of mankind against the gods, especially Zeus.

54. In 1787 Ligne received a grant of land from Catherine II at Parthenizza, which he sold in 1795 to the empress's last paramour, Platon Count Zubov (1767–1822). The mythological Iphigenia, after being delivered from Chalcas's sacrifice in Aulis (eastern Greece), became a priestess of Diana, the Virgin Goddess, in this locale, where King Thoas sacrificed to her all strangers who approached the fane by casting them from atop the high cliffs.

harbor with a pretty little village halfway up the hill dominating this amphitheater is called Parthenizza and, excepting the view of two other mountains, enjoys all the advantages I have mentioned. Here I am almost "Sur les bords fortunés de l'antique Idalie / Lieux où finit l'Europe et commence l'Asie" [On the favored shores of ancient Idalia, / At the confines of Europe and Asia (Voltaire, *La Henriade*, 9:1–2)]. I am resting at the foot of the most venerable walnut tree, on the site where, perhaps, Ovid in exile wrote his elegies from Pontus.[55] As I glance about me, I tell myself that nothing is wanting in this best of natural gardens but a temple with twelve columns on a perfectly shaded plateau, two-thirds as high as Iphigenia's cliff. I would dedicate this folly to the empress with this inscription:

> *Dans ce lieu si tranquille, autrefois si vanté*
> *Des Dieux et des Héros, la fable a fait la gloire:*
> *Peuple, voyez notre Divinité*
> *Tirer ici la sienne de l'Histoire.*

> [In this tranquil spot, formerly so renowned,
>     Fables told the glory of gods and heroes.
> Note, people, how our goddess
>     Here creates hers from history.]

On the spot where I wrote this, where two streams flowing past my feet with unequaled swiftness empty into the sea twenty feet farther on, I shall erect an altar to friendship, with the following inscription dedicated to the marvelous governor of this wonderland, Prince Potemkin:[56]

> *De la Baltique à la Mer Noire*
> *Ton génie et ton coeur travaillent de moitié.*
> *Que l'Empire te place au Temple de Mémoire:*
> *Je t'offre un simple autel: il est à l'Amitié.*

> [From the Baltic to the Black Sea
>     Your genius and your heart labor in concert.
> Let the empire erect a memorial temple to you;
>     My offering is more simple: an altar to friendship.]

55. The place of Ovid's exile (ca. A.D. 10) at Tomis on the shores of the Black Sea, though uncertain in Ligne's time, is now thought to have been near the mouth of the Danube at Kustendji, Romania.
56. Ligne's friend Gregory-Alexievitch Potemkin, Prince of Tauris (1739–91), a well-known favorite of Catherine II's and a clever but unscrupulous politician who received great grants of land for his services to the Crown; died in Catherine's Second Turkish War (1787–92) and was buried at Kishinev (Moldavian SSR).

95   If you are tired of admiring, if by dint of thinking of the wonders of past time and of those of the present, your heart, your eyes, and your senses are in need of rest, settle your estates and seek the beautiful Vale of Bedjary. The waters there rush headlong from the mountains to the lawns and the precious trees below and divide the scattered fields of Tartar shepherds—perhaps more frightening than those of Virgil and Theocritus, because of their beards and turbans, but certainly much more handsome.

96   I shall not speak of the rich depression of Karasubazaar, or of the smiling, flowery hillsides of Achmetzet. Yet how can I describe the great surprise when after more than one hundred leagues of desert you descend into an enchanted hollow full of orchards, natural waterfalls, mosques, minarets, tall white and narrow chimneys, and a sort of poplar tree that rises in a pyramid with dense branches? At the same time, what teeming and harmonious contrasts! That is where I found gardens just as the Crimean khan left them, with forests of long white columns and gilded kiosks.[57] That is where I saw rich divans around basins of white marble and where twenty pretty fountain jets showered water on sultanas who used to stop there before they went from baths for cleansing to those of sensual delight. The pavilions in which they were located, as well as those of the Sultan of Tauris, were made of colored glass surrounded by roses and jasmine. Everything seemed to come from the *Thousand and One Nights*, including an old gardener who encouraged the loves of the odalisques. The harem had three or four secret courtyards, with trelliswork in purple, gold, and azure; marble fountains; inscriptions in gilded Turkish characters everywhere; seven or eight little stairways; arched corridors made of vines and honeysuckle. Everything seemed designed to hide, to surprise, or to reveal love, perhaps to encourage jealousy, but certainly to inflame desire and to renew pleasure. At least everything was so prepared to arouse the senses that I, staying overnight in the apartment of Circassian slave girls, could not sleep a wink.

97   And that is the country of wonders, the land of marvels that are not merely cold quotations or imitations. It is the place of origins that produces elsewhere inspired or monstrous copies. That climate is hap-

---

57. Selim (or Sahim) Geray (d. 1787), the last Tartar khan of the Crimea, died a prisoner of the Turks at Rhodes for having surrendered this rich and important province in 1783. His palace at Bakhchisarai was occupied by the Russians, who then set about redecorating the apartments in which Ligne pretends to have slept, which still exist. Charles Cameron (1743–1812) was the chief architect.

piest where you can find what you need in brooks and plantations that protect you from the excessive heat. That whole country of gardens, therefore, justifies my system, which is to have none. It seems that Heaven wished to recompense Mohammedans for not being able to enter in by giving them here below—and in abundance—all that is best in Nature.[58]

58. See Lady Craven, *Journey through the Crimea*, 244–83, and compare Casanova's comment on III.97 (*Quelques Remarques*, 9):

> The whole surface of our globe is most certainly a garden all the more beautiful as it could not be more irregular than it already is. My soul is made for that garden par excellence, Paradise. But to be absolutely sure, I would have to go to Belœil or Mon Refuge, for in truth, I am bored when walking around my surroundings at Dux. Goodbye, Le Nôtre! Until now I thought it was my fault that you were boring me; hereafter, I shall be a proud dissident. I was not really amused at the Tuileries, except by the irregularity of the women I saw there. . . . After all, good or bad, I prefer my own taste. Variety in everything, even the seasons, which I prefer to be irregular. The crazy climate of Paris pleased me more than that of Rome. An irregular life cannot be approved by a wise man and yet is more instructive than its opposite. What I learned by experience forces me to like my escapades. I would wish for regularity only in temperament.

*Fig. 76.* M. Ivanov, *Palladian Bridge at Tsarskoye Selo,* Russia. Watercolor, 1793, from Likhachev, *Poeziia Sadov.*

An imitation of the Palladian bridge in Figure 75, illustrating the far-reaching influence of the model and confirming Ligne's appraisal in IV.13.

strollers and make them believe in a danger that is nonexistent (even without the railing) but charms them (without alarming them). Women like to be deceived; perhaps that is why sometimes they also like to have their revenge. Busy yourselves in your garden. Invite, promenade, and amuse the charming sex. Above all, let the paths be well beaten lest the ladies wet their pretty feet. Through winding arbors, narrow and fragrant with roses, jasmine, violets, and honeysuckle, lead the ladies to the bath or to sofas where they will find their embroidery frames, their knitting, their netting, and above all their black writing cases, from which the sand or something else is always missing—though secrets, ignored by husband and lovers, are always hidden there. Those desks, resting on their knees, will serve them as they tell white lies with crow quills.

14  Sometimes I see plantings of thickets and brambles with thorns; I see people caring for thistles, protecting reeds and rushes; I see moorlands preferred to gardens: that is not loving Nature as we ought. Nor should you believe, my atrabilious lords, that all has been said—and done—once you have determined on a thick wood or a wild landscape as a setting for your castle. You wish to call it a park, while farther on you call a garden what would be a mere orchard in our land. So I once judged the Duke of Beaufort's country house[5] and another where, according to what I was told, the princes of England had been raised [Fig. 77].[6]

5. Badminton House (Avon), site of a fine castle and park, remodeled by Kent in 1745. See Emil Kaufmann, *Architecture in the Age of Reason,* 21–22.
6. Probably either Burford House (or Lower Lodge), Windsor (Berkshire), now destroyed, but formerly near the castle and the Long Walk, a favorite residence of George III (1738–1820) and his family, or the so-called White House at Kew (Greater London), now destroyed.

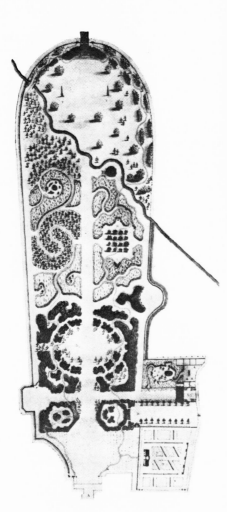

*Fig. 77.* Thomas Wright, *Plan of Badminton House*, Avon. Drawing, 1750, from *The Garden*, ed. Harris.

This plan shows a nice arrangement of classical and natural designs for a flower garden covering only a modest area of an estate comprising some fifty thousand acres, typical perhaps of what Ligne admired in gardens he was able to visit in England in 1766.

*15* I detest rough sketches of great things; once they are begun at all, they must not fail. No ruins of Palmyra in the manner of General Conway;[7] their whiteness, their short columns set a bad example; crumbling arches too well kept become ridiculous. Ruins should convey the idea of places of dignity that have passed away with the celebrated persons who inhabited them. But when one sees the Greekery of certain Englishmen and M. Walpole's Gothick,[8] one is tempted to believe that the delirium of a bad dream contrived the work. I much prefer Walpole's *Castle of Otranto*[9] to that on the Thames, which is quite as distraught, and not nearly so gay [Fig. 78].

*16* Temples ought either to inspire sensuous pleasure or to recall the secret awe that used to be felt on entering them in days of old. But what can we feel on beholding one after another? Their number spoils with templomania those that, like the Temple of Friendship,

---

7. "I imagine that this will not be so easily recognized from my description, written more than twenty years ago, as I have already mentioned. Nonetheless, that will not stop me from playing the pedant, as if it were still standing, and will serve to illustrate the faults I would avoid. I think I have said that, too, if I must defend myself" (Ligne's note).

Park Place (Berkshire), not far from Henley-on-Thames, the seat of Henry Seymour Conway, politician and major general (1721–95), was decorated with follies inspired by the ruins of Palmyra, revealed by Robert Wood in 1757; now a school. See Chase, *Horace Walpole, Gardenist*, 219–25.

8. Strawberry Hill, Twickenham (Greater London), was probably the most famous example of Gothick taste in the eighteenth century. Begun, continued, and practically completed by Horace Walpole (1717–97); now a religious training center. See Walpole's own *Description of the Villa . . . at Strawberry Hill*.

9. Famous Gothick novel by Horace Walpole (1765).

*Fig. 78 (left).* Paul Sandby,
*View of Strawberry Hill,*
Twickenham. Gouache, 1774(?),
from Hunt and Willis,
*The Genius of the Place.*

A general view of Walpole's villa
at Strawberry Hill, displaying the
somewhat attenuated Gothick of
the whole. Contrast with Figure 58
from the same estate.

*Fig. 79 (above, right).*
Jacques Rigaud,
*View of the Queen's
Theater from the Rotunda,*
Stowe. Engraving, 1739,
*Jardins et paysages.*

The arrangement of space is
important in this creation of
areas for two different purposes
(as also in Fig. 131) that lacks
the separations Ligne would
perhaps have preferred.

deserve better. Milord Temple[10] was too much carried away by his
name [Fig. 79].

17  I should esteem the seat of Lord Botetourt near Bristol,[11] but it
has no water, save that which comes down from Heaven. In vain do
we build Chinese bridges over hollows, making believe that water
flows beneath; no one is long the dupe of that. And what I saw of my
lord Mansfield's from the windows of his house[12] is only one instance
of an unfortunate lack in many of the finest gardens in England.

18  The English might overcome this difficulty if it were not a mania
with them to get away from the Thames; they do not know how to
profit by it. The Duke of Marlborough has supplied the want by

10. Richard Temple, Viscount Cobham (1669–1749), creator in 1713, with
Charles Bridgeman (d. 1738), of Stowe (Buckinghamshire), famous as one of the
earliest and most extensive "English" gardens of the eighteenth century. See Benton Seeley, *A Description of the House and Gardens . . . at Stow;* also Peter Willis's
study, *Charles Bridgeman.*
11. Norborne Berkeley, fourth Lord Botetourt (1717–76), the next-to-last royal
governor of Virginia, whose seat was at Castle Blaise, Henbury (Avon), now one
of the city of Bristol art museums. See *The Genius of the Place,* 359–65, as well as
chap. 11 of Jane Austen's *Northanger Abbey.*
12. Kenwood (or more properly Caenwood) estate at Hampstead, near the center of London, decorated for the Earl of Mansfield (1705–93) by Robert Adam
(1728–92) in 1769, with a famous garden begun ca. 1760. See Daniel Lysons, *The
Environs of London.*

*Fig. 80.* Henry Wise,
*Plan of Blenheim*, Oxfordshire.
Drawing, 1710(?),
from Fleming and Gore,
*The English Garden.*

This original plan for Blenheim shows the formal garden to the south of the palace, with walks and bastions (now destroyed) symbolic of fortifications encountered in Marlborough's campaigns providing a base for the building. The whole design has a military air. The grand approach is now supplemented by the Brownian vistas through the triumphal entry from Woodstock. The plan makes clear what was lost—and what was gained—in 1763 with the creation of a larger lake, the flooding of the bridge, and the addition of the grand cascade, among other noteworthy features. Despite all, however, nothing holds the newer parts together, and Thomas Jefferson's strictures still hold: "The water here is very beautiful and very grand. the cascade from the lake a fine one. except this the garden has no great beauties. it is not laid out in fine lawns and woods, but the trees are scattered thinly over the ground, and every here and there small thickets of shrubs, in oval raised beds, cultivated, and flowers among the shrubs. the gravelled walks are broad, art appears too much. there are but few seats in it, and nothing of architecture more dignified. there is no one striking position" (quoted in *The Genius of the Place,* p. 336).

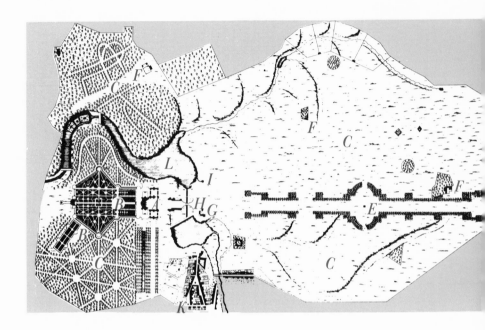

turning a river through his park,[13] where with a roar it becomes both broad and quick flowing [Fig. 80]. I cannot forgive Lord Pembroke for letting his run sluggishly, like a canal.[14]

*19*  Wimbledon[15] does not seem worthwhile to me, despite all the good I hear about it. The house should have been made taller and

13. Blenheim Palace (Oxfordshire), built in 1705–22 by John Vanbrugh (1664–1726) for John Churchill, Duke of Marlborough (1650–1722), at the expense of the state for his victories abroad, especially at Blenheim (Blindheim, Bavaria) in 1704; one of the most magnificent English estates. The effect of water Ligne mentions in this paragraph dated only from 1763 when Lancelot "Capability" Brown (1715–83) dammed the waters of the River Glyme, flooding Vanbrugh's monumental bridge and creating the lake, considered to be his masterpiece, along with the grand cascade. See William F. Mavor, *A New Description of Blenheim.*
14. Wilton House (Wiltshire), seat of the earls of Pembroke, remodeled in 1732. See the anonymous *Aedes Pembrochianae.*
15. Wimbledon (Greater London), site of an important Renaissance house and garden belonging to the Cecils, in the eighteenth century the seat of the earls Spencer; now destroyed. See R. J. Milward, *Tudor Wimbledon.*

A The house
B The gardens
C The park
E The avenue
F The lodges
G The remains of
the old manor
H The bridge
I Rosamond's Well
K Woodstock Town
L The lake

*Fig. 81.* Dorothy Boyle, Countess Burlington? William Kent? *Pope in His Grotto* (meditating on *Man?*) Drawing, 1730. Devonshire Collection, Chatsworth. Reproduced by permission of the Chatsworth Settlement Trustees (photograph Courtauld Institute of Art).

Although it is difficult to imagine that Ligne saw this drawing, the pose and general feeling seem a nice complement to his comment in IV.19.

the coppice more dense. Everything there seems thin and paltry. That is not natural beauty!

The English like grottoes, it seems. To be sure, Lord Tylney's[16] cost him too dearly for the pleasure it gives. I like the one at Twickenham only because I imagine Pope engaged there on *Man* [Fig. 81].[17] He was almost as successful at working on gardens, for his own, though small and today the property of Madame Stanhope, is quite pleasing [Fig. 82].

20   Nor do I like half-foreign things. The Duke of Devonshire brought back from his travels objects of virtu that do not suit his country.[18] And the bits of France and Italy to be found at Chiswick[19] did not please me at all [Figs. 83–85].

16. Wanstead House (Greater London), celebrated for its garden with a grotto dating from 1762, seat of Ligne's friend John Child, the second Lord Tylney (d. 1784); destroyed in 1823.

17. Twickenham (Greater London), Thames-side village, site of the celebrated villa of Alexander Pope (1688–1744), author of the *Essay on Man*, whose garden was considered a major achievement; now occupied by a religious school. See Maynard Mack, *The Garden and the City;* Peter Martin, *Pursuing Innocent Pleasures;* and the catalog *Alexander Pope's Villa,* ed. Morris R. Brownell.

18. Not Chatsworth (Derbyshire), since Ligne's journey of 1766 was in an almost straight line from Dover to London to Bristol and back; rather, Chiswick House (see note 19 for details), at the time of Ligne's visit a recent acquisition by marriage of the fourth Duke of Devonshire. See *The Genius of the Place,* 333.

19. Chiswick (Greater London), Thames-side borough, site of a famous Palladian villa (1729) by Richard Boyle, third Lord Burlington (1695–1753) and William Kent. See Lysons, *The Environs of London,* and Peter Murray, "L'Architecture de Burlington et Kent," 49–54.

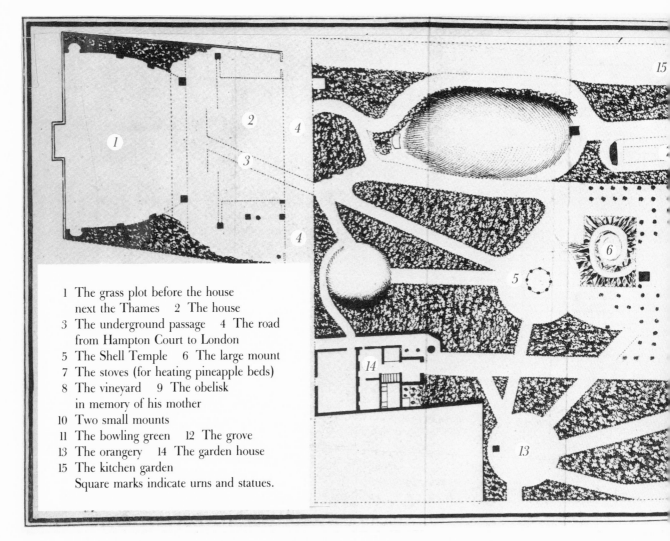

1 The grass plot before the house
next the Thames   2 The house
3 The underground passage   4 The road
from Hampton Court to London
5 The Shell Temple   6 The large mount
7 The stoves (for heating pineapple beds)
8 The vineyard   9 The obelisk
in memory of his mother
10 Two small mounts
11 The bowling green   12 The grove
13 The orangery   14 The garden house
15 The kitchen garden
Square marks indicate urns and statues.

*Fig. 82.* John Searle, *A Plan of Mr. Pope's Garden,* Twickenham. Engraving, 1745. Photograph courtesy University of California Libraries, Berkeley.

A well-known plan of what was probably the most important and influential garden of the eighteenth century. Within a limited space all sorts of polarities are suggested, from spiritual (reason/sensibility) to physical (high/low, exterior/interior,

But what is more beautiful than King's Weston and the view over the Severn and the whole of Wales?[20] What more superb than Windsor?[21] What a forest! What majesty!

21   Such were the oaks that uttered oracles in Dodona's forest [in Greece] of old. I was tempted to consult those of Windsor in like

20. King's Weston (Gloucestershire), created ca. 1713 by Vanbrugh for Edward Southwell (1671–1730), whose grandson Edward, Baron de Clifford (1738–77), was a friend of Ligne's; now much altered.

21. Windsor (Berkshire), site of the most imposing royal castle in England, dating from at least as far back as the twelfth century, with extensive forest and gardens. See Sacheverell Sitwell, *Great Palaces of Europe,* 24–33.

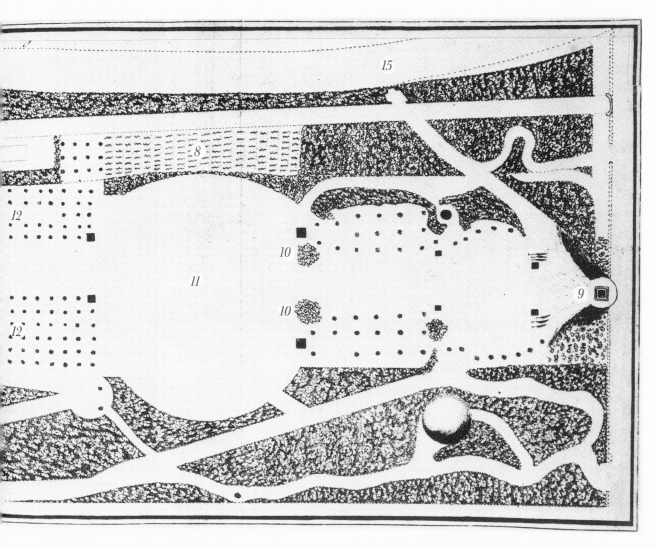

light/dark, etc.) to anagogical (aspiration/dejection). Although the varieties of experience thus set forth are manifold, encompassing both nature and the imagination in subtly orchestrated forms and colors, the later excesses of the picturesque garden are strictly controlled. A remarkable achievement, never equaled elsewhere, either in gardens or in theory.

fashion, for they inspired that awe that used to overcome true believers as they approached the Deity.

22    Blenheim and Kew[22] are best for flower beds and rare shrubs [Figs. 86, 87]. Wilton next, for the sake of its bridge, its mill, and its busts, too numerous even in the house, though I would rather see

22. Kew (Greater London), a royal residence on the Thames, much improved in the eighteenth century by Sir William Chambers (1726–96); see his *Plans, . . . of the Gardens and Buildings at Kew* and *An Explanatory Discourse by Tan Chet-Qua;* Chase, *Horace Walpole, Gardenist,* 158–61; and John Harris, *Sir William Chambers.* For Blenheim, see part IV, note 13; for Wilton, IV.13–18.

*Fig. 83. Plan of Chiswick House*, London. Anonymous engraving, 1780(?), from Lerouge, *Détail des nouveaux jardins à la mode*, cahier 1.

A noble but unsuccessful effort, within a limited space, to adapt the garden to the terrain. There is no central focus, and the awkward architecture of the house, with statuary and decorative elements scattered hither and yon, does nothing to unify the different parts and validate this garden's reputation.

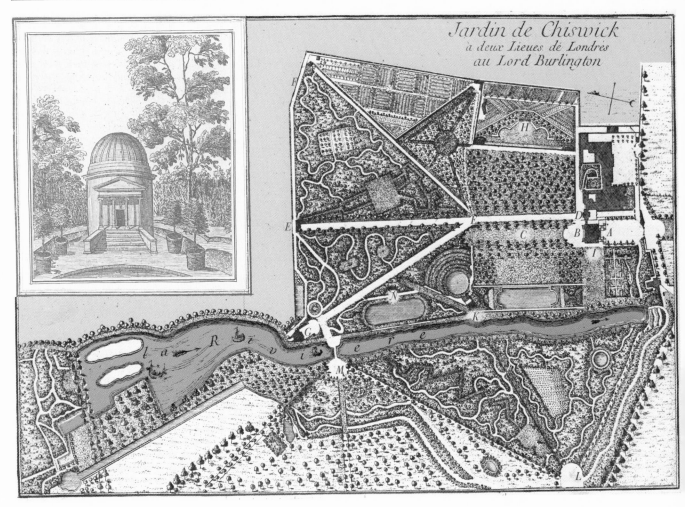

A Entrance court    B House    C Exedra    D Summer house, or banqueting house    E Folly    F Folly with statue in a niche    G Riverside pavilion

H Orangery    I Lawn    K Pavilion    L Obelisk

M Bridge    N Temple    The second E in the middle of the path shows the location of a goosefoot. The river ends at the right in a cascade and grotto.

*Fig. 84.* William Kent, *The Exedra at Chiswick House,* London. Drawing, 1730. Devonshire Collection, Chatsworth. Reproduced by permission of the Chatsworth Settlement Trustees (photograph Courtauld Institute of Art).

A classic example of "bits of France and Italy" in the landscape, as criticized by Ligne in IV.20.

them in the gardens. Lastly, the lodge of the Duke of Cumberland.[23] These are what gave me the greatest pleasure in England.

23    I do not speak here of the architecture of the country. The heaviness of Sir John Vanbrugh is as well known as his epitaph, which is an excellent joke.[24] Inigo Jones, noble and simple in his work, is the last to have done honor to England in this style. He has imitated the antique rather too closely in his narrow doors and windows. Greenwich[25] would have done him more credit, it seems to me, if he had joined the two wings in a wood representing the Elysian Fields at the lower end, with a superb temple cum mausoleum, filled with urns to receive the ashes of the brave sailors who are the honor and substance of the kingdom and the admiration of foreigners.

23. Cumberland Lodge (or Byefield House), in Windsor Great Park, some two miles from the famous castle, was long the home of William Augustus, Duke of Cumberland (1721–65), third son of George II, who, with Thomas Sandby (1721–98), laid out nearby the romantic lake called Virginia Water ca. 1760.
24. Sir John Vanbrugh, celebrated dramatic author and architect, whose epitaph by Abel Evans (*not* by Swift) runs: "Lie heavy on him earth, for he / Laid many a heavy load on thee." His own dwelling, Vanbrugh Castle, still stands near Blackheath, London.
25. Inigo Jones (1573–1652), celebrated classicizing architect and decorator, worked on the Queen's House, Greenwich (Greater London), from 1617 to 1637.

*Fig. 85.* Peter Rysbrack, *Canal and Bridge at Chiswick House,*
London. Engraving, 1730(?), from *Jardins et paysages.*

A more conventional view of the gardens at Chiswick, which satisfied Ligne no better than the statuary in Figure 84.

24    I have said nothing of Syon House,[26] formerly a Catholic convent, then the residence of Cardinal Wolsey, and now the property of the Duchess of Northumberland. It is not yet finished, but when it is, it will surely be deserving of praise. It stands on the bank of the Thames, with a splendid view of Richmond and the little house of Milady Harrington.[27]

25    Those who can call to mind the sublime and stupendous scenes of Shakespeare and the grotesques by the author of *Hudibras*[28] will have some idea of them in the gardens of England, as well as in her morals, medicine, and philosophy. We have a great obligation to the English; even their faults are virtues. I defy anyone to work really well with Nature who has not been in England, if only to learn neatness. Go into the finest palace precincts of France or into the residences of the empire, for instance; I think more highly of the suburban pleasure garden of a London cobbler, where the furniture is polished like

26. Syon House (Greater London), formerly a Brigittine convent, escheated to the earls of Northumberland in 1557; renovated by Robert Adam (1728–92) in 1762, with gardens by "Capability" Brown dating from the same period. See Sacheverell Sitwell, *Great Houses of Europe*, 258–67.

27. From 1756 to her death, Caroline Fitzroy, second Countess Harrington (1725–84), dwelt at Petersham Lodge, Richmond (Greater London), across the river from Pope's villa at Twickenham. It is a moot point whether even at the time of Ligne's visit this estate could be viewed from Syon House, as Ligne suggests here. See Walpole's letter to George Montagu, 23 June 1750, and Lysons, *The Environs of London*, 1:399–400. This information was kindly supplied by Professor Morris Brownell, University of Nevada, Reno.

28. *Hudibras*, a long satirical poem against the Puritans by Samuel Butler (1612–80).

*Fig. 87.* William Chambers, *View of Kew Gardens.*
Engraving, 1763, from Chambers,
*Plans . . . of the Gardens and Buildings at Kew.*

A classic view of Kew Gardens in the eighteenth century with the Moorish Pavilion, Pagoda, and Mosque, prototypes that were to be the undoing of gardenomania with their heteroclite combination of exotica. Ligne criticizes them indirectly in IV.22.

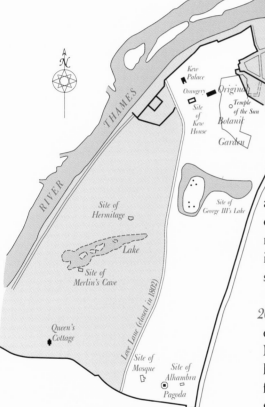

*Fig. 86.* After E. Goldring, *Plan of Kew Gardens,* London. Drawing, 1908(?), based on Bean, *The Royal Botanic Gardens, Kew.*

The screened area is the new portion of the gardens.

a snuffbox, the turf like a billiard table, and the shrubs like the combed hair of a pretty woman. It is neatness that I commend the most. Without it, a man should quit the fields, which he is not fit to inhabit, and contribute to the increase of filth in great cities, where some will rub off on his soul, which will thereby lose its purity.

26  If it were not so damp, England would perhaps be the country of eclogues. There I was tempted to seek Tityrus, the bad example for Menalchas and Meliboeus.[29] It seemed to me I could hear their challenges to learning and love. I could have lent my ear to inaudible flute concerts, while on their handsome greens I might have wished to see them sing to shepherds about the faithfulness of their mistresses . . . and their dogs. But in England, shepherds are not so meek as their sheep, and the tender trilling of the flute was not made for these insular creatures. Only in more favored climes can the flame of Corydon and the demands of Alexis be sung. The heat of the day brings a sort of voluptuousness to the respite love requires: it is almost pleasurable to suffer for love. To it alone are due those feelings that do not suit other zones.

29. Characters in Virgil's *Eclogues,* or *Bucolics,* as are, later in this paragraph, Corydon and Alexis.

*Fig. 88.* G. Coronelli, *Casa Giovanelli on the Brenta,* Venice. Engraving, 1730(?), from Coronelli, *Ville del Brenta.* Photograph courtesy Archivo Fotografico Correr, Venice.

One of several villas on the Brenta whose gardens Ligne criticized in IV.27 for their too-rigid formal layout.

27  Italy is the country where once they most understood this phenomenon. But what are they doing there now? No more turf; no more Sabine valley, as in the days of Horace;[30] even charming Tiber is no more! What has become of the spot that he paints so well as a natural garden?

> *Quo pinus ingens, albaque populus*
> *Umbram hospitalem consociare amant*
> *Ramis? Quid obliquo laborat*
> *Lympha fuga trepidare rivo?*

> [Where the pine tree, raising its proud head,
> And the white poplar like to mingle their hospitable shade,
>     And the brook struggles to flee,
> Murmuring, from the constricting bank.]
>                                        [Horace, *Odes,* 2.3.]

Perhaps it was this ode that suggested the idea of their gardens to the English, for they all have Horace in their heads as well as Homer and Virgil. It seems as though the climate must have changed. The Romans owed their carpets of green—which have since disappeared—to the snow. *Solvitur hiems* [The winter is thawing], sang Horace at one time; *diffugere nives* [the snow is gone], at another.[31] But in Italy I saw only tracks between French flower beds, with burned lawns and misshapen trees in the Colonna gardens near

30. See Horace's *Epistles* 1.16.
31. Horace, *Odes* 1.4 and 4.7.

YEKATERININSKY PARK:

1 Yekaterininsky Palace   2 Circumference
3 Agate Pavilion   4 Cameron Gallery
5 Ramp   6 Grotto   7 Large Orangery
8 Hermitage   9 Admiralty and Aviary
10 Rostral or Chesmé Column   11 Turkish Bath
12 Palladian Bridge   13 Tower Ruin
14 Milkmaid Fountain   15 Monument to Lanskoy
16 Concert Hall   17 Creaking Pavilion
18 Large Folly   19 Chinese Village
20 Cross Bridge   21 Aleksandrovsky Palace

*Fig. 89. Plan of Tsarskoye Selo*, Russia. Anonymous drawing, 1970(?), from Kennett, *The Palaces of Leningrad.*

It is almost impossible to imagine the challenge to the designer(s) of this park. On a small plan, the project appears nicely coordinated, and some of the individual parts, as Ligne says, merit consideration. But in extent and disparateness the ensemble outstrips all but the largest estates, like the Esterházy's in Hungary (see IV.113), making it something of a *monstre sacré.*

Parma or at the Case Pisani, Giovanelli, and so forth on the Brenta.[32] The Italians, magnificent in their lodgings, no matter how uncomfortable, build handsome façades fit only for sightseers [Fig. 88]. They create naught but staircases and peristyles. I have said elsewhere[33] what their fathers did for pleasure and convenience in a countryside they loved as dearly as the present generation detests it.

32. The Palazzo Colonna (Parma) is an imposing heteroclite pile in seemingly neoclassical style, with parts dating from the Renaissance and formal gardens; perhaps Ligne is thinking, rather, of the grounds, designed by Ennemond Petitot (1727–1801) in 1762, adjoining the elegant Casino of Charles de Wailly (1729–98). There are several Case Pisani. Undoubtedly Ligne refers here to one by Girolamo Frigimelica (1653–1732) and Francesco-Maria Preti (1701–74) on the Brenta at Strà (1730), with imposing colonnades, reflecting pools, and stables; see Nigel Nicolson, *Great Houses of the Western World*, 220–27. Casa Giovanelli refers to a country seat by Giorgio Massari (1686–1766), not far from the Casa Pisani at Noventa Padovana, renovated in 1738, with a superb park; recently destroyed. See Vincenzo Coronelli, *Ville del Brenta*, 160; and M. Muraro, *Venetian Villas*, 358–476. Information kindly provided by the late Professor Arnolfo Ferruolo, Berkeley.

33. The references to Italian patriotism and creativity are vague in the 1795 edition of the *Coup d'Œil*, but see III.2; and Casanova, *Quelques Remarques*, 6–7.

*Fig. 90.* Vorobiev, *Cameron Gallery,*
Tsarskoye Selo. Lithograph,
1820(?), from Kennett,
*The Palaces of Leningrad.*

One of the grander features of
the palace at Tsarskoye Selo,
mentioned by Ligne in IV.28.

28    Indifference to the god of taste in the south of Europe has determined him on a rash act. Although sensitive to the cold, he has
passed to the north. On arrival, he had an audience with the Empress of Russia. They understood each other on the spot. He became
her bostangi-pasha;[34] or rather, the conqueror of the Turks is herself
the gardener of Tsarskoye Selo [Fig. 89].[35] The legislatrix of the greatest of empires, the support—or the terror—of her neighbors, sows
her own lawns. The homage her great spirit renders to those who
have extended her glory even to the gates of the Orient is as great an
honor for her as for her glorious generals. Tsarskoye Selo, which
contains what the empress calls her fancies, presents on all sides the
most charming of pictures. These fancies, so-called, are water and
optical effects, well imagined and varied, such as a bridge of Siberian
marble in an architecture styled by Palladio, baths, a Turkish pavilion, the Admiralty—a sort of town that has been set up—iron gates, a
ruin, monuments to the victories of Roumianzov and Orlov, a superb

34. From the Turkish for "keeper of the garden," a term later designating the
Ottoman captain of the palace guard, used here ironically by Ligne.
35. Tsarskoye Selo (modern Pushkin, USSR) is a vast assemblage of palaces and
outbuildings with two extensive parks. Founded by Catherine I, some thirteen
miles south of Leningrad, it was developed as it now is by Bartolomeo-Francesco
Rastrelli (1700–1771) and Charles Cameron for Catherine II from 1765 to her
death in 1796. For this and the Russian estates that follow, see Kennett, *The
Palaces of Leningrad,* 120–233 passim.

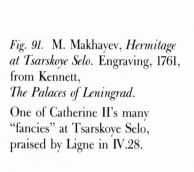

*Fig. 91.* M. Makhayev, *Hermitage at Tsarskoye Selo*. Engraving, 1761, from Kennett, *The Palaces of Leningrad*.

One of Catherine II's many "fancies" at Tsarskoye Selo, praised by Ligne in IV.28.

rostral column in the middle of the lake to commemorate Chesmé;[36] on the bank a charming building; agreeable contours everywhere, quantities of flowers and exotic shrubs, lawns as well kept and as fine as those of England, Chinese bridges and kiosks, a temple with thirty-two marble columns, a colonnade, and, above all, the grand staircase of Hercules on the garden side—all of which makes this the most interesting park in the world [Figs. 90, 91]. It is here that the great princess, dropping for a moment the reins of government, takes up a pencil, a rake, a pruning hook, which, however, she does not handle as she would a sword if destiny had not made her, for the honor of her sex, a woman.

29 Peterhof[37] is two leagues from Tsarskoye Selo [Fig. 92]. It is the most imperial dwelling of all the summer residences of the court, consequently the least gay. The pretty Dutch style in which Peter the Great began it is visible as well as the enlargement of his ideas from

36. Famous generals under Catherine II. Peter Roumianzov (1735–96), renowned for his victory over the Turks at Kinburn (Ukrainian SSR) in 1774, and Alexis Orlov (1737–1808), for his naval victory at Chesmé (near Chios, Greece) in 1770.
37. Peterhof (modern Petrodvorets, USSR), a palace and park on the Gulf of Finland, about thirteen miles west of Leningrad; the main castle built for Peter the Great in 1720, enlarged by Catherine II, and destroyed in World War II, though now happily rebuilt with its marvelous statues and fountains.

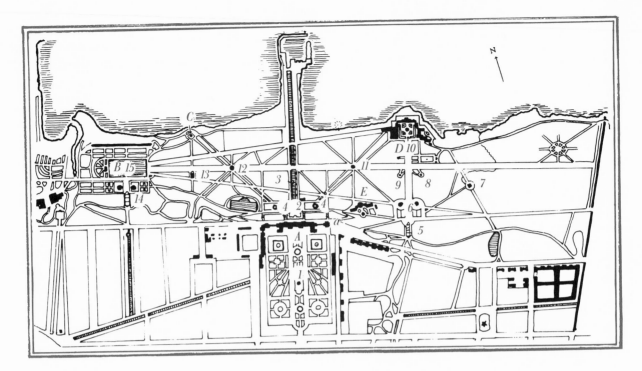

A  Great Palace
   (*a*: church)
B  Marly
C  Hermitage
D  Monplaisir
E  Orangery

1  Neptune Fountain
2  Samson Fountain
   and Cascade
3  Canal (ending
   in harbor)
4  Italian Fountains

5  Chessboard Cascade
6  Roman Fountains
7  Pyramid Fountain
8  Parasol Trick Fountain
9  Oak Sapling Trick
   Fountain

10  Bell Fountains
11  Adam Fountain
12  Eve Fountain
13  Lion Cascade
14  Marly Cascade,
    or Golden Hill
15  Marly Lake

*Fig. 92. Plan of Peterhof*, Russia.
Anonymous drawing, 1970(?),
from Kennett,
*The Palaces of Leningrad.*

Still basically Peter the Great's handsome complex, Peterhof overlooks the Gulf of Finland with charming vistas and formal gardens. Despite Ligne's strictures, despite excessive gilding, and despite some questionable elements like joke fountains, this garden presents a combination of styles remarkable because of the scope and ingenious siting.

what he had seen during his travels. It was in the first manner that he built himself on the shore of the Baltic a house called Monplaisir, where in arbors ill designed and ill planted there are traps, clocks, harpsichords, chimes, organs, musicians, ducks, hounds, deer, all set in motion by waterwheels.

30  Thus, in the second style, the cascades are better than those at Versailles, always flowing and furnishing the greatest volume of water I have ever seen. If all the canals were edged in granite or, rather, with grass instead of brick, which makes the garden look most bour-

geois; if the pedestals of two water columns imitating two marble ones in Rome were likewise of marble; if to the pyramid basin whose waterspout were likewise meant to imitate the finest Roman obelisk; if the drainage ditches were set to winding through a forest of orange trees so as to surround them in a sort of amphitheater where there is now a wretched cascade falling over wood; if the hedgerows were removed and all the roads planted in grass; if a mill for minerals were set out so as to create a pleasant and useful structure; and if all this were done in the new natural garden now being built on the other side of the castle, old Peterhof would become as interesting as it is now admired. In the new garden there is a hideaway in the form of a hayrick. A few bundles of hay, which must be removed to enter, block the door and windows and fool the visitor, who easily forgives such trickery on entering a room decorated in the latest Parisian taste. The Baltic, which waters the garden of old Peterhof and may be seen afresh from each new vantage point, diffuses an inexpressible charm over all.

*31* In the midst of a wood near Tsarskoye Selo, Pavleskoye,[38] which belongs to the grand duchess, is worth noting. Nature has not been opposed but made to contribute to this marvel where everything is agreeable because the unevenness of the terrain has been used to great advantage. A small ruin, a seemingly ancient bridge, a chalet that appears to be a cottage from the outside contains, within, a lounge in the most decorative and exquisite fashion of private homes in Paris, a Temple of Union—all of which does honor to the taste of the grand duchess [Figs. 93, 94].

*32* Two versts from Tsarskoye Selo, Prince Potemkin has a small Gothick house[39] with an English garden in which reign simplicity, grace, ease, and pleasure. There is neither prettifying nor pretension, though the two cascades, one outside, the other in, and his Russian bath, are noteworthy. The latter, in particular, is unique in its kind and exudes freshness everywhere in that time when the Sun takes revenge for not being able to remain longer on a horizon worthy of him. Russia has always sacrificed to the Sun. They plant, they sow, they have taste . . . Why can they not have clear skies and fine ter-

*Fig. 93.* V. A. Jukhovsky, *View at Pavlovsk.* Drawing, 1843, from Likhachev, *Poeziia Sadov.*

A charming nineteenth-century drawing of a scene at Pavleskoye, seemingly in accord with Ligne's appreciative remark in IV.31. Starting with the near-perfect design and siting of the palace, this garden illustrates the possibility of giving sentimental expression to the picturesque and fully deserves Ligne's praise for its tastefulness.

38. Pavleskoye (modern Pavlovsk, USSR), a palace and park some two miles southeast of Tsarskoye Selo, built in 1777 by Charles Cameron for the Grand Duke Paul-Petrovitch (1754–1801); after 1788 inhabited almost exclusively by his second wife, the Grand Duchess Sophia-Dorothea of Württemberg (1736–1826).
39. Babalova, Potemkin's small and unoriginal country seat, adjoining the park at Tsarskoye Selo, one mile west-southwest of the castle, reverted on his death in 1791 to Paul-Petrovitch, who because of his great personal animosity proceeded to misuse, then sell the property, as he did most of the favorite's residences; now destroyed.

rain? Prince Potemkin, for example, is genial and has a definite penchant for beauty and grandeur. He renders Nature her due, though the superb Anichkov colonnade in the high style of Athens proves that he understands art and the arts; his Moldavian dwelling at Cherkassy is graceful.[40]

*33* On the road to Peterhof, the two Naryshkin gardens are proof once more of the excellent taste to be found in Russia.[41] The one, thanks to the charming contours of the greensward, the streams, and islets; the other, thanks to the surprises in the wood, which are nothing short of magic. They both deserve the greatest praise for their buildings, temples, and well-kept bridges. If the second is more pleasing to me, it is undoubtedly because of the most beautiful creature in the world who often strolls in the garden there that bears her name,[42] making the visitor wish he were the genius loci in order to receive her in his sanctuary. He is not proud; he can easily make one anywhere, and a hollow oak is ofttimes preferable to a divan.

*34* Gatschina [Fig. 95], which belongs to Prince Orlov, is an imitation of several gardens in England and contains important attractions.[43]

*Fig. 94.* V. A. Jukhovsky, *Another View of Pavlovsk.* Drawing, 1843, from Likhachev, *Poeziia Sadov.*

40. The Anichkov colonnade is a feature of the palace of the same name on the Fontanka in Saint Petersburg, given to Potemkin by Catherine II in 1776. Cherkassy (Ukrainian SSR), 115 miles southeast of Kiev, on the west bank of the Dnieper, capital of the Don Cossacks, where Potemkin was rewarded with a large grant of land for his exploits, including a palace built in 1765; now destroyed. See Ligne, *Lettres à la Marquise de Coigny*, no. 3, and Lady Craven, *Journey through the Crimea*, 172–73.

41. These two gardens were Baba and Nana (Hirschfeld, *Théorie de l'art des jardins* 5:339–42, says "Haha" through a misreading of the Cyrillic; information kindly supplied by Professor S. Karlinsky, Berkeley). They were located near modern Ligovo, halfway between Leningrad and Peterhof, and formed but part of a huge estate, Krasnaya Myza (The Red Grange), comprising, among others, Dutch, English, Chinese, and classical gardens, the property of the Naryshkin brothers, Alexei (1726–95) and Lev (1733–99). Baba, "the ladies' (garden)," was the more southerly, occupied rising ground, and was the more "natural" of the two; now completely destroyed. Nana was more "artistic," containing a pavilion in Moldavian style; there a brilliant reception honored Mme de Staël in 1812; now destroyed. See her *Dix Années d'exil*, pt. 2, chap. 18, and Vassily Kirbatov, *Sadi i Parki*, 599.

42. Nana, so named for the eldest daughter of Lev Alexandrovitch, Natalia (1762–1819), in 1781 Countess Sologuba, a great beauty of the time (see her portrait by Mme Vigée-Lebrun in the collections of the Hermitage, Leningrad).

43. "In the time since my description, Gatschina has become the property of the present grand duke [Paul-Petrovitch]" (Ligne's note). Located some twenty-five miles south-southwest of Saint Petersburg, this estate was built in 1766 by Rinaldi for Gregory Orlov (1734–83), a favorite of Catherine II's and brother to the victor of Chesmé; it reverted on his death to Grand Duke Paul-Petrovitch; partly destroyed in World War II.

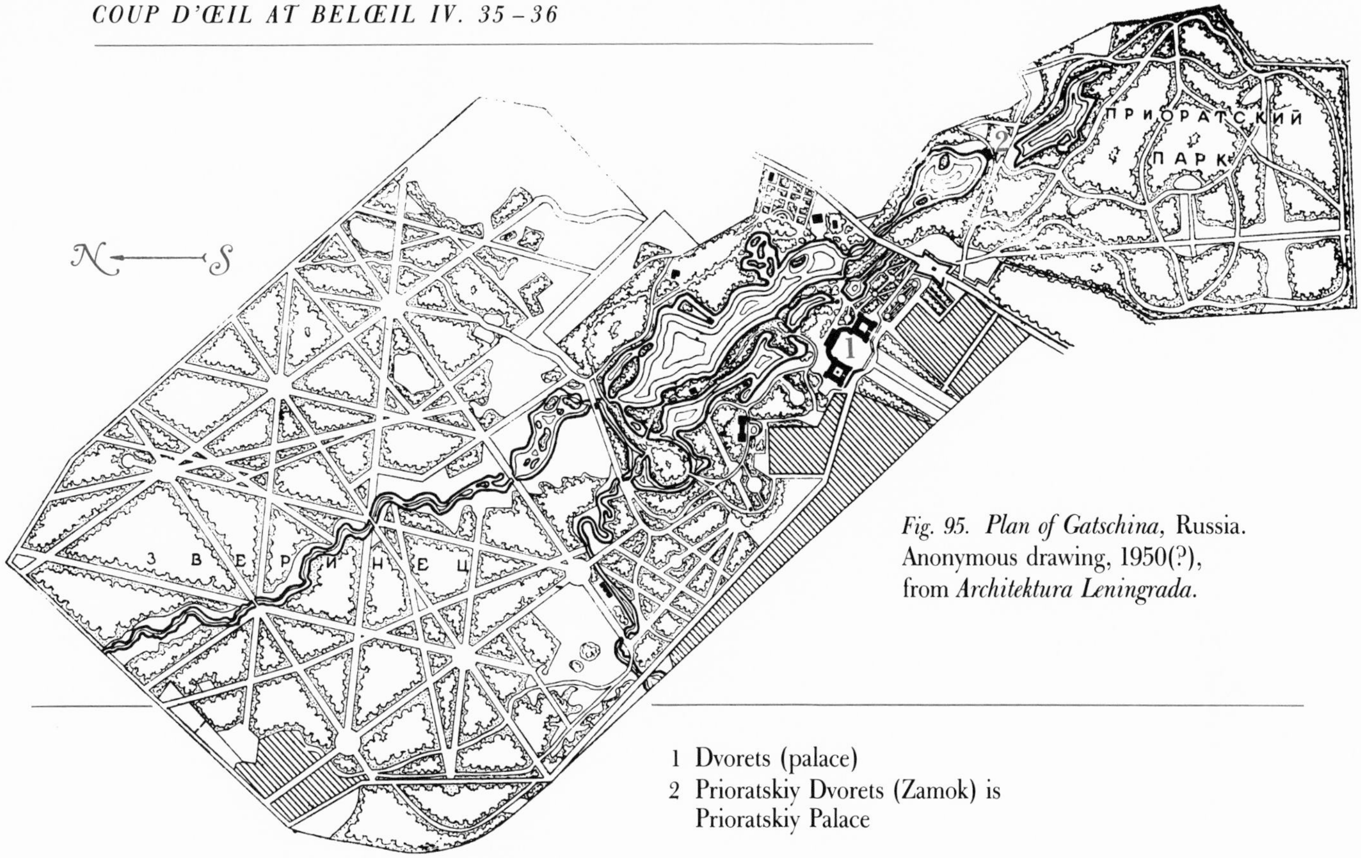

*Fig. 95. Plan of Gatschina*, Russia. Anonymous drawing, 1950(?), from *Architektura Leningrada*.

1 Dvorets (palace)
2 Prioratskiy Dvorets (Zamok) is Prioratskiy Palace

Gorod Gatschina is the town of Gatschina; Zverinets (lower left) is the deer park; Prioratskiy Park is at the upper right.

Although only a few features are indicated on the plan, other staples from the garden repertory were included, such as memorial columns and statues. By omitting these other details, the artist underlines the landscape garden qualities of Gatschina, where the countryside and its vistas take pride of place. Nature has been encouraged to be artistic (Ligne's "jardins de l'art") rather than artful. This considerable layout thus deserves attention more than, say, Peterhof or Tsarskoye Selo. Largely destroyed in World War II, the garden is now being slowly restored.

*35* There are winter gardens in Russia that could be better treated.[44] They construct immense buildings for them. Trelliswork with mirrors and barrel vaulting would lend them an air of truthfulness, of all airs the most precious.

*36* There is more merit in the gardens around Saint Petersburg than in those I saw in all the governments of Moscow, Pultava, Tula, Kursk, and Kharkov (which enjoy more sunshine and trees), for they have only the sad pine and the leafless birch to plant. But they know how to arrange them especially well. Nature is a little more generous in Poland, though for want of blessings from Heaven, people there redouble in invention and create gardens that either amuse or fascinate. There is proof of what I say at Schoulé,[45] where Prince Casimir

44. See, for instance, the enormous hall in the Tavrichesky Palace, Leningrad, once the property of Potemkin. As in I.7, Ligne's idea of long galleries ending in mirrors was later taken up by no less than Humphry Repton; see Nikolaus Pevsner, "Humphry Repton," in *Studies in Art*, 153.

45. Schoulé (Szulec) is the site of a palace and garden called Książęce (Princely Domain), built in 1772–82, some six miles southeast of Warsaw, for the grand chamberlain, Casimir Poniatowski (1721–99), brother to King Stanislas Augustus (1732–98), by Szymon Zug (1733–1807). For more detailed information concerning Polish gardens, see Zbigniew Domchowski, *The Architecture of Poland*, and especially Gerard Ciołek, *Gärten in Polen*, 189–92.

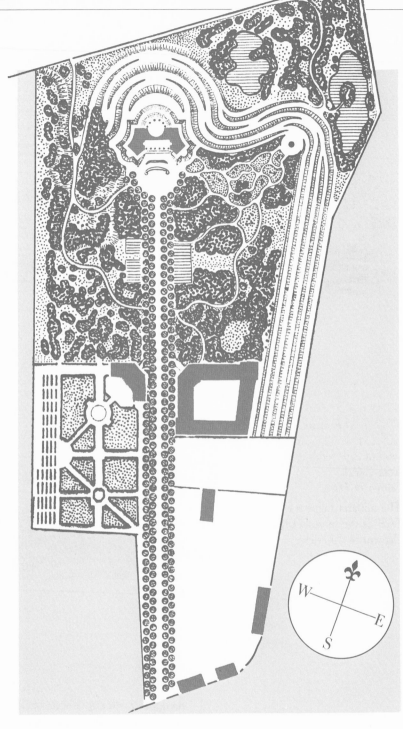

*Fig. 96. Plan of Książęce, Szulec, Poland. Drawing after Simon Zug, 1949, from Ciołek, Gärten in Polen.*

It is difficult for the modern reader to imagine within this seemingly exiguous layout a garden as rich and varied as the one Ligne describes. Yet by a judicious use of follies and other picturesque elements and by careful arrangement of the parts leading imperceptibly from one to another, the garden provided genuine inspiration for a variety of moods and emotions (see Figs. 97 and 98).

Poniatowski has produced charming effects by a considerable rearranging of the terrain [Fig. 96]. Hillocks surround saloons of perfect taste. You come upon one by chance, yet you cannot avoid this "chance." You descend into a grotto so deep you need a torch to come out [Fig. 97]; you think you catch a glimmer of light and, advancing, find a room marvelously decorated, painted, and furnished

*Fig. 97 (left).* Simon Zug, *View of Książęce*, Szulec, Poland. Gouache (end of eighteenth century), from Ciołek, *Gärten in Polen.*

Only part of the charm Ligne discerned in this garden (IV.36) can be divined from this illustration.

*Fig. 98 (right).* Simon Zug, *Minarets at Książęce*, Szulec, Poland. Gouache (end of eighteenth century), from Ciołek, *Gärten in Polen.*

The minaret Ligne mentions in IV.36 is the most distinctive element in this view.

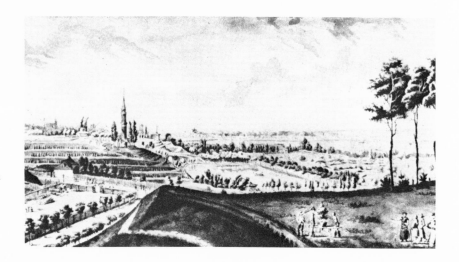

magnificently with stucco columns, bas-reliefs, and so forth. There is another on a steep incline where a large body of people may assemble without crowding. There are two stories: one for those who like to game, another for those who like to chat. This sort of arrangement is quite novel, and I should hope to imitate it sometime. The light in the rocaille saloon seems to come from behind a rock. The estate also contains a very beautiful minaret [Fig. 98]; this is a Turkish tower with prayer bells. Temples are also to be seen there, along with a superb colonnade and nearby an exquisite theater whose exterior is decorated like a Gothick church. I might wish there were also a bridge to cross over the highway and so link the two parts of this garden, each so beautiful, which it is wrong to separate. There is also

*Fig. 99. Temple*, Powąski, Warsaw. Anonymous engraving, 1775(?), from Ciołek, *Gärten in Polen.*

A picturesque view of a garden Ligne greatly admired.

an island containing a children's village that must not be missed; it is the prettiest fancy in the world. The prince assembles there all those who people his pleasures, and the seriousness with which they go about their work—prescribed by different tradesmen's costumes that they wear—is most amusing. There are, for example, a garrison and clergy. The parish choir is a marionette theater. That gave me the idea of an island where I might imitate this establishment. I am thrilled in advance at the idea of my people's robes and uniforms. Each day I see some that are not so colorful as mine will be, and which I do not want. It seems to me that I can already imagine them receiving visitors. Long and light chains [marking the bounds] will put a limit to some of their politeness; only their gallantries will be difficult to contain.

*37*   Let me cast aside this image and wild tableau for a moment in order to enjoy a picture of true sensibility: Powąski[46] formerly calm, now saddened, is the Temple of Regrets [Fig. 99]. Each day the tears of Princess Czartoriska water the garden of the little house where her unfortunate daughter died a victim of the flames. Unfortunately, she ought to have known only those of love. There are cypresses, roses, and sad inscriptions on the spot where stood the cabin destroyed in this misfortune for which the Graces and the god who follows in their train will never be consoled. The glory of this site is the perfect image of Nature, who is not thwarted here [Fig. 100]. Every guest has his dwelling, looking perhaps a little too peasantlike from the outside (since those of this region have nothing agreeable to offer), though the interiors are charming. Partitions separate the family and company entering the central pavillion into several little groups. I think they used to gather to make love; now it is only to weep. I was tempted to do so myself on seeing in this same spot the intriguing and unfortunate beauty of the princess [Fig. 101]. I am like "Love" in *Le Devin du village*, who expects both laughter and tears;[47] but I hope I am never bored.

46. Powąski is a famous estate northwest of Greater Warsaw, destroyed in 1794, known at one time as the Polish Trianon, created ca. 1775 by Princess Isabella Czartoriska, née Flemming (1746–1835); now the site of a national memorial. See the princess's treatise, *Myśli różne o sposobie zakładania ogrodów* (Reflections on the planting of gardens). No reference I have been able to consult mentions a Czartoriski daughter. Assuming Ligne was correct in identifying the victim of this tragedy, this girl would have been born after 1761, the date of her parents' marriage, dying before Ligne's visit to Warsaw in 1781. See Brian Knox, "The English Garden in Poland and Bohemia," 101–11.

47. Couplet 6, sung by Colette in the last vaudeville of Jean-Jacques Rousseau's *Devin du village* (1752). The opera was an immediate success when first produced, leading to a command performance at Fountainebleau. See Rousseau's *Confessions*, bk. 8.

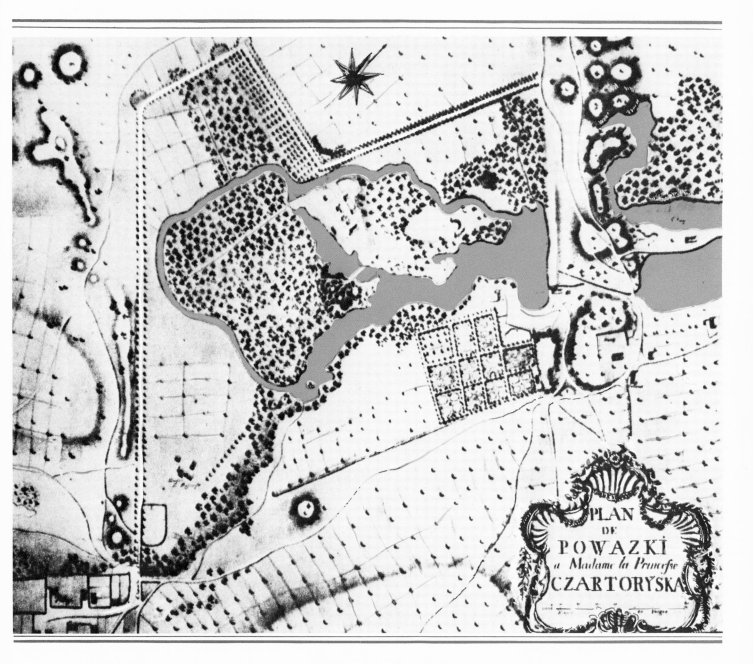

*Fig. 100. Plan of Powąski*, Warsaw. Anonymous engraving, 1775(?), from Ciołek, *Gärten in Polen*.

This extensive picturesque garden was arranged around a lake created by the damming of a small stream. Despite the irregularity and the inclusion of diverse appurtenances common to this type of garden, the effect was undoubtedly less natural and less attractive than that of, for example, Rheinsberg (see Fig. 143).

Fig. 101. *View of the Lake*,
Powąski, Warsaw.
Anonymous engraving, 1775(?),
from Ciołek, *Gärten in Polen*.

Since Ligne wrote, this garden
has been completely
transformed; it is now a national
memorial.

*38*  Werky, the seat of the Bishop of Vilna,[48] is a happy reflection of
Nature. One large stream, three little ones; a range of hillocks separating two vales; four or five cascades; three islets; constructions; castles;
a mill; a harbor; a ruin; two convents with fine façades that create a
handsome effect; natural inclines; the Temple of Vulcan, one to Bac-
chus, another to the Union,[49] which was supposed to be built on
pilings; a sort of bridge over the confluence of three pretty rills; an
obelisk; a cabin for fishermen and one for workmen; some decorated
bridges, and others [that are] rustic serve to guarantee the pleasures
of this residence, where I was a consultant and became almost ac-
tively engaged in building what I have just described.

*39*  In the advice that I distribute without being asked (for the worst
little author, or maker of gardens, thinks that he at least has no need
of any), I always say: "It is by doing, reflecting, walking about, and
noting down that you will see what persons with fitful notions cannot
see. Let your eye never weary of wandering over the beauties of Nature, and you will learn from her how to combine them." I have
looked long at open fields, and I have learned that the red of poppies, the blue of cornflowers, the yellow of turnips make the best of
palettes; unite them with the tender green of flax, the honeygrass, the
mottled buckwheat, the pale gold of wheat, the vivid green of barley,
and many other species that I do not yet know and you will have an
enchanting effect. To me, not liking walls and satisfied with hedges
and canals, this picture is one joy more in a country home.

48. "Hanged three months ago by those who love liberty, equality, justice, and
happiness" (Ligne's note). Ignaz Massalski, Bishop of Vilna (1728–94), related to
Ligne by marriage, had a summer palace at Verkhiai (Lithuanian SSR), some
three miles north of Vilna, built in 1780 by Wawrzyniec Gucewicz (1753–98);
now an agricultural college. See Wilhelm Hentschel, *Die sächsische Baukunst des
18. Jahrhunderts in Polen*. Ligne's note helps date the passage.
49. Allusion to the union between Poland and the Grand Duchy of Lithuania,
dating from the time of the Jagellonians (1386).

*Fig. 103 (left).* Jouanne, *Plan of Ermenonville* (Oise), France. Engraving, 1808(?), from Laborde, *Description des nouveaux jardins.*

This vast undertaking is remarkable, like its creator, a parvenu attempting to imitate and profit by the various passing modes and fancies of his time. Not least among these was an admiration for Rousseau, who died on the estate in 1778 and was buried there until 1794, when his remains were transferred to the Panthéon in Paris. There are other effects of Rousseaumania dotting this landscape, for example, at 19, 20, 32, and 33. But there are also echoes of the rebirth of an interest in the Middle Ages (at 8, 21, 42) and in wild nature (10, 28, 44), not to mention the literature of passion (27), exoticism (35, 36), and the arts (43, the tomb of Georges Mayer, a painter from Strasbourg who died on the estate). Ligne's criticism is not far from the mark. Everything tends to create the same effect of kitsch as in Figures 124 and 126, but less noticeably here because that effect is spread over a larger expanse and because of the abiding presence of the unfortunate Jean-Jacques. (Not all elements listed in the key appear on the plan.)

*Fig. 104.* Demonchy, after Bourgeois, *Gabrielle's Tower,* Ermenonville. Engraving, 1808(?), from Laborde, *Description des nouveaux jardins.*

One of several follies on this important estate northeast of Paris.

liard green; the trivial, or pedantic, or unfortunate, or innumerable, or ill-sited inscriptions—none of which was able to satisfy the demands of this beautiful location.

57   Everything had a surprising effect on me. Only a long time after did I recall that "the desert" was nothing but an odd and insignificant moor on which the sightseers to Ermenonville might take their exercise [Fig. 107]. But aside from that, let me go over those other attractions again, I said to myself. I returned to Ermenonville. I went, thinking only of Julie.[57] I think I wept for her, while blessing her historian. I sat on her bench. I saw the ducks that had been fed by her own hand. It seemed to me that their noise was more pleasant than before, though still not on pitch. I began again to think of Julie. I refused to utter again my remark about the lack of resemblance between this Clarens and the real one that I knew. But unfortunately,

57. *Julie; ou, la nouvelle Héloïse* (1761), an important epistolary novel by Jean-Jacques Rousseau, whose hero and heroine are Saint-Preux and Julie d'Etanges; see Ligne's comments on this work elsewhere in his writings, as well as Basil Guy, "The Prince de Ligne, Laclos, and the *Liaisons dangereuses*," 260–67.

Perhaps the most important monument at Ermenonville, where Rousseau died in 1778 and was buried until 1794. Popular pilgrimages caused the ruin of the first tomb on this site, consisting of an urn atop an almost square pedestal (see the engraving by Moreau le jeune). This second tomb, designed by Hubert Robert in 1781, was likewise almost ruined by the enthusiasm of sightseers and souvenir hunters. The sarcophagus is now empty, Rousseau's remains having been enshrined in the Panthéon, Paris, by the Revolution.

*Fig. 106. Rousseau's Tomb*, Ermenonville. Anonymous engraving, 1780(?), from Girardin, *Promenade; ou, itinéraire des jardins d'Ermenonville.*

*Fig. 105 Philosopher's Hut*, Ermenonville. Anonymous engraving, 1776, from Lerouge, *Détail des nouveaux jardins à la mode*, cahier 3.

Here the ever-popular hermitage has been transformed into a philosopher's dwelling, as Ligne would have done at Belœil, a sign of the increased secularization of ideals before the French Revolution.

O Saint-Preux! I envied you your lot. Your letter fifty-five made me forget the bitterness of number fourteen [Fig. 108]. Happy! O a thousand times happy are those who have been exposed to it! [Fig. 109].

58   Here is a spot perhaps more to my liking—and nearer to Paris. One day, abandoning the vain whirl of the capital and following my own whimsy, I lost sight of Paris at Moulin Joli [Fig. 110][58] and found myself (possible only in Nature). Whoever you may be, unless your heart is hardened, sit down in the fork of a willow by the riverside at Moulin Joli. Read, look around, and weep—not from sadness but from a delicious feeling of sensibility. The panorama of your soul will appear before you. Past happiness (should you have known it), happiness to come, and the desire to be happy—a thousand thoughts revolving around this one thought, regrets, joys, desires, all will rush upon you at once. Struggles . . . your indignation . . . the heart . . . memories . . . the present . . . Go away, unbelievers! Reflect upon the

58. Property with an important "English" garden arranged in 1754 on three islands in the Seine between Colombes and Argenteuil (Greater Paris); now destroyed. See Claude-Henri Watelet, *Essai sur les jardins;* Hirschfeld, *Théorie de l'art des jardins* 1:45–54; Walpole's letters to William Mason, 7 August and 6 September 1775; and Wiebenson, *The Picturesque Garden in France*, 15–19.

*Fig. 107.* Perdoux, after Bourgeois, *The Wilderness,* Ermenonville (with an admiring Jean-Jacques Rousseau). Engraving, 1808(?), from Laborde, *Description des nouveaux jardins.*

This illustration from the early nineteenth century displays one of the attractions of the estate, with a sentimental reminder of Rousseau's sojourn there.

inscriptions that Taste has placed there. Meditate with the wise man, sigh with the lover, and bless M. Watelet.[59]

59 Frenchmen, in their prejudice, criticize the wildness of the island. Too much grass, they say, too many trees, too much irregularity. No bowers, no flower beds . . . Those Frenchmen (who are not French enough) speak ill of the two goosefoots, but these grow out of the treatment—they do not repeat the design—and are necessary to appreciate three different points of view. There is little grace in wanting to do without them; and the contrast between water and foliage to be observed at the end of these three avenues should form part of the calculations of Anglomaniacs.

60 I have never seen anything quite like the two bridges at Moulin Joli. The Dutch bridge, leading to the second island, and the other, which is a suspension bridge edged with flowers, have a fairy-tale quality [Fig. 111]. Yet the treatment is not reasonable, for there is no explanation why there should be cases, shrubs, and the semblance of orange trees. But it is the prettiest unreason in the world. These non sequiturs par excellence are the specialty of the Chinese. Their gardens are full of them, as are their designs, and in the same way their paintings are often filled with men riding horseback over water and ships on mountainsides.

59. Claude-Henri Watelet (1718–86), receveur-général des finances under the Old Regime, the dilettante artist and decorator who created Moulin-Joli and was painted by Greuze.

*Fig. 108.* Hubert Gravelot, *Love's First Kiss.* Engraving, 1761, from Rousseau, *Julie; ou, la Nouvelle Héloïse.*

Rousseau proposed the following legend to accompany this plate, referring to part 1, letter 14: "The scene takes place in a grove. Julie has just given her friend a kiss, *cosí saporito*, and has nearly fainted. We see her in a languorous position, leaning, flowing almost, on the arm of her cousin, while the latter welcomes her with an eagerness that does not prevent her from smiling as she looks to the friend out of the corner of her eye. The youth stretches out his arms toward Julie. He has just held her in one arm, and with the other is attempting to support her. His hat is on the ground. His gesture and his face reveal how transported, or even ravished, he is with pleasure and alarm. Julie should be fainting but not unconscious. The whole scene must breathe a feeling of voluptuousness that a certain modesty makes all the more touching." An illustration from Rousseau's famous novel, recalled by Ligne in IV.57.

61   After viewing the works of M. Watelet and M. de Girardin, I almost gave up working. After reading their treatises, I almost gave up writing. How could both of them say so many new, gallant, philosophical, and sublime things? M. Watelet is almost as inspired as Robertson;[60] he finds in gardens the antiquity of feudalism and the spirit of a personality later modified according to the age. M. de Girardin is less of a metaphysician and perhaps more of a gardener. The first is more of a poet and more costly to follow, the second, more of a slave to Nature. The first would subject her to the power of his imagination if there were treasures that might aid him. The second seems to prescribe a surer progress. Which of the two has more soul and spirit? Find out about one from the woman he loves;[61] as for the other, I know not who is capable of deciding. What I know best is that I was enchanted first by reading them both and later by asking myself what I had learned. I do not wish to enchant anyone— nor can I. But I trust my gardener will understand me. Undoubtedly because Abbé Delille praised modern gardens in very harmonious poetry, the pride of the French language, M. Fontanes, to draw atten-

60. Ganay, in his edition of *Coup d'Œil*, 217, states that this allusion is to a famous aeronaut of the eighteenth century—more properly, the Robert brothers; on the basis of a later remark concerning feudalism, it would seem instead to refer to the famous Scots historian, William Robertson (1721–93).

61. Watelet's paramour, who lived with him at Moulin-Joli, was Mme Leconte, wife of a procurator in the Paris Parlement. See *Coup d'Œil* (ed. Ganay), 218 n. a; Hautecoeur, *Histoire de l'architecture classique* 5:10; and Elisabeth Vigée-Lebrun, *Souvenirs* 1:182.

*Fig. 109 (left). Memorials to Past Loves,* Ermenonville. Anonymous engraving, 1780(?), from Girardin, *Promenade; ou, itinéraire des jardins d'Ermenonville.*

Proof, if it were needed, of the widespread influence of Rousseau's *Nouvelle Héloïse* (see Fig. 25) even in gardens, where the visitor was expected to be intelligent and literate and to make the correct associations.

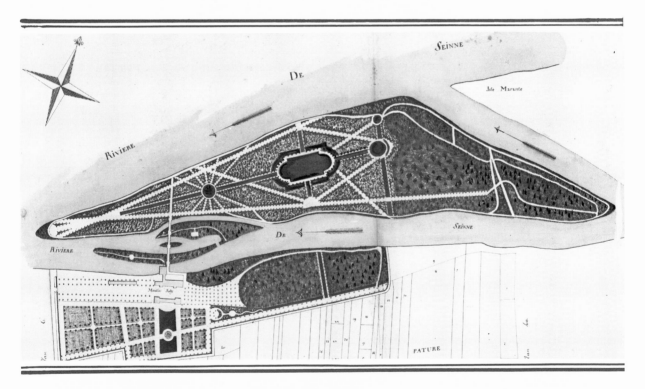

*110. Plan of Moulin Joli.* Anonymous drawing, 1786(?). Courtesy Archives nationales, Paris.

Moulin Joli is one of the more original sites and treatments of a picturesque garden among the many examples Ligne mentions. Its creator was a wealthy dilettante whose inspiration here was Netherlandish landscape painting. The swinging bridge—the most noteworthy feature—was oriented on the central axis of the house, going as far as the banks of the Seine on the main island. This island and the aits were cleverly planted not with flowers but with willows growing naturally. The lush verdure added considerably to the pleasure of a visit like the one Ligne describes.

*Fig. 111.* Jean-Claude de Saint-Non, after Le Prince, *Mill with Suspension Bridge* (at right), Moulin Joli. Engraving, 1774. Courtesy Cabinet des Estampes, Bibliothèque nationale, Paris.

One of the more spectacular features of this garden was the suspension bridge connecting the island with the mainland, mentioned by Ligne in IV.60.

tion to himself, took the part of ancient gardens in pretty but inferior verse and defended his unfortunate cause with grace; but his editor brings him up short with a note on every mistake. Another poet-gardener, M. [Lezay-] Marnésia, does not choose between the two sides; his poem is likewise not without merit.[62]

62    Duke Harcourt wrote earlier—and better—than the others, uniting precept with example.[63] They say gardens are like his work. Before us he was acquainted with Nature—better acquainted than we. Scattered throughout his book are the delicacy, the grace, the taste that formerly were to be found only at court. He is as learned as a gardener, as authoritative as a great lord, as poetic as Anacreon, and as colorful as Albano.[64]

62. Undoubtedly Ligne is here referring to Watelet's *Essai sur les jardins* and René de Girardin's *De la Composition des paysages*. But see Delille, *Les Jardins*; Louis de Fontanes, "Fragment d'une lettre sur la nature et sur l'homme"; and C-F-A. de Lezay-Marnésia, *Essai sur la nature champêtre*.

63. François d'Harcourt (1726–1802) was the author of the *Traité de la décoration des dehors, des jardins, et des parcs*, written ca. 1775; Wiebenson, *The Picturesque Garden in France*, 124, assigns the date 1774.

64. "His works have been praised by the infamous Cerutti who, despite awful constitutional notices, nonetheless composed a charming poem on the gardens at Betz" (Ligne's note). Joseph-Antoine Cerutti (1738–92), a former Jesuit and partisan of the Revolution, wrote *Les Jardins de Betz* ca. 1785 about a property near Senlis (Oise) belonging to Louise d'Aumont, Princess of Monaco (1759–1826), which at one time contained an important "English" garden, designed by Jules-David Leroy (1724–1803) and Hubert Robert (though Ganay in his edition of *Coup d'Œil* claims this for d'Harcourt, 227 n. d); now transformed; see Alexandre de Laborde, *Description des nouveaux jardins*, 116–17.

For Anacreon, see part I, note 5; Francesco Albano (1578–1660), an Italian artist, "the Anacreon of painting."

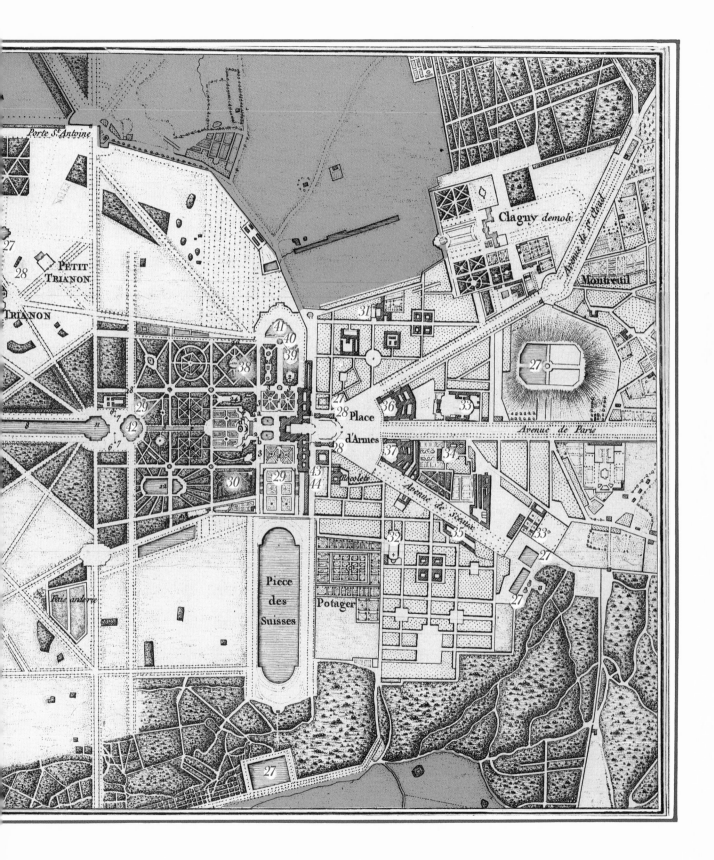

78    Today the best part of this so-vaunted Versailles is the one that is not—that is, the surroundings [Fig. 120]. Although they are not so manicured [as the rest], we can recognize there all at once the delicate touch of the hand of the Graces, especially in one part.[78] Fortunately, the Petit Trianon is not yet completed, [else] I would have too many things to say [Fig. 121]. Meanwhile, visitors to it breathe the air of happiness and freedom. The greensward seems more handsome, the water more clear, the guests so contented there that they never utter a word of complaint. Yet even if they did, they would be forgiven; and unless they made a determined effort, I am sure that the power of the waters would prevent them from leaving this enchanted garden. As encomiums are jaded, one day I amused myself with a bit of satire at the queen's expense.

I had just come from the Grand Trianon. Unfortunately for me, the water is flowing fast and sounds wonderful; nor is its murmur, which I had not expected, able to linger longer in this happy retreat, which can be left behind only with regret. You think you are one hundred leagues from court. Nevertheless, the contents of this pretty garden are so well arranged that it seems to include everything and appears ten times larger than it really is. The great trees of the park at Versailles form a precious frame for it without the least formality. The deity seems to reign over a great area that does not belong to him, just as he governs those who were not born 'neath his laws. There is perhaps some sorcery here.

79    I know of nothing more handsome or better executed than the Temple [of Love] or the Pavilion.[79] The colonnade of the one [Fig. 122] and the interior of the other are the peak of perfection, of taste, of sculpting. I wager that the trees will hurry and grow tall to hide a rock outcropping that I don't like—an enormous white mass too close to the house. The brook may be seen to advantage where it straightens out momentarily near the Temple. The rest is, of course, hidden—except where it is intended to be seen. The clumps of trees

78. "I would still prefer to water this article with my tears and wash it away. Great, sublime, beautiful, adorable, and unfortunate daughter and sister of my masters, behold, wherever you may be, in recognition of your virtues, the eternal regrets of those, like me, who were witness to them and who are still filled with the most tender admiration and the keenest grief." (Ligne's note)
    This touching testimonial to Marie-Antoinette (1755–93) is another witness to the late date of this paragraph. The statement that "the Petit Trianon is not yet completed" is copied directly from the first edition of the *Coup d'Œil;* by 1795 it was obviously incorrect. Ligne does not finish the anecdote that follows.

79. According to Nolhac, "Le Prince de Ligne à Trianon," 115–19, Ligne had a direct role in creating the Temple of Love in the garden of the Petit Trianon. See Alphonse Dupront, *Les Lettres . . . dans la société française* 4:309–11.

*Fig. 121.* Johann Carl Krafft, *Plan of the Petit Trianon,*
Versailles. Engraving, 1812(?),
from Krafft and Ransonnette,
*Recueil d'architecture civile aux environs de Paris.*

This retreat from the formalism of Versailles and its
routine is noteworthy, especially the Hamlet around the
lakes. The picturesque effects, like so many stage
props, symbolized the potent desire for a return to
nature (but of what kind?) and the reinforcement of
social consciousness at the end of the eighteenth
century. Both found an almost perfect echo in Ligne
and—a sign of their popularity—in the Hamlet at
Chantilly, Figure 112.

E  Cascade
F  Gardener's house
G  Emperor's Hall
1  Petit Trianon
2  Victuallers
3  French pavilion
4  Union Bridge
5  Individual garden
6  Stables
7  Dairy
8  Theater
9  Icehouses
10  Gardener's house
11  Reservoir
12  Nurseries
13  Orangery
14  Belvedere
15  Small lake
16  Tilting rings
17  Grotto
18  Temple of Love
19  Large lake
20  Observation tower
21  Cottage
22  Gateway
23  Grill

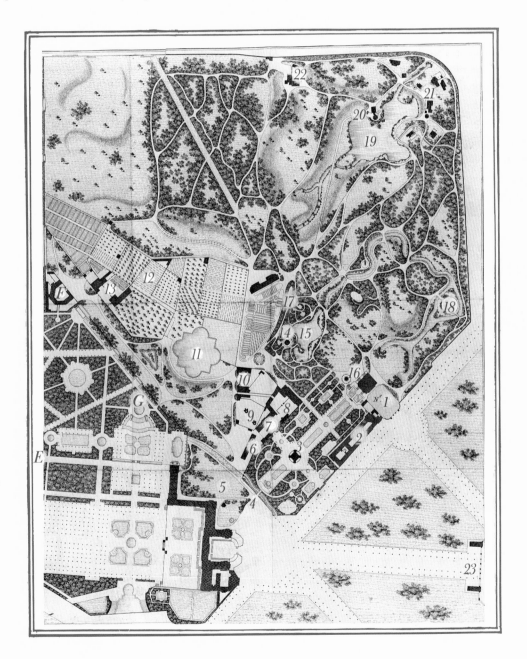

*Fig. 122.* Née, after Lespinasse, *Petit Trianon with Temple of Love*, Versailles. Engraving, 1780(?). Courtesy of the Boston Athenaeum.

See Figure 6 for another view of the Temple of Love, which was supposedly Ligne's invention.

are effectively placed to separate elements that would be too close to one another. There is a perfect grotto, well located and quite natural. In my opinion, the hillocks are too much, and one flower bed that I think looks too ribbonlike will soon be changed, according to what I have been promised. The three or four faults I have noted prove that although the Petit Trianon is capable of arousing my enthusiasm, that is not what excites me about it: there is nothing modish, nothing too refined, nothing strange. Every form is pleasing. The ensemble is appropriate and simply perfect. Apparently the Graces are also exact and still exercise this advantage over all those who shall ever adore them.

80    Near Neuilly there is a garden that would be quite handsome if it were not already so and if it were a garden.[80] If M. Saint-James had spent 400,000 francs less, he would have been more successful. Too many buildings in close quarters do him a disservice [Figs. 123, 124]. But he deserves to be forgiven because of the spirit that, despite everything, holds sway in his works.

80. Saint-James's folly (properly Sainte-Gemmes's), the property of a wealthy financier, Claude Baudard de Vaudésir, Baron Sainte-Gemmes (1738–87), was created at no. 16, avenue de Madrid, Neuilly (Greater Paris), by the architect François-Joseph Bélanger (1744–1818) in 1784; now transformed. See Thiéry, *Guide des amateurs* 1:33–39, and Jean Stern, *A l'ombre de Sophie Arnould* 1:133–47.

*Fig. 123.* François-Joseph Bélanger, *The Rock*, Saint-James's, Paris. Gouache, undated. Courtesy Cabinet des Estampes, Bibliothèque nationale, Paris.

One of the most famous grottoes in France, still standing, though in a garden greatly reduced in size. As in Pope's grotto, the interior was to house the owner's extensive mineral collection, thereby illustrating the necessary connection between interior and exterior.

*81*    But taste controlled by judgment, seemliness, tact, refinement, and delicacy, acquaintance with all the fine arts; the simplicity of a noble, and sometimes necessary, splendor—all are to be found at Gennevilliers.[81] I notice that I am speaking of this garden as if I were addressing its owner. I seem to be sketching his portrait. But he is too great a friend for me to speak directly of him. Besides, I would never be finished praising his high-mindedness, his sensitivity, his chivalric loyalty, and the ancient and modern graces of the happy days of his country. His Gennevilliers is charming and his rock outcroppings a fit subject for artists.

*82*    There are still a few barbarian imitators of old-fashioned taste in Europe. Leaving capital cities, I sometimes see these nouveaux-riches to whom Providence has given mangificence in order to punish them for fortunes they have frequently amassed at the expense of great lords. Happily, bad taste makes them share their treasures with people who might deserve them better than they. It was on you, poor country folk, that Fortune should have rained her benefits. You might not then have been so proud or hard-hearted. You would have extended your hand to the unfortunate, assisting the poor, doing good to your brethren. They might not have made you blush. You would have raised your children properly. And that priest of Plutus, who has not even the merit of having any, makes his entry into his village with the luxurious trappings of an Oriental satrap. People bow before this idol. Happily, as I have said, there is no taste; and if this idol orders one hundred workmen for the next day, it is to disfigure Nature, not to assist her. It is not to help a spring gush forth but to have it rise so high that it is lost forever. It is not to decorate a valley but to fill it in and to level lands that used to be embellished by distinctive features. In this valley your different brooks should have been brought together, for that is where they were so necessary for refreshing the lawns dried out by the rays of the sun, intense and burning. That is where a Temple to Unity should have been built. The parvenu ought to say, let us help one another all we can. Let us render to Humanity the tribute that is her due; later on, I shall return to Poverty that which is hers by right. Let us relieve Misery, but also let us refrain from representing her in oils—it would make her blush too much. But let happiness and comfort preside here. This is the Vale of Tempe.[82] Here, when he has finished his labors, the harvester will

81. As Ligne mentions in a note, this estate belonged to his boon companion, Joseph, Count Vaudreuil (1740–1817), in the Paris suburb of Gennevilliers and was created by La Brière ca. 1780; site of the premiere of Beaumarchais's *Mariage de Figaro* in 1783; now destroyed. See Vigée-Lebrun's *Souvenirs* 1:97–103, 210–15.
82. See part III, note 26, and, for Guillot and Colette, part III, note 5.

1 Entrance court
2 Dwelling
3 Poultry yard
4 Stables and carriage house
5 Menagerie and aviary
  (from drawings by
  M. Choffard, architect)
6 Cooling room
7 Well and hydraulic system
8 Kennels
9 Compost yard
10 Seedling beds
11 Kitchen garden
12 Hothouses
13 Flower gardens
14 Italian trellis
15 Pool surrounded by urns
16 Trellis with statues
17 Chinese vases
18 Antique vases
19 Icehouse and
  Chinese pavilion
20 Pavilion at entrance
  to *sala terrena*
21 Exit from the *sala terrena*
22 Chinese pavilion
23 Ashlar bridge
24 Bridge of Love in brick
25 Isle of Love with statues
  of Psyche and Eros,
  decorated with a marble
  fountain and vases
26 Antique column
27 Pavilion with statue
  of Venus and putti
28 Sphinx's Bridge of wood
29 Drawbridge
30 Chinese bridge
31 Trap shoot
32 Tightrope walk
33 Rock bridge over a waterfall
34 Statue of Rousseau
35 Antique sculpture
36 Statue of Diana
37 Chinese pavilion
38 Tilting rings
39 Swings
40 Fountain at entrance
  to Turkish pavilion

41 The Rock
42 Upper canal
43 Large wooden bridge
44 Spring to supply the canal
45 Underground passage
  leading to the English
  garden next the Seine

46 Waterfall
  from upper garden
47 Wooden bridges
48 Grotto where water
  disappears
49 Cottage
50 Hydraulic pump for
  the canal and Rock

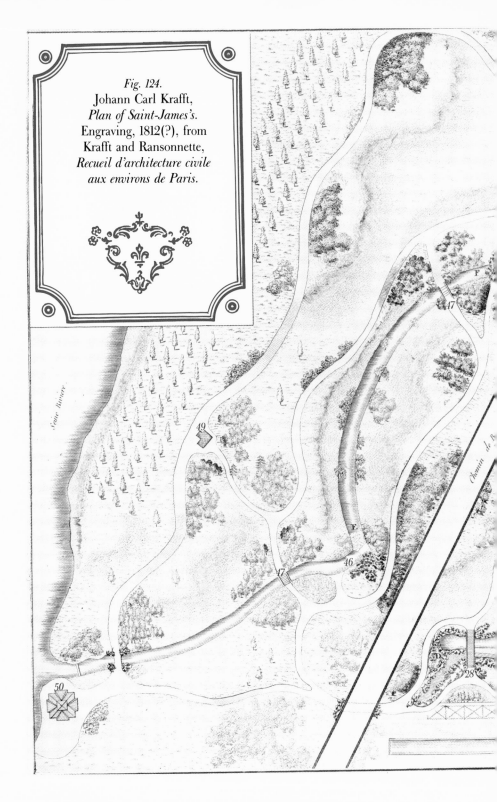

Fig. 124.
Johann Carl Krafft,
*Plan of Saint-James's.*
Engraving, 1812(?), from
Krafft and Ransonnette,
*Recueil d'architecture civile
aux environs de Paris.*

The detailed key (Krafft provides no key to the letters) demonstrates how even on large estates the day-to-day exigencies of life had to be recognized and practical problems solved (here, a sufficient supply of water) before the decorative effects of the picturesque garden could be put into place. The plan makes clear the heteroclite nature of this assemblage, with practically all the features of the ideal model acknowledged (at least in passing—see no. 34, the statue of Rousseau). The resulting creation, however, had nothing significant about it except, perhaps, the Rock (almost the only feature remaining today), which is remarkable for its grotesqueness. Seventeen acres, developed at a cost of some fifty thousand louis! As Ligne says—in another context—Money cannot buy Taste.

*Fig. 125.* Antoine Cardon, *Village Gathering.*
Engraving, 1781,
from Ligne, *Colette et Lucas.*
By permission of the Houghton
Library, Harvard University.
The frontispiece to Ligne's own play,
illustrative of his remarks in IV.82,
underlines again the lessons
of morality implicit in the garden.

come and tell me his doings; the laborer his hopes; youths their amorous escapades; the aged, who have served under the colors, old battles; and mothers the tricks they played on their husbands in the first year of their marriage. Here, an alfresco collation will relax, restore, console, and revivify everyone. I shall hold audiences. The prior will render an account of births, promises of marriage, betrothals. I shall commend love's children to him. He will tell me that he has already taken care of them. I shall unite in holy matrimony those who are ready to wed [Fig. 125]. I shall reassure those girls who are not rich enough to marry their lovers. I shall found in my village a hospital for old soldiers and for laborers who can no longer work. I shall give linen and hemp for spinning to elderly mothers. I shall make the young dance. I shall laugh at the slow and awkward minuet of Guillot and Colette, their arms outstretched; and the story of how they were surprised in a barn will amuse me more than the latest novel I shall have brought from Paris.

Undoubtedly, but very few. One will carve his name there, along with mine; another will plant a few cypresses; another will afford shelter with some weeping willows in order to weep with them; she who is more beautiful than anything in the world will write a romance on the loss of him who was the most amorous; one of her friends will sing it; another will trace its words on the green around my tomb.

*89*   Why do I no longer enjoy that intoxication where my imagination led the way? I would willingly forgo its uncertainties if I could still delight in it for a long time to come. Everything the poets, troubadours,[86] and writers of songs have told me about country life and the simplicity of its ornaments, which they extol without knowing it, did not turn my head. They speak to me about the fernwood and all the delightful activity that goes on there. I have never even been able to sleep there. Yet without possessing that precious exaltation of youth, love of the countryside increases with age, inspires, fulfills, consoles, and makes life worth living.

*90*   That fountain concerning which too pastoral a feeling in my heart caused me to digress recalls to my mind another not far from Lunéville that was treated in the modern manner before Anglomania was the fashion and before travelers just embarked at Calais exclaimed, "How handsome" as soon as they espied the wretched castle at Dover. The fountain bore the name Fontaine-Royale.[87] It was all that remained of the realm of a kinglet who created charming little things in his little province. At Fontaine-Royale we understand how he guessed at what he did not know and how he worked wonders with what he did not know. I did not wish to say anything about his palaces at Chandieu, Jolivet, or La Malgrange, or about his water

86.   Troubadours: use of this word by Ligne points clearly to that renewal of interest in the Middle Ages so nicely studied by Henri Jacoubet in *Le Comte de Tressan et le genre troubadour* and Lionel Gossman in *Mediaeval Philosophies of the Enlightenment.*

87.   Fontaine-Royale, at Lunéville (Meurthe-et-Moselle), was once part of the castle and gardens of the dukes of Lorraine (and later of Stanislas Leszczynski, from 1738 to 1766), along with the lodges Chanteheux (or Chandieu) and Jolivet, built in 1739 by Emmanuel Héré de Corny (1705–63); now destroyed. See the latter's *Recueil des plans, élévations, et coupes.* There subsists only a part of the once-imposing castle of La Malgrange near Nancy (Meurthe-et-Moselle), built in 1712 by Germain Boffrand (1667–1754) for the dukes of Lorraine, the rest having been torn down by King Stanislas in 1738. The gardens of the enormous estate at Commercy (Meuse), some twenty-three miles northwest of Nancy, have been destroyed, leaving only the castle, built for the dukes of Lorraine by Boffrand and Nicolas d'Orbay (1679–1742) in 1708. For details regarding these estates, see Emmanuel Rostworowski, "Stanislas Leszczynski et les lumières," 15–24; Jean Fabre, "Stanislas Leszczynski," 25–42; D. Ostrowski, "Tschifflik, la maison de plaisance du roi Stanislas," 315–22; and Wiebenson, *The Picturesque Garden in France,* 10–13.

towers, his rock outcroppings, his *tableaux mouvants*,[88] his kiosks, or his bridges [Fig. 127]. Because they were a perpetual enchantment, they were delightful. The fairies were outraged to see their labors brought to naught. I have sworn not to talk about them at all, yet his handsome compositions with water, his landscapes were perhaps a trifle airy. They are sketches that would have created a better effect if they had been better executed. There was more wit than genius in his work; but the detail was amusing. I have never been bored in the gardens at Lunéville or Commercy.

*91*  Every nation prizes the sun, I notice, and every gardener worships it like the Incas. But the Dutch are the only ones to have made a mechanical being of it. There is not one of its rays from which they do not receive some good. Go and see how they treat it in their country like a thing, a workman, a lowly craftsman subordinate to the industry and avarice of a heavy-handed gardener who, deprived of philosophic insights, without being an eagle, nevertheless stares at the sun. In his greenhouses, with the help of several vents with windows and mirrors, he knows how to attract and seize on it the very moment it comes out from behind a cloud, to keep it and make it work like a galley slave on his peach trees and ranunculuses.

*92*  What a luxury to recommend to the rich of every country! I would go even further and recommend attention in marrying perfumes just as I have in marrying the colors of a flower bed. Why not create a bouquet in a bosquet, or a sachet, a potpourri, or a large censer? By mixing carnations with roses, orange blossoms, and jasmine, I would attempt to satisfy the sense of smell as others have that of sight. A little field of well-chosen blooms would create an excellent pomander ball or a bottle of cologne or honey. A bosquet would be redolent with grapes known as sultanas. The new way of interesting two senses at the same time would do honor to those Dutchmen who have the means of essaying everything possible in every genre. Then we would go to their country to admire them [Fig. 128] instead of

---

88. *Tableaux mouvants*, depictions of a scene or scenes peopled with mechanically operated figures, were popular among the wealthy in the eighteenth century. Héré de Corny describes what was undoubtedly the most famous example of garden automata (at Lunéville) in his *Recueil des plans, élévations, et coupes*:

> There are eighty-six life-size figures whose movements are so perfectly adjusted that they do not seem to be at all the effect of artifice. . . . At the heart of this composition you may see and hear with pleasure a flute player who appears more alive than aught else. . . . [Also] a goat rearing up against a tree to munch on the tendrils and the new growth; its head and feet move in such a way as to make you think it is a real animal, so natural does it seem. (2:97)

See also Robert Niklaus, "*Tableaux mouvants* as a Technical Innovation," 71–82, and especially Reed Benhamou, "From *Curiosité* to *Utilité*."

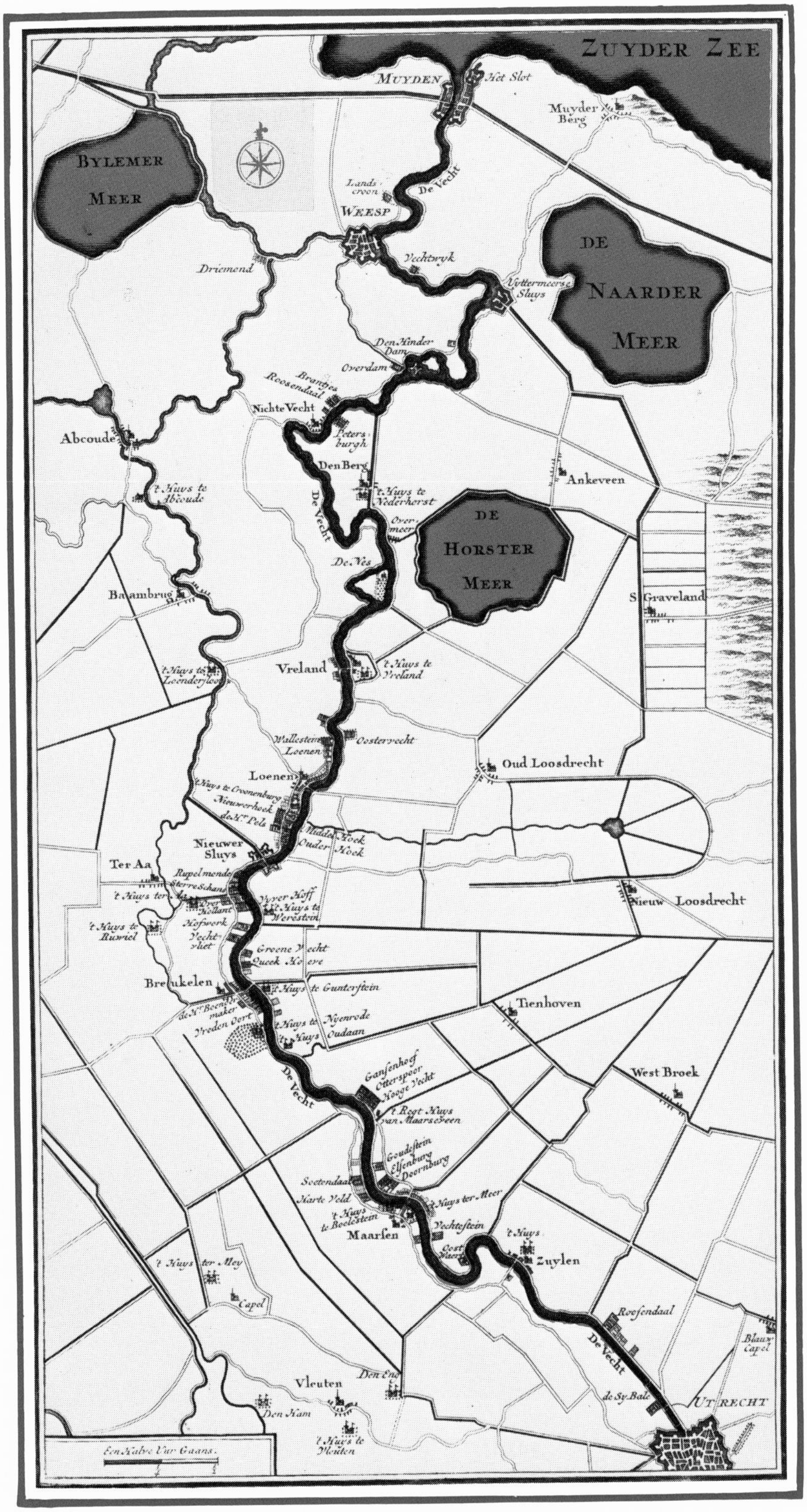

*Fig. 128. Map of the Vecht in the Eighteenth Century.* Anonymous engraving, 1730(?), from Rademaker, *Hollands Arkadia.*

Several of the Dutch estates Ligne mentions in his text were located on the canal from Utrecht to Amsterdam. An important and beautiful waterway in the eighteenth century, the Vecht still flows from Utrecht (*at bottom of map*) to near Amsterdam (*top left*), passing through Maarsen and Breukelen (Brooklyn); and there are still elegant country-house properties along several stretches of its course.

*Fig. 129. Over-Holland on the Vecht, with Teahouse and Pleasure Craft.* Anonymous engraving, 1730, from Rademaker, *Hollands Arkadia.*

An early eighteenth-century view of a famous estate, along with the kind of elegant yacht that made visiting it (and other estates along the canal) more pleasant.

going to make fun of gardens like the one belonging to a M. Beck near Rotterdam.[89] His is the acme of unreasonableness, with little golden birds; tortoiseshell basins; glass fountains; red, white, yellow, and black flower beds. The garden of an Anabaptist near Haarlem is slightly less Dutch than others, but two large pointed mounts make it look ridiculous. The garden in the silk manufactory near Utrecht, all those located along the canal between Utrecht and Amsterdam [Fig. 129], the gardens of van de Smet, those at Ter Meer, and those of a wealthy Jew are in their way detestable above all. None of their owners knew how to spend enough money in their different efforts. They all look alike [Fig. 130], with very expensive urns too near one an-

89. Ligne's references to estates in Holland are so vague that positive identification is difficult. Was he perhaps following Delille's *Jardins* (canto 1, verses 145–54, and canto 4, verses 97–104), where much the same order is followed for a similar effect? Beck's garden near Rotterdam was attached to the castle at Rhoon, south of the city on a branch of the Oude Maas; that of "an Anabaptist" was probably Marquette, to the north of Haarlem, the work of Ligne's countryman Daniel De Hartaing; the garden "in the silk manufactory" at Utrecht was Zijdebalen, near the Weertpoort. Established in 1681, it was already famous in Ligne's time for its shellwork grotto, as witness the anonymous *Description of Holland* (1743), 395. Of van de Smet's several gardens along the Vecht, Ligne undoubtedly refers here to those at Gansenhof (between Maarssen and Breukelen), established in 1655; the baroque gardens, laid out by Daniel Mawt around 1725 at Ter Meer or Zuilenberg in Maarssen, were likewise renowned; see Abraham Rademaker, *Hollands Arkadia.* The Jewish property is impossible to identify, but see J. Zwarts, "Portugeesche Joden te Maarsen en Maarsseveen," 48–65. Information kindly supplied by Dr. Christine van Ronnen of the Rijksarchief in Utrecht.

*Fig. 130. "Typical" Dutch Garden.* Anonymous engraving, 1730(?), from Rademaker, *Hollands Arkadia.*

The sort of clutter in a garden that Ligne, blithely forgetting his own plans for Belœil, decries so loudly in his condemnation of everything "Dutch" (IV.91–95).

other; with tiny inventions that suit not at all their sad-faced gardeners who, unsmiling, water the envious visitor; and with grottoes on which is lavished all the wealth of the seas and of the Indies.

93    Apropos of which: I remember my grotto at Klosterneuburg[90] in Austria, part of a pleasure garden that I sold. It cost huge sums of money. Water no longer flowed through it; frogs had blocked all the waterpipes. There was so much in it of shellwork, mirrors, paintings, almost-fine gems, little tiles, sirens, gods, seasons—and a ceiling!— that I wager a pensioner or scrivener of the [Dutch] Republic would have given 60,000 francs for it.

94    There are grottoes near Utrecht that cost more than that. Pinto's[91] cost much more. It contains a hunting scene. The quarry is atop the waterfall, while the dogs and men chasing it are made of the most

90. See part III, note 18.
91. Isaac Pinto (1715–87), a famous humanitarian, known to Voltaire and Diderot as an economist and moralist; according to available information, he did *not* own property near Utrecht; see Jacob S. Wijler, *Isaac de Pinto, sa vie et ses œuvres.* It may be that Ligne had in mind another famous and wealthy landowner, Jakob Poppen, whose estate still exists at Over-Holland (between Breukelen and Loenen, though somewhat altered from this description); it was for a time the scene of Linnaeus's research (as was Pinto's estate near Amsterdam, whence perhaps this confusion); see Zerbe and Connolly, *Small Castles and Pavilions of Europe,* 52–53.

valuable shells. In that country it is not rare to find carnelian eyes, emerald noses, topaz cheeks, and agate brows. Unfortunately, I have missed seeing only coral lips and pearly teeth. Everything that is so boring to examine in collections of natural history is used for those figures. What passes with the Dutch for countrified or improper costume consists of aquatic plants, herbaria, and petrified woods. You would think it a deliberate insult to the poverty of other nations. But Taste, whose history I seem to be writing, and Chronology, that charming god without whom all the others would be unable to please us and who is always warring with the god of wealth, avenge us properly.

95  Taste is never cheated. In Holland, people wish to succeed in this field by purely superficial cleanliness. But Taste is wary of appearances; it pierces coppices, goes into homes, plumbs the depths of canals, and when it finds them muddy or the air heavy and unhealthy, it jumps into the swim and lands wherever possible. That is why, no longer able to stand the dampness and the pettiness of the land of the Dutch, Taste came to seek its fortune in the Austrian Low Countries.

96  I have already spoken of the refuge I tried to offer Taste at Belœil. Not far from the shores of the handsomest canal, bordered with meadows, fences, and agreeable dwellings and framed with the most beautiful trees, which proclaim the felicity and wealth of this country, there is a retreat in good taste on a fine lawn with lattice-work pavilions. Something about it amused passersby who stopped along the highway to see a noble and pleasing amphitheater; but after amusing the sightseers, M. Walckiers wanted to amuse himself.[92] Without disturbing the arrangement of a seemingly French garden, he astonishes by revealing, in what we take for an ordinary clump of trees, coppices to the right, while to the left there are others, cleverly linked across the lawn to the natural garden. From whatever angle we view this perfect picture, its creator is always right. His grotto is correct because it serves to link one scene with another, and the visitor is astonished at the end to discover the ruins of Tivoli.[93] The great bridge that improperly occupies the whole valley in a second

92. Edouard, Viscount Walckiers (1758–1837), a politician and wealthy financier of the Low Countries, had a pavilion built by Antoine Payen the Elder (1749–98) and Louis-Joseph Montoyer (1750?–1800) ca. 1781 to the north of Laeken, now known as the Belvédère and home to the Princes of Liège. See Zerbe and Connolly, *Small Castles and Pavilions of Europe*, 57–59.
93. The ruins of the Temple of Vesta at Tivoli (Italy) were a commonplace of the picturesque garden. See *Jardins en France*, no. 112A–G, and Thacker, *The History of Gardens*, 12, 100.

scene will be modified, I trust, just as will the tortuous watercourse of the stream it spans, which looks like a knotted ribbon. It is annoying to be so oneself when forced to go either up or down in strolling. Everything is charming to remark, but not at all agreeable to use. The handsome greensward with greenery of the four seasons, the choice of some of the most precious shrubs from all countries, the plantings, the most careful cultivation—all are good examples to follow. It was clever to have the domain seem more spacious than it is; I've already said so. But this desire for illusions must not be pushed too far. M. Walckiers should have curbed his megalomania from time to time with great coppices, without which we have to say that he who proves too much proves nothing. I dislike vagueness, whether in expression or in gardens. The canal, the stream, and the meadows that do not belong to M. Walckiers swear fealty to him. You might say that Nature laughs at him who knows how to treat her so well and that she would wish only to depend on him.

97    Duke Albert of Saxe-Teschen[94] imagined and designed by himself and created like an artist the handsomest saloon in the Christian world, [one that is] completely in keeping with the style of the ancient world, more magnificent still. Surely he would have gloried in the superb construction of a shape and proportions so beautiful, so balanced, noble, daring, rich, elegant, majestic, agreeable, and perfect in effect and ornament. The society of a very fine château does him a disservice; even that of Versailles would be unworthy of him. We are allowed to wrong ourselves. And it is a fine wrong to have sacrificed so much to taste and wealth together; a rarity, say I. The true spot for this august temple is in the midst of the forest of Dodona or at a junction of twelve highways amid a marvelous forest. And if Diana, in her way, had wished to give a party on Olympus, I would have advised her on the wedding celebration of one of her nymphs.

98    From this saloon, which it pains me to leave, you go down by a lawn that extends the whole length of the castle and by well-designed slopes to a perfectly conceived stream watered from another level via a very lovely waterfall that can work, unfortunately, for only a few hours at a time, since it is powered by a wood-burning machine, but would be one of the wonders of the world if the course of recycled

94. Duke Albert of Saxe-Teschen (1737–1822) and his wife, Archduchess Marie-Christine of Austria (1742–98), sister of Marie-Antoinette, were the last regents of the Low Countries before the French Revolution; from 1786 to 1794 they occupied an estate at Laeken (Brussels) designed by Payen ca. 1784, which, modernized and enlarged, has become the home of the Belgian monarchs.

water through this immense rock were never ending. Someday, I hope, all the water will link up with the grand canal (which flows into Dutch territory), so that boats may pass under the roadway on its border. That is very necessary and would make the river much more interesting, for at present it is too broad for so short a distance. To the right and left of the lawn there are very agreeable walks amid plantations of precious shrubs, where tall trees sometimes conceal completely the pretty surroundings of the capital. To the left is an open temple—perhaps too open but marvelously located on a rise from which one can view the city [Fig. 131], along with the forest [of Soignies] behind it and the meadows [bordering the Senne] before. To the right, at the end of the lawn, near the canal, is an enclosed temple with a salon and four private rooms. Above that is a cottage very artistically built by Baron Seckendorff,[95] who sometimes resides there. The magnificent Chinese pagoda, the orangery, and other objects of curiosity, whether serious or lighthearted, create variety while offering learned details and interesting observation points.

*99*    Farther along on the same left bank of the same canal, there may be seen a house, belonging to M. Gamarages, that strikes a simply perfect note of elegance.[96] Besides a fine specimen of a garden, it offers the spectacle of correcting errors each time they are made. And it is impossible not to make mistakes when working along these lines. I am guilty of errors; or, rather, I take pride in not being perfect. A picturesque garden is like a work of literature, but it is more difficult to move mountains that were ineptly created or to move a bridge or to fill in a valley than to erase a dozen verses. Yet we must all learn this lesson and examine the work from afar, from near to hand, from the rear, from all sides, calculating the effect of meadows, water, woods; perhaps of a bust; and even of changing light, which we must foresee. M. Gamarages should remove, if he can, a little eminence; he will hide a temple that seems to be too much like a chapel and will set out plantings between the river and the canal. Yet there is nothing to be desired in the way of vantage points (the ones here are ingenious) to make visitors believe that the property is still more extensive.

95. About 1780, Lieutenant Colonel Baron von Seckendorff, a member of the famous family of Austrian diplomats, owned a "natural" garden adjoining the once-extensive royal domain at Laeken, near the corner of the present rue de Tivoli and rue Olivier Brunel (Brussels); now destroyed. See the *Plan perspectif de la campagne de Scoonenberg* by Cardon and Landerer, ca. 1781; reference kindly supplied by Professor Jeroom Vercruysse, Brussels.
96. Until the time of the French Revolution, Alexandre Richardot, Count Gamarages, a wealthy member of the Ostend Company, trading in slaves, had a country seat known as Tournhout between the Koekelberg and the present Gare des Marchandises in Laeken; now destroyed. See Alexandre Henne and Alphonse Wauters, *Histoire de la ville de Bruxelles* 3:640–47.

under his windows and would see as close and as often as those who have business there a great lord and a great minister in one person—and that is only to the good.

*115* The Danube even comes to pay homage to him there, for Lan(d)schütz is admirably located. There is a handsome castle, a small stream, a great ravine, fine carpets of greensward, the most varied sorts of view. Yet what is most extraordinary is a wood one-half league thence that you would swear is an island while you are there; you cannot imagine or recall that you got there by buggy. Everywhere—from the cross-paths, from the transverse and angled roadways, from the goosefoots—you can always glimpse the Danube near at hand or far away. It is easy to imagine all kinds of celebrations possible there (at one time I arranged for a very nice one for the master of the place, complete with hunting, fishing, and illuminations, all together), and if the magic of the woods and water were summoned up in turn more cleverly, it would give to them a quality that could not be matched anywhere. There is an island with a bridge, a Chinese parasol under which people may gather, a park with foreign ducks and rare birds; in the midst of the river a rabbit warren, enclosed by walls whose foundations are very deepset; a menagerie whose every niche has a waterfount; and in the center of a spacious crossing where it is located, a handsome pavilion. I disapprove of a new colonnade that has no reason, no design, and improperly backs up to a coppice of no account.[109]

*116* You whom the Creator has so well and so comfortably situated, do not blaspheme against uniformity. Do not consider interrupting it with prodigious expense in order to rise up against God in a daring fountain. Waters that for your convenience are placed at your level will soon fall down on you with all your buildings. Your hydraulic machines and your castles will know the fate of Babel. Have your water running if you can. If you have marshy land, dig out lakes. Still waters, if plentiful, do not stagnate. Wind moves them more readily than the current of a stream. If you do not have the means, create fish ponds to be decorated with flowery borders. As regards profit,

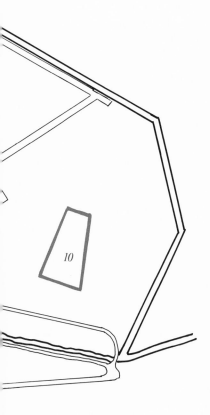

109. "Since then, Count Zichy, Prince Bathiány at Komárom, Baron Véczey, and several counts Esterházy have embellished the kingdom [of Hungary] with gardens in the modern manner" (Ligne's note). The references here are to the Zichy estates at modern Nagyvásöny and Osöny, Cziffer, and Zichyfalva; Bathiány's at Komáron, Körmend, Güssing, Czakány, Gyandfalva, and Szabad-Battyán; the Véczey estates at Hainácskeö and Szatmár; and the lesser Esterházy estates at Fráknovár, Galántha, Totis, Szered, Devecser, Pápa (Táta), and Czákvár. See Ligne's *Nouveau Recueil* 2:137, and Anna Zádor, "The English Garden in Hungary," 79–98.

say you like fishing and aquatic birds. Construct baldachins on pilings, fishermen's cabins covered with rushes and draped with garlands of nets; several open-sided structures do marvels. Let some be traps for the amusement of hunters, others for possible collations. Set up duck preserves whose vaulting is agreeable. Make goosefoots in your canals, beds of water, clumps of reeds; let there be something to recall the loves of Pan and Syrinx.[110] But again, enclose neither your water, nor your gardens, nor your forests.

117  It is sad to watch wealth and workmanship go to waste. Schönbrunn,[111] for instance, which cost so much and has so often been changed, is badly situated. The gloriette above it looks moribund. But the temple, which looks as if it belonged; the needle; the menagerie; the hothouses; the botanical garden—all are superior to all others, and the august vaults of those most majestic of lanes are remarkable.

118  Laxenburg[112] would be too, if it could be approached from the mountains [Fig. 134]. Joseph II had wished to build there for his court, half in the woods and half on the green, separate houses. Each one would have been in the style of a different kingdom or country under his dominion, from the Black Sea almost to the ocean, and from the Adriatic to the Rhine. It was a new, piquant, and different project that would have been fun to carry out. And the irregular little squares or circles enclosing each house would also have been treated in exotic fashion.

119  Joseph II made some errors in embellishing the Prater,[113] of which I have already spoken [Fig. 135]. The goosefoot is too much. What pleasure is there in seeing Heaven via a direct line through the aperture of two short and broad lanes? I should leave but one of

110. That is, the illusion of love. In ancient mythology, Pan attempted to possess the chaste nymph Syrinx, but at the crucial moment she was transformed into reeds that sighed as they rustled, giving him the idea for his pipes, thereafter called Syrinx.

111. Schönbrunn is the famous imperial palace, two and one-half miles southwest of Vienna, begun ca. 1695 by Fischer von Erlach (1656–1723), with extensive gardens; now within the city limits. See Sitwell, *Great Palaces of Europe*, 212–21.

112. Laxenburg is the site of an imperial hunting lodge with a superb park some eight miles south of Vienna.

During his reign, Joseph II (1741–90), emperor from 1765, formulated controversial policies involving the multinational empire yet retained Ligne's complete devotion. See Roger Bauër, "Remarques sur l'histoire," 107–12.

113. The Prater, the Augarten, and Brigittenau were once popular pleasure gardens and important green spaces between the inner city of Vienna and the Danube; now within the city limits. Only the Prater retains anything of its former function. Ligne mentioned it earlier (III.63).

*Fig. 135.* L. Janscha,
*Coffee Houses in the Prater,*
Vienna. Tinted engraving, 1790(?).
Courtesy Graphische Sammlung
Albertina, Vienna.

One of the attractions of
the Prater was this sort of
restaurant, where people
of every nation and condition
came to relax, as evidenced
in the variety of costumes
shown here.

these last and I should fill the great circle with the biggest trees I
could find so that the insignificant void would not diminish part of
the charm of this unusual forest by predisposing people against it.
Through two curved lanes I would then be able to go without being
discovered, on the one side to the suburbs, on the other to the
Augarten. By thus linking it to the Brigittenau in a more obvious
manner, I would create the most handsome of gardens, half-groomed,
half-natural. To draw the Prater and the city even closer, I would
plant tall trees on both sides of the main street of Leopoldstadt, almost against the houses. By similar plantings on each side of the
street that leads from the city to the Augarten, I would have the forest
extend into Vienna itself [Fig. 136].

120    If I were a great lord of Austria or Bavaria, I would purchase
ready-made gardens in Upper Austria or in the area near Salzburg,
which combines surprising features with the gentlest effects. To be
sure, we can do without such combinations when we have the courage to sacrifice so many natural beauties to gardens, like Count Prosper von Sinzendorf at Ernstbrunn, a few leagues from Vienna.[114] He

114. Ernstbrunn (Greater Vienna), an estate belonging to Count Prosper von
Sinzendorf (1751–1822), from which his branch of the family took its name, located between the Wienerwald and the capital, today in the seventeenth ward of
the city but greatly transformed.

created even the setting for his garden. His plantings had picturesque objectives favored by the elevation and irregularity of the site, which he improved at every point. I like his huge ruin. I like broad expanses heralding a grander construction than others that are marred for want of several stories. His temple is disfigured no more than necessary and is in the grand style. The obelisk to Marshal Laudhon is handsome and daring. The ancient gateway is in excellent taste, while the wooded portions have charming greenswards in inviting hollows. This fine country seat is unique and quite unlike other domains of *servile imitatorum pecus* [the herd of servile imitators].[115]

*121* Almost everywhere in Bohemia, instead of battlefields we now see fields of flowers, thanks to the absence of war. The country is again glorified by Schönhof, where the gardens of Count Czernin are none at all.[116] Nor are they a park. Nor a forest. They are neither quite artistic nor yet quite natural. They are rather a mixture of all that makes owning them a pleasure and the owner quite happy. They are the only garden that has the extraordinary merit of not being enclosed. Hares, foxes, boar, travelers, the sick who leave the baths at Karlsbad for those at Toeplitz—all go there, enter, and stroll about at their leisure. It is blessed for such openness, and the strange thing is that there is no danger or destruction. The very animals seem more discreet than elsewhere. They eat nothing, they spoil nothing, they steal nothing, and they are delighted with Count Czernin. The beginning of the visit is a bit tiring: there are too many ups and downs. But the first scene to be observed is a quiet one where a very handsome saloon in a mysterious and severe temple is located beneath tall old timber trees. Then there is a wild scene in the hollow of a draw. Next, a rustic and religious scene near the house, or rather the rockpile, of a hermit at the foot of a hill atop which sits the hermit's church. From there, you pass over a bridge that begins amid several large trees and links two ravines before descending to a cavern with a tomb and a fountain. On leaving this almost-wild setting, you are surprised to find a broad avenue, like a terrace, from which you view the surrounding area. To the left, as you go up a stairway cut into imitation cliffs, you are even more surprised to find an extensive ornamental lake, above which is a sort of cave, topped in turn by a Chi-

---

115. Horace, *Epistles* 1.19, adapted. Marshal Laudhon is Gideon, Baron Laudhon (1717–90), Austrian field marshal, famous for his victory over the Turks at Belgrade (1789).

116. Around 1785, Count Rudolf Czernin von Chudenitz (1757–1845), a Bohemian noble, created Schönhof (modern Krásný Dvůr) with magnificent gardens some thirty-two miles northwest of Prague. For this and some of the following gardens in modern Czechoslovakia, see Knox, "The English Garden in Poland and Bohemia," 111–16, and Ligne, *Mélanges* 21:196 (1801).

*Fig. 136.* J. Ziegler,
*Entrance to the Augarten,*
Vienna, with the Prince
de Ligne in his cabriolet.
Tinted engraving, 1790(?).
Courtesy Historisches
Museum der Stadt, Vienna.

After the loss of his fortune
in 1794, Ligne was reduced to
using this one carriage, which
was soon dilapidated and easily
recognized, becoming the talk
of Vienna.

nese house. Continuing on, you climb steadily but imperceptibly to a
Gothick church now under construction, from which you can view
the whole countryside. Farther on, there is a Dutch farm, separated
by coppices from a new plantation. In returning to the main house,
after crossing a small enclosure with a few tame animals, you are
delighted to come upon a handsome open saloon, with eight columns
calling attention to its magnificence, after you have passed through
regions that were by turns Alpine or agricultural, Gothick or mandarin. Then you come to a small lake with a very beautiful waterfall,
ending on one side with a fisherman's shack in perfect taste. From
there, a pleasant roadway leads through a wooded dell to an immense
meadow of the greatest beauty, where a superb, high, long, tortuous,
and abundant cascade falls with the greatest swiftness from the height
of a mountain and seems to be visible through the trees. It comes to
an end in a closed temple of a very handsome architectural order,
opposite a sort of basin, supplied with water for as long as desired, to
which, I believe, changes should be made. Finally, two paths that
follow the course of a wide and flowing brook, agreeably babbling on
(with neither too many nor too few pebbles), lead the satisfied stroller
to the castle. The richness of the exotic plants and the follies and the
maintenance of the paths exceed by far the best I once saw in England and France. We must admit that the estate of Count Czernin is
very extensive.

122 As a good patriot, I feel obligated to mention those who support grace, taste, and the fine arts in our kingdoms. Countess Bucquoy has labored in their name at Gratzen.[117] I would be mistaken for a writer of novels or idylls and the rival of Gessner or Berquin,[118] the author of eclogues, Arabian nights' entertainment, and poems if I were to mention Vallon Chéri and all that makes this creation divinely interesting. Go there and see for yourselves the lawns, the monument, and the brook with its first enchanting waterfall before you discover, after a short walk, the majestic and overflowing cascade that, thanks to the clouds, appears to link Earth and Heaven.

123 Dux, the Chantilly of Bohemia, is as yet incomplete.[119] But it will be even more lovely when the rustic part is extended at the cost of two roads with hedgerows, unfortunately so attractive that it is difficult to condemn them. By removing thirty or forty lengths of wall and by planting four rows of trees around an immense pond, I would have that rustic part become one with the park, which would then be the rival of the three most handsome ones I know in the whole world.[120]

124 I like projects whose realization seems to be the result of magic; and I admire those who know how to create magic. For instance, a traveler I know arrived at one of the estates of Count Chotek, called L'Isle,[121] which he had not visited in more than three months. He believed it had been mislaid or that inadvertently the name of another place had been given to the postilion. He found neither the canal that

117. Vallon Chéri (Czech. Terčino údolí) was partly the creation of an outstanding beauty at the court of Leopold II, Countess Marie-Thérèse de Bucquoy, née Paar (1746–1818), at Nové Hrady, Czechoslovakia, not far from Budweis; see her portrait by Mme Vigée-Lebrun in the Liechtenstein Gallery, Vienna, with one of several cascades on the estate flowing in the background. Situated in a valley about 1.5 kilometers by .5 kilometer, the site was part of a larger "friendship garden" (Czech. *zahrada přátelství*) conceived of as an illustration of picturesque sentimentality.

118. Salomon Gessner (1730–88), the Swiss poet and painter, author of *Idyllen*, famous in the history of the return to nature and the development of the "natural" garden at the end of the eighteenth century; Arnaud Berquin (1747–91), the French author of children's books and elegies now remembered only for their saccharine quality.

119. "The property of Count Waldstein" (Ligne's note). Joseph, Count Waldstein (1775–1814) was Ligne's nephew, in whose castle at Dux (modern Duchcov, Czechoslovakia) Casanova was librarian, dying there in 1798.

120. These were Versailles, Belœil, and Wörlitz.

121. Count Johann-Rudolf Chotek von Chotkowa (1748–1824), Austrian chamberlain and Ligne's companion, created an extensive landscape garden at L'Isle (modern Veltrusy), some ten miles northwest of Prague, designed by Rudolph Födisch (fl. 1780–1800) in 1783.

he had been used to crossing at a ford, nor the avenue that had led to the garden, nor the garden itself. The avenue of willows, the flower beds, the terrace, the ramps, the balustrade of sculptured stone—all had disappeared. The whole extent of the garden has now been replaced by a fine lawn that rises imperceptibly from the canal to the castle. There you can enjoy a view uninterrupted by any intermediate object. The uneven ground rising to the terrace that used to form an eminence of several rods is completely leveled and now offers only a vast even surface, covered with a superb carpet of green.

125   The widened canal has become a magnificent lake ending in a semicircle that, on the one hand, leaves the smiling banks of the greensward and, on the other, is blocked by a raised dike, covered with grass and crowned with charming groves. The drive that used to lead directly to the castle winds through these groves and after a few detours crosses a handsome wooden bridge high above the bed of the canal, set upon stone piers that also serve as retaining walls and are linked to another dike that has been terraced and grassed over. Crossing this bridge, whose location and construction are truly picturesque, the eye is drawn to the expanse of water and notes everywhere a spectacle as striking as it is unexpected.

126   At that spot, from which we are most likely to embrace in a single glance all the beauties of the landscape, a grassy couch has been created, shaded by two enormously tall and leafy poplars that seem to raise their proud heads to the heavens. While resting quietly on this rustic seat, capable of accommodating twenty persons, we can discover at our feet a sort of quay along the canal leading both left and right to the pheasant run. Opposite, in all their beauty, lie the lake, the greensward, and the castle, reflected in the liquid crystal. A few trees, isolated or in clumps, planted here and there with discernment and several other new objects created by a clever hand have made the fortune of the landscape gardener who knew how to utilize them [Fig. 137].

127   That is the secret merit of those who work at garden painting. If they create an ensemble that a painter might imitate without changing a single detail, they are the high priests of the temple of gardening. But do not imitate paintings in order to make gardens, else you will often make mistakes. Those objects that painting assembles are sometimes out of place in the garden. I have seen people led astray by following too closely in the steps of [Hubert] Robert.[122]

122. Hubert Robert, French landscape painter and garden designer, important for the history of taste at the end of the eighteenth century. See Pierre de Nolhac and Hubert Burda.

*Fig. 137. View of Veltrusy,*
Czechoslovakia.
Anonymous lithograph,
1820(?), from Dokoupil,
*Historické zahrady.*

Veltrusy, one of the great Czech
gardens in the picturesque
manner, still exists
in its original state.

*128*   Toeplitz is where you must go to see the wisest re-creation after destruction. Prince Clary, according to those who take the waters, had the most nobly fastidious garden ever.[123] But he declared war on the stones, the walls, the stairways, the terraces, the arbors. And though full of respect for the most ancient trees, by condemning enough of them to destroy their straight lines, he has nevertheless skillfully known how to preserve enough of them, intermingled with irregular plantations, to create the most majestic wood. He has artfully separated two immense ponds, one of which is indeed a lake while the other contains a Moorish temple on a charming island.

*129*   Without trickery he has called forth genuine prodigies, locating the masses of green where they create the best effects with no exaggeration. You find your own entertainment at Toeplitz. You are not busied, despite yourself, by a lord who wants you to see one hundred things at once, so that you end by seeing none. He once had an orchard. Well and good. But it was spiritless. He has now enlivened it with cabins and a herd. A quite lovely assembly house for those who go to take the waters, warm and healthful, demanded a sort of regularity, but it can be seen from only one vantage point. The rest of the garden has the same sort of contour, whether greensward or

123. Toeplitz (modern Teplice, Czechoslovakia), spa and seat of the Clary-Aldringen family in northwest Bohemia, where Ligne was a frequent guest after 1794, thanks to the kindness of his connections, and where, around 1806, Mont Ligne, a folly, was created in his honor. See Ligne's *Nouveau Recueil* 2:101, and *Fragments* 2:99.

*Fig. 138. Panorama of Toeplitz.*
Anonymous engraving, 1814(?),
Courtesy Historisches Museum
der Stadt, Vienna.

Mont Ligne is the terraced
hill to the left of center, and
the Clary Palace is to the
right of the church steeples in
this view of a typical middle-
European watering spot.
See also Figure 10.

highway, blurred in outline beyond accidental banks of flowers or the
lawn that is opposite his very pretty theater. A greening room there,
decorated on the inside but outside a temple, successfully situates his
castle in the garden; otherwise it would be merely in town. This
building, which appears detached, is nonetheless the end of one wing
of the castle; and this temple, at the edge of the town square and
overshadowed by trees, turned the trick. There is no logic in all this
but a discernment that I shall ever cite as a model worthy of imitation. And I would like to see someone in England solve like Prince
Clary this problem of creating from an old garden an agreeable new
one, whose plan would be sent by post.

130   His park is separated from the valleys of Switzerland and from
the meadows of England by six or seven parks for game where there
are saloons of verdure, benches beneath immense oak trees, handsome roads for tracking, little paths for strolling, some dwellings—or
at least, shelters—sited in picturesque fashion on rock outcroppings,
with natural waterfalls, swift brooks, and incomparable vistas everywhere [Fig. 138].

*131*　With time and patience (the only virtue I advocate) there will be roads, bordered by trees, linking the seven wild gardens to the decorative park at Toeplitz, which will then become a metropolis for them. One joy more will be having in the midst of this fine valley—which, with its quincunxes of fruit trees added to what I have just described will make a garden of the whole estate—a mountain on which, thanks to the daring of the Swedes [in the Thirty Years' War], there will be the most august ruin of an ancient fortress, where you can view the Elbe and Saxony.

*132*　That is what I offer to true connoisseurs for their serious consideration of the way in which the whole country has been treated. And I wager that on seeing the labors of the lord of Toeplitz, you may well imagine it to be full of taste, tact, wit, and judiciousness.

*133*　You have to have seen many countries to have an idea of a site like Toeplitz. You frequently want the genre to be to your own taste, yet you cannot imagine it. Lakes, dark trees, decorative heaths covered with cattle, decorated columns scattered among the cultivated fields would have suited Potsdam.[124] Instead of that, Frederick II, who traveled only in the company of a hundred thousand men, was improperly magnificent, having seen but imperfect old engravings of Versailles and the paintings on the walls of some cabaret where, after a battle he had won, he perhaps had his headquarters. He thought that with the strength of his genius he could force Nature as he had forced victory, war, politics, population, finance, and industry. But Nature does not care two whits for heroes. She prefers a farmer from Somerset to them.

*134*　At barren Sanssouci[125] there are only two agreeable things—both rather wild—which, luckily, have been forgotten or neglected until the present time [Fig. 139]. On the one hand, there is a temple of a rather severe order that contains a treasure trove of medallions and rarities from the collections, partly at Charlottenburg, which I saw mutilated or destroyed by the Cossacks during the Seven Years' War.[126] On the other, as a sort of pendant, there is the handsomest,

---

124. Potsdam, a town southwest of Berlin, practically the capital of Brandenburg-Prussia under Frederick II (1712–86), whose megalomania Ligne criticizes in this paragraph; see Guy, "The Prince de Ligne and the Exemplification of Heroic Virtue," 79.

125. Sanssouci, a pleasure palace with extensive gardens in Potsdam, built to plans of Frederick II in 1745–53 by Georg von Knobelstorff (1699–1753). See Sitwell, *Great Palaces of Europe*, 94–104.

126. Charlottenburg, a castle and garden in West Berlin, in a bend of the river Spree, built from 1695 to 1788 and occupied by Ligne and his troops 9–12 October 1760. See Sitwell, *Great Palaces of Europe*, 78–85.

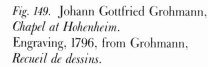

*Fig. 149.* Johann Gottfried Grohmann,
*Chapel at Hohenheim.*
Engraving, 1796, from Grohmann,
*Recueil de dessins.*

One of the several structures
described by Ligne (IV.141–
46) that is still standing at
Hohenheim.

less organized than Europe. This first stage would suffice to honor its creator, but the wealth of his imagination and his fortune demanded another. To have an excuse for turning this presentation to advantage, the duke has backed each of his monuments with a small house, seemingly the dwelling of a peasant in which are all his tools, his resting place, his kitchen, and, amid all that, where you least expect it, a saloon of the greatest richness and—sometimes—taste. Among some ruins there is an aqueduct with five rows of arches, cabins nestling in the most picturesque manner with baths, boudoirs, studies, and charming saloons, and, ever-present, the peasant's little house. All the roads leading from one dwelling to another are bordered with beds of the most precious flowers; everywhere there are delightful masses of them and the best-maintained carpets of green. The program for all that and the details elaborated by the duke are most ingenious. He has imagined that pioneers, having discovered in this plot of ground the remains of buildings from a Roman colony, have elected to use them for their own lodgings. I deem it would have been better to have installed his own court there, instead of leaving idle and useless the decorated saloon, the kitchen, and the supposed ovens of his imaginary peasant, whose house would prove to be an excellent place for select company, while his sort of estate would add great piquancy to such an assembly.

*143* Although all this might satisfy the richest of imaginations, the duke has seen fit to try his hand at still other effects. He has come down to our own times. Mythology has yielded to martyrology, the latter brought to mind by catacombs fashioned artistically out of a cliff. The early Church has become a congeries of sects, with Gothick buildings and windows [Fig. 149], a curacy, statues of saints of ill repute and worse construction, a hermit, and so forth.

*144*   The Turks and the Chinese have not been forgotten. Even the Japanese have their place there. The English too, although you cannot say it is truly an English garden, since there is only the meadow treated in the style of this nation, from which practically nothing else has been borrowed. The plot is meager, but you can walk for four or five hours around it before realizing it to be so, and you need time to discover all the parts. Since, unfortunately, it must all come to an end sometime, there are, to conclude, two waterfalls beyond a few cairns to the right, and to the left another superb cascade falls from a prodigious height onto immense boulders, of which the most handsome and the largest supply the needs of still more grottoes, saloons, stairways, and the most agreeable vista I know.

*145*   Here, lest the enthusiasm this fine site inspires in me become insipid, I shall reveal two faults that may be easily rectified. First, the large building, or barracks, located next to the cliff has plaster of a white so unworthy that it dishonors the pungency of the cliff. I requested that it be hidden (and the duke has promised that this will be done) with huge plantings, which by surrounding the cliff with a separate view will give it a suitably somber and austere appearance. Through the shady top of thick and leafy trees on the other side of a small ravine a large village will be visible, admirably suited to the scene since it seems to be part of a lovely picture. The other fault is irremediable: the lack of water. This spot needs it. This water exists, but for how many minutes? Before the duke can show his garden, which he alone can do (for an inexpert guide would merely underline the fact that each folly is only twenty steps from the next), the visitor has to wait for the river as if for actors dressing for the stage. The river is ready. Here it comes! But it is more swift and strong than any kindly Nature could ever create. At full tilt it comes to kiss your feet, the flowers, and the buildings: you might just as well exclaim *Transivit* [Gone]! and bid it goodbye for twenty-four hours.

*146*   I cannot praise enough the artful and daring execution of the vaults and crevasses or the cleverness of placing in the buildings of all those supposed peasants mutilated statues, stones bearing inscriptions, trunks of columns that, in combination with birch and wattle, seem to have been collected only to support such frail edifices. Everything has the shade of color that it ought; everything has the patina of age. The temples are sited mysteriously, and sometimes it is a pleasure to see rising to left or right a superb ancient monument or the wings of a new one, as if the lord of the hamlet had followed the plans of the colony. For instance, what they call the town hall, where the fathers of this wretched little village meet, with marvelous ruins in the back-

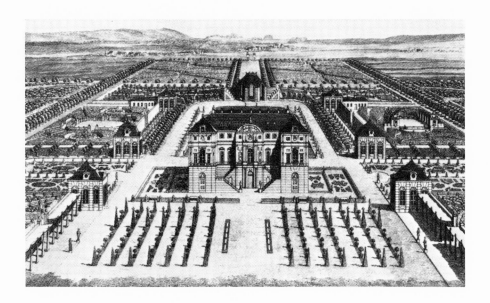

*Fig. 150.* Johann Starke, *Palace in the Grosser Garten*, Dresden. Engraving, 1719, in Hennebo and Hoffmann, *Geschichte der deutschen Gartenkunst.*

An eighteenth-century view of the castle where Ligne had a narrow escape in the Seven Years' War and which is still the centerpiece of a restored and revitalized Dresden.

ground, is of the most desirable modern kind possible. Thus are both imagination and erudition intrigued at the same time. Go there and study. Admire and imitate if you wish. Do better if you can.

147   Saxony, for a long time satisfied with her Elbe and its rich banks, green or hilly, admired especially the handsome Dresden basin without working at it.[142] The only familiar public promenade was the superb Grosser Garten, which I spoiled when occupying it with my regiment [Figs. 150, 151]. Because at that time I was raked by a few cannon, which carried off the arm of a statue next to me, I have since had perhaps no use for straight avenues. The palace and the pavilions would recall to mind Marly, insofar as August II, the Louis XIV of

142. In Dresden (East Germany), the Grosser Garten, laid out ca. 1730 under August II the Strong of Saxony (1670–1733), is somewhat reduced in size since the eighteenth century. Ligne refers here to an incident that occurred during the Seven Years' War (20 August 1759).

   Prince Max (1759–1838), fifth son of Duke Frederick-Christian (1730?–63) and father of King Frederick-August II (1780?–1854), renounced his dynastic rights in 1830. He inherited the castle and park of Elsterwerda, about seventeen miles northwest of Dresden on the Schwarzer Elster, begun by Matthäus Daniel Pöppelmann (1662–1736) in 1732 and mentioned by Ligne in the *Coup d'Œil* of 1786 (III.33). Meanwhile, he occupied the Prince Max Palace in Dresden (destroyed at the end of the nineteenth century).

   From 1768, Prince Anton (1755–1836), King of Saxony in 1827, fourth son of Duke Frederick-Christian and brother to Prince Max, resided at Pillnitz on the Elbe (East Germany), seven miles southeast of Dresden, built ca. 1723 by Pöppleman with a cleverly combined "French" and "Chinese" garden, later celebrated as the scene of the Declaration of Pillnitz, 27 August 1791 (against the French Revolution).

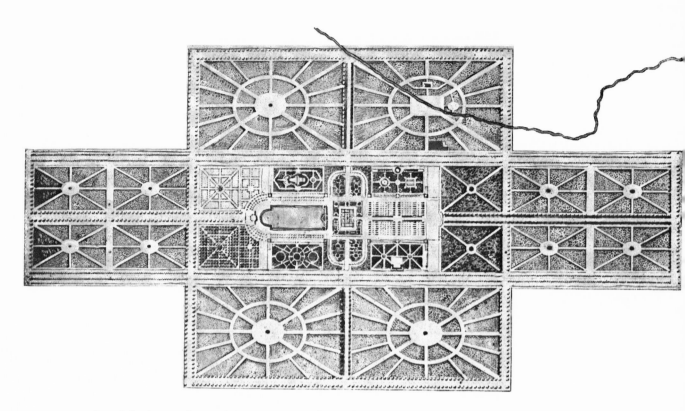

*Fig. 151. Plan of the Grosser Garten.* Anonymous engraving, 1719, courtesy Sächsische Landesbibliothek.

This early plan shows the garden as it was approximately in 1759, when during the Seven Years' War Ligne was nearly killed in a skirmish along one of the walks. In the later eighteenth and early nineteenth centuries the garden was developed much more extensively into a park not unlike the Prater in Vienna. Although it suffered considerable damage in World War II, it has been restored and serves once more as one of the world's great pleasure gardens.

Germany, recalled the French king. Right now there is nothing so agreeable as the huts in the vineyards, backing on to the forest, though they do have the inconvenience of four or five hundred steps if you are to go down to the river's edge. The country house of Prince Max is built in a charming style, both inside and out. His stairway is a masterpiece; but his garden is mediocre and ought to be redone, since it is either too open or too closed. Prince Anton's is much better and has some fine parts [Figs. 152, 153].

148    In the suburbs a model garden, the essence and example of pretty things assembled in a few hundred square feet, is worthy of a visit. It belongs to Baron Adlersthal,[143] who, in the limited space at his disposal, has included a French garden, a Chinese garden, an English garden, a temple, a belvedere, a cliff, a waterfall, baths, caverns, a grotto, a pavilion, a kiosk, a colonnade, a brook, a fountain

143. Although difficult to identify as a person, Baron Adlersthal is known to have possessed a famous "English" garden at Briesnitz to the east of Dresden, now destroyed and the land incorporated into the city limits. See Heinrich Koch, *Sächsische Gartenkunst,* 234. Information most kindly supplied by Dr. Harald Marx, Dresden.

*Fig. 152.* Matthäus-Daniel Pöppleman, *Elevation of the Water Palace, Pillnitz, from the Elbe.* Engraving, 1720, courtesy Sächsische Landesbibliothek.

The chinoiserie of this structure is delightfully subdued and enhanced by its combination with and proximity to the Elbe River.

*Fig. 153.* A. Zingg, *View of Pillnitz.* Engraving, 1800, courtesy Sächsische Landesbibliothek.

A picturesque presentation of the ensemble at Pillnitz as seen from a distance.

jet, a portico, a saloon, a cabinet, a *sala terrena*,[144] a Gothick tower, a bridge, an aviary, a picturelike vista, bark walls, a mausoleum, a pyramid, an obelisk, groupings, monuments, statues, rivers, an orangery, greensward, trees, flowers, a pretty house, sumptuous inside and elegant out—you could fill more than one hundred acres with all this. No garden is more amusing.

144. A *sala terrena* is a grotto (sometimes a garden house or gazebo) intended for alfresco social functions, especially dining. See E. Herget, *Die Sala Terrena im deutschen Barock.*

149   Why not create a new genre? We think all has been said when we are sad and when we depict sad subjects. There is not one false melancholic who does not think he is capable of drawing a garden with two or three winding pathways along which to indulge in deep reflections, they say. But not everyone who wants to be melancholy can be. All these gardens à la Young[145] are often but the work of lovers who for want of imagination hurl themselves into a boring and simple task, like those German and English authors who insist on putting skulls and bones in their plays, being inept at stirring the heart like Rousseau and Voltaire. Sometimes I have also said that you must address the soul, but my friends, by dint of repeating this phrase, have made me disgusted with it. At one point in the present work I said that you must speak to the nose, for I recommend a mixture of perfumes. Here I will add: Speak to the eyes. Refresh them with amiable nothings. At this time I will also say, Speak to the ears; do not leave the bells hanging useless from your Chinese pavilions. Arrange them with graduated tones so that the breeze in blowing makes them chime like a tuneful carillon. Go even so far as to make music with the murmur of your waters, if you can. Metaphysicians, I defy you to get lost in an amusing little garden of a quarter acre, you and your ideas. Wits who see neither mountains nor sea, you have neither space nor time to meditate. Take the air; do not lose yourselves in reflection; have a good time; make fun of the whole world. Or else let it go its own way.

150   Since it is midway between Dresden and Wörlitz, I owe it to the surroundings and still more to taste, which will be ever present in the following descriptions, to mention Thalwitz,[146] on the slope of a most pleasant hillside. The heavenly owner will certainly never create aught but Heaven there. It has a brook, a river, ponds, the handsomest meadows, the most attractive copses, the greatest number of exotic trees that an old ignoramus of a gardener was once barbarous enough to prune as if they were his measly espaliers. What material for grace and wit! There I discovered that two fine French ideas escaped his reforms. They have only to be hidden and set amid plantings. One is a circular bed that appears to be an island from which only the bowers need to be removed. The other is a large pool in the form of a parallelogram paved with arabesque mosaics from which shoot up high two fountain jets that a natural waterfall, sheltered in part by a rather well-proportioned rock, supplies night and day. I can under-

145. The pictures of horror and desolation in *Night Thoughts* by Edward Young (1683–1765) are important for the development of European Romanticism.
146. Thalwitz, village on the Mulde some fifteen miles northwest of Leipzig (near Eilenberg, East Germany), formerly the site of a hunting box and garden belonging to the elector of Saxony.

*Fig. 154.* C. Kunz,
*Palace*, Wörlitz.
Tinted engraving, 1797,
from Hennebo and Hoffmann,
*Geschichte der deutschen
Gartenkunst.*

In an almost perfect example of
the union of opposites, the
classical façade of this palace
belies the charm of the extensive
gardens that still surround it.

stand how people might not want to create similar attractions, but
this one really exists and charmed me into special pleading to estab-
lish that (1) you should destroy as little as possible, as I have already
said; and (2) part of the garden must be in the French style, just as
you create a Chinese tableau to assure thereby a variety that I consider the soul of gardens.

151   It is neither the jealousy of an author, the smugness of an owner,
nor the spirit of contradiction that has so often made me criticize,
desire, or advise for those gardens in Europe that I have frequented
and reviewed. I needs must admire too. And I have just satisfied that
need. Gardeners, painters, philosophers, poets, go to Wörlitz.[147] You
too will enjoy this pleasure there. But do not expect me to break into
an encomium. First, because I want to surprise you. Second, because
Abbé Delille has done so quite unwittingly. He correctly divined
everything that the sovereign of the most beautiful country and of the
happiest subjects in the empire has created in this splendid place
[Fig. 154]. If you seek proof of this, read Abbé Delille.[148]

153   Despite the fine principles of Abbé Delille and the prince, who
were walking abreast of each other in the same career [as gardenists],
the prince could very well go astray, since he carried in his hand
neither pen nor brush but an axe, a shovel, a hoe, and a spade.

147. Wörlitz, some six miles east of Dessau (East Germany), is the magnificent
creation, including the Louisium, Oranienbaum, and the Sieglitzerberg, begun in
1768 by Friedrich-Wilhelm von Erdmannsdorf (1736–95) for Leopold-Franz,
Duke, then Prince (1806) of Anhalt-Dessau (1740–1817), who was a relative of
Catherine II of Russia. See Franz Reil, *Vater Franz, sein Leben und sein
Lebenswerk.*
148. Paragraph 152 is omitted here because it contains only references to quotations from Delille's *Jardins.*

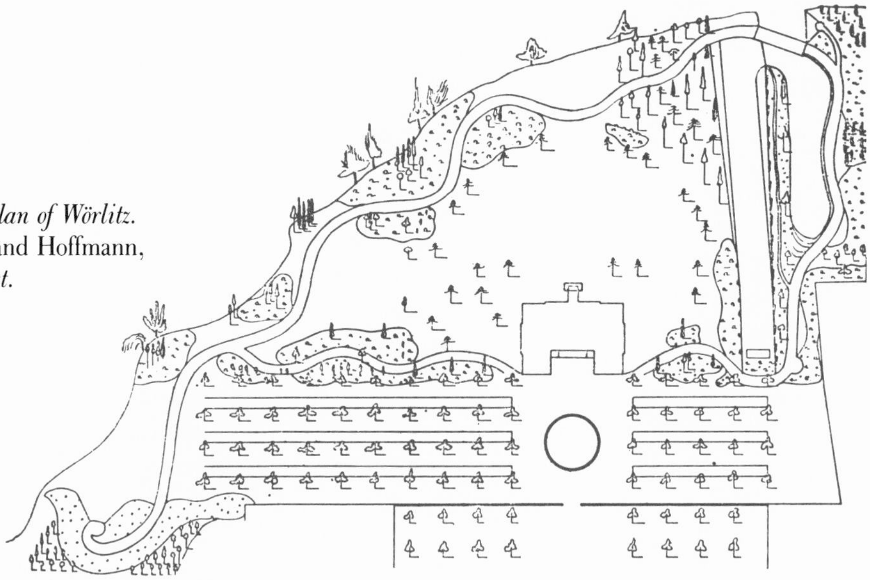

*Fig. 155.* Franz Eyserbeck, *Sketch Plan of Wörlitz.* Drawing, 1763(?), from Hennebo and Hoffmann, *Geschichte der deutschen Gartenkunst.*

This plan is still the basis for the extensive garden layout at Wörlitz. It continued to be developed until about 1820. The famous lime-tree walk, for example, was planted in 1768, starting from the site of a hunting lodge (now destroyed) to the right of the castle and going straight to the top of this sketch.

Before his time, no one had created this sort of garden in Germany or even in France. Scarce had the imaginings of the Chinese become somewhat civilized in England either. At an inn near Wörlitz, a pleasant and comfortable hostelry built by the Prince as part of the decor and vista, is a large old book in which the visitors write what strikes their fancy. Here is what I have just added:

> *J'ai vu Wörlitz. J'ai deviné son maître*
> *L'âme comme l'esprit se peint dans ce qu'on fait.*
> *Dieu le créa dit-on pour nous faire connaître*
> *En vertus, en jardins, un modèle parfait*

> [I saw Wörlitz and guessed the master's name.
> Our actions bespeak both our soul and mind.
> God created this to have us know, they say,
> The perfect example of gardens and virtue].[149]

154  Here is what I hope to prove: Wörlitz would have cost Louis XIV at least twenty million. The prince, who does not want to create the slightest hardship for his subjects, was so sparing in the creation and upkeep of his gardens that you have yourself to be a past master to appreciate his talent as an administrator and to believe how little all that cost him. I am mistaken in calling a garden what he has treated as if it were a whole country, extending even from the residence at Dessau as far as Wörlitz [Fig. 155]. For his canals, his superb fields, and the masses of oak, sycamore, Lombardy poplar, pines, and so forth link the two seats. You need at least three days to see everything. For convenience, Wörlitz can be divided into five cantos with

149.  For Ligne's habit of inscribing guest books with verse, see "A. M. Elliot" in Ligne's *Nouveau Recueil* 1:106.

*Fig. 157.* F. von Laek, after Matthey, *Temple at Wörlitz.* Lithograph, undated, from Hennebo and Hoffmann, *Geschichte der deutschen Gartenkunst.*

Not just another picturesque view but an example, along with Figure 156, of the wide variety of structures and spaces, not to mention topography, in the extensive gardens at Wörlitz that contributed so much to Ligne's delight and admiration.

with ours and frequently taking advantage of their weakness, increases daily in strength and is excellent for gardening. Garden tools are well suited to those arms that the tanning of the sun has only mellowed. Whatever is not too hard to do may easily be entrusted to the village maidens, who, singing at their work, can earn enough to help an elderly mother—a scolding mother, perhaps, but one who at heart is as tender a parent as he who merely consults Love and Nature without inquiring about the means to support their productions.

167   Let us take care and remember the children too. Each morning, if they are seven years old, they can gather up the leaves that have fallen at night, or pull the weeds the dainty sheep refuse upon the lawns.[158] The luxury of neatness that I have stressed will employ a score of people, great and small, from your village. And five or six hundred ducats thus spent each year will ensure you a neat and beautiful garden, a proper tribute paid by wealth to poverty. Employ all ages, but without fatiguing the old soldiers banished to their cottages by wounds and age. They can do something: they can keep the little ones from quarreling, the girls from giggling and chattering instead of working, the laborers from lingering too long over their dinners. They could even wheel a barrow with steps slow but sure and fill the ruts that deface the roads beyond the park. On Sundays they can

158. Ligne is specific about the children's age because of the laws regarding vagabondage and vagrancy (which were said to begin applying to children at seven years), before the days of compulsory education.

watch the visitors and see that they do not gather flowers or trespass through the shrubbery and that their lively children do not disturb the concerts in preparation beneath a brood hen on her nest.[159]

168    The policy of a wise government should include protecting the art of gardens and those who cultivate them and inducing the lord of a village to live upon his property, at least for six months of every year. But no, the government sends him to his regiments, never to his estate, where he might be far more useful. He could, for example, redress wrongs, reconcile the vicar and the bailiff who have quarreled about the former's niece or about cheating at cards. He could check the zeal of the young doctor who is experimenting on the hapless villagers, biding time till he acquires a city practice. He could say to the apothecary (receiver of city chemists' trash), Do not prescribe those dangerous mixtures of American barks and juices; come into my garden and gather for yourself indigenous and wholesome herbs. Above all, he could entreat the vicar to read less theology and practice more charity; to explain and paraphrase it, not interpreting it according to his own notions but (finding there a mystery too great for him to solve) preaching from its pages the rewards of duty, harmony in the parish, and obedience to the sovereign, to fathers and mothers, the lord, the parson.

169    While strolling, or hunting, or going to see his people, this lord or gentleman who lives in the country can perhaps relieve the suffering of an entire family with a gift of coin or surprise some of his poorer charges by depositing, unknown to them, a sum in a corner of their cottage, then refuse the blessings they would pour on him from a distance as he quickly makes good his escape.[160]

170    Through physical advance to mental peace and from that to physical calm, I advise others, from my own experience, to love gardens to the point of dreaming about them. May Heaven preserve you from thinking as you go to rest of women, war, or the court or of evildoers, fools, or fortune. But if some plan of a bower, an orchard, or a brook goes to bed with you, you will surely pass an excellent night. Your ideas will be lulled by the undulating water, by the golden grain of Ceres, by flowers softly trembling on the breath of a gentle zephyr.

*Fig. 158.* Daniel Chodowiecki, *Family Scene.* Engraving, 1790(?).

A sentimental vignette that corresponds almost exactly to the feelings Ligne frequently expresses, most notably in IV.166–70.

159.  Here Ligne seems to be a precursor of Charles Fourier (1772–1837) and his vision of a controlled economy/society for the improvement of mankind. See Jonathan Beecher, *Charles Fourier.*

160.  Ligne is a typical representative of his own age with this awkward scene of benevolence, a sine qua non for French novelists, at least from the time of Rousseau's *Nouvelle Héloïse,* pt. 5, letter 2. See Fargher, *Life and Letters in France,* 16–27, and Rosenblum, *Transformations in Late Eighteenth Century Art,* 55–60.

How happy I shall be who have so often claimed that men should make a code, and even a regime of happiness, if I have now held out a branch to be seized by some about to drown in the ocean of the great world. Happy indeed is it to guard from storms, to offer a hospitable shade to those who are flung into the vale of tears, to teach them to plant with flowers the little distance that separates, as I have shown in my garden of allegory, the cradle of infancy from the sanctuary of death [Fig. 158].

*171*   Yes, happy if I have succeeded, if, in embellishing Nature; or, rather, in bringing her closer; or—better still let me say—in making her *felt*, I have imparted a taste for her. From our gardens, as I have said, she will lead us elsewhere. Our spirits will have recourse to her power in all things; our purified hearts will be the most precious temple we can dedicate to her; our souls will glow with her beauties. Truth will return to live among us. Justice will come down from above. And one hundred times more happy than on Olympus, the gods will beg mankind to let them dwell on earth.

# Appendices

## Comparison of the 1786 and 1795 Editions

The 1786 edition of the *Coup d'Œil* had three parts, 269 paragraphs, divided as follows: part I, 31 paragraphs; part II, 31 paragraphs; part III, 207 paragraphs.

The 1795 edition, with 332 paragraphs, was organized as follows: part I, 33 paragraphs plus author's note; part II, 31 paragraphs plus author's note; part III, 268 paragraphs, divided into two sections, with 97 paragraphs in IIIa and 171 paragraphs in IIIb.

The ordering of the original paragraphs in the 1795 edition, compared with that of 1786, is as follows, IIIa becoming III and IIIb becoming IV:

PART I —1, 2, 3, 4, 5, 6, 7, 8, four new paragraphs, 12, 13, 17, 18 plus second half of the author's note at the end, 19, new paragraph, 26, 27, 28, three new paragraphs, 20, 21, 24, new paragraph, 29, 30, 31, two new paragraphs, new paragraph plus first half of note to paragraph 31
      —omits 9, 10, 11, 14, 15, 16, 22, 23, 25, 32, 33
      —subdivides 31
      —adds 12 new paragraphs

PART II —1, 2, 3, new paragraph, 5, 6, 7, 8, 9, 10, 11, 12, 13, 14, 15, 16, 17, 18, 19, 20, 21, 22, 23, 24, 25, 26, 27, 28, 29, 30, 31, author's note
      —omits paragraph 4
      —adds one new paragraph

PART III —twenty-one new paragraphs, 100, 101, 102, twenty-six new paragraphs, 72, six new paragraphs, 28, seven new paragraphs, 9, 69, 46, 47, 48, 49, 50, 51, 52, 53, 54, 55, 56, 57, 58, 59, 60, 61, 62, 63, 64, 65, 66, 67, 119, seven new paragraphs

PART IV —nine new paragraphs, 105, 106, 108, new paragraph, new paragraph plus 14, 11, 13, 15, 16, 17, 18, 20, 21, 22, 23, new paragraph, 24, 6 plus 25, 118, 120, 121, 122, 123, 124, 125, 126, 148, 149, 150, 158, 159, 160, 161, 162, 163, 164, 165, 166, 167, 168, 169, 170, 172, new paragraph, 177, 178, 180, 182, 128, 129, 130, 181, 184, new paragraph, 91, 92, 185, 186, 187, 189, 190, 191, 192, two new paragraphs, 90, new paragraph, 99, two new paragraphs, 195, 196, 138, 139, 140, 113 plus 115, 203, 204, 205, new paragraph, 146 plus 147, new paragraph, 36, new paragraph, 37, new paragraph, 74, 75, 76, 77, two new paragraphs, 133 plus 134, 135, new paragraph, 110, 111, two new paragraphs, 80, 82, 83, 84, 85, 86, 87, 88, seventeen new paragraphs, 29, 30, 31, 32, 33, two new paragraphs, 40, 41, 42, 43, 44, 45, twenty-four new paragraphs, 207
      —omits 1–5, 7, 8, 10, 12, 19, 26, 27, 34, 35, 38, 39, 68, 70, 71, 73, 78, 79, 81, 89, 93–98, 103, 104, 107, 109, 112, 114, 116, 117, 127, 131, 132, 136, 137, 141–45, 151–57, 171, 173–76, 179, 183, 184, 188, 193, 194, 197–202, 206, 208–68
      —subdivides 185
      —combines 6 and 25, 113 and 115, 133 and 134, 146 and 147
      —adds 138 new paragraphs, 67 to Part III and 71 to Part IV

# Gardens in the Coup d'Œil (1795)

The following list is intended to enable the interested reader (perhaps also the tourist) to identify and locate the gardens mentioned by Ligne. French articles (*le, la, l', les*) are not taken into consideration. All information is subject to modification or correction. Modern place names are given in parentheses.

| Garden or Site | Nearest Town | Date of Creation | Architect(s) | Present Condition |
|---|---|---|---|---|
| Adlersthal's villa | Dresden, E.Ger. | ? | ? | destr. 19th cent. |
| Baba | Ligovo, USSR | 1770? | ? | destr. |
| Babalowa | Tsarskoye Selo (Pushkin), USSR | ? | ? | destr. 18th cent. |
| Badminton House | Badminton, U.K. | 1745–70 | Kent, Wright | residence |
| Bagatelle | Paris | 1775 | Blaikie, Bélanger | public garden |
| Baudour | Mons, Belg. | 1776 | Ligne | destr. ca. 1785 |
| Belœil | Mons, Belg. | 1754–71 | Bergé, Bélanger, Ligne | residence |
| Belvédère | Brussels | 1781 | Payen, Montoyer | residence |
| Betz | Senlis, Fr. | 1780 | Harcourt, Robert | transformed |
| Blenheim Palace | Oxford, U.K. | 1705–65 | Bridgeman, Wise, Brown | residence |
| Boufflers's folly | Paris | 1773? | Countess Boufflers | residence |
| Casa Giovanelli | Noventa Padovana, It. | 1738 | Massari | destr. 1960 |
| Casa Pisani | Strà, It. | 1735–56 | Frigimelica, Preti | residence |
| Castle Blaise | Bristol, U.K. | ? | ? | museum |
| Chandieu | Lunéville, Fr. | ? | Héré de Corny | destr. 1738 |
| Chanteheux (see Chandieu) | | | | |
| Chantilly Castle (see le Hameau) | | | | |
| Charlottenburg Palace | West Berlin | 1741? | Godeau | museum |
| Chatsworth House | Derby | 1706–65 | Wise, Archer, Brown | residence |
| Chiswick House | Greater London | 1715–81 | Bridgeman, Kent | public garden |
| Cobenzl's (see Reisenberg) | | | | |
| Commercy Castle | Commercy, Fr. | 1708 | Boffrand, d'Orbay | destr. 1738 |
| Constant's villa | Geneva | ? | ? | destr. |
| Cumberland Lodge | Windsor, U.K. | 1751 | ? | residence |
| Les Délices | Geneva | ? | ? | museum |
| Le Désert | Chambourcy, Fr. | 1774 | Barbier, Robert, Ligne? | being restored |
| Dieburg Castle | Dieburg, W.Ger. | ? | ? | town hall |
| Dux Palace | Dux (Duchcov), Czech. | ? | ? | museum |
| Eichwald (Dubí) | Toeplitz (Teplice), Czech. | ? | ? | ? |
| Elsterwerda | Dresden, E.Ger. | 1732 | Pöppleman | ? |
| Enghien | Hal, Belg. | 1783? | de Wailly | residence |
| Ermenonville | Ermenonville, Fr. | 1766–76 | Girardin, Morel, Robert | being restored |
| Ernstbrunn | Vienna | ? | ? | transformed |
| Esterháza Palace | Fertöd, Hung. | 1766–84 | Moreau?, Gruss | being restored |

| Garden or Site | Nearest Town | Date of Creation | Architect(s) | Present Condition |
|---|---|---|---|---|
| La Favorite | Mainz, W.Ger. | 1696–1724 | Max von Welsch | destr. 1794 |
| Fontaine Budé | Yerres, Fr. | ? | ? | town hall |
| Fontaine Royale | Lunéville, Fr. | 1730? | Héré de Corny | destr. 1738 |
| | | | | |
| Gansenhof | Utrecht, Neth. | 1655 | ? | residence |
| Gatschina Palace | Gatschina, USSR | 1766 | Rinaldi | partly destr. 1942 |
| Gémenos | Aubagne, Fr. | ? | ? | town hall garden |
| Gennevilliers | Paris | 1785 | La Brière | destr. |
| Greenwich | Greater London | 1617 | Webb, Mollet | public garden |
| Grosser Garten | Dresden, E.Ger. | 1715–33 | Pöppleman | public garden |
| Guiscard | Compiègne, Fr. | 1774 | Morel, Robert | transformed |
| | | | | |
| Le Hameau | Chantilly, Fr. | 1773 | Le Camus de Mézières, Leroy | museum |
| Hampton Court | Greater London | 1689–1768 | Marot, Wise, Brown | public garden |
| L'Hermitage | Valenciennes, Fr. | 1747 | Marshal Croÿ | residence |
| Hingene | Antwerp, Belg. | 1789 | Payen | residence |
| Hohenheim | Stuttgart, W.Ger. | 1785 | Fischer | school |
| L'Isle | Veltrusy, Czech. | 1783 | Födisch | school |
| Jolivet | Lunéville, Fr. | ? | Héré de Corny | destr. 1738 |
| | | | | |
| Kamenets Castle | Kamenets-Podolskiy, USSR | ? | Sophie de Witte | destr. |
| Kenwood | London | 1760? | ? | museum |
| Kew | Greater London | 1730–57 | Bridgeman, Kent, Chambers, Brown | botanical garden |
| King's Weston | Gloucester, U.K. | 1777 | Brown | museum |
| Klosterneuburg Manor | Klosterneuberg, Aus. | ? | ? | sold in 1767 |
| Knauthain | Leipzig, E.Ger. | 1770? | Schatz | ? |
| Komárom Palace | Komárom, Hung. | ? | ? | ? |
| Książęce | Szulec, Pol. | 1776–79 | Zug | destr. |
| | | | | |
| Laeken Palace | Brussels, Belg. | 1781 | Payen | residence |
| Lan(d)schütz | Bratislava, Hung. | 1781 | Moreau | school |
| Laxenburg | Vienna, Aus. | ? | ? | museum |
| Łazenki | Warsaw, Pol. | 1784–93 | King Stanislas Augustus, Schuh, Merlini | museum |
| Lichtenberg | Toeplitz (Teplice), Czech. | ? | ? | ? |
| Louveciennes | Louveciennes, Fr. | 1771 | Ledoux | govt. property |
| Lunéville Castle | Lunéville, Fr. | 1739 | Héré de Corny | govt. property |
| Luzancy | La Ferté-sous-Jouarre, Fr. | ? | ? | hospice |

| Garden or Site | Nearest Town | Date of Creation | Architect(s) | Present Condition |
|---|---|---|---|---|
| Machern | Leipzig, E.Ger. | ? | ? | park |
| La Malgrange | Nancy, Fr. | 1712 | Boffrand | transformed |
| Marly | Versailles, Fr. | 1679–1794 | Hardouin-Mansart | destr. 1794 |
| Marquette | Haarlem, Neth. | ? | de Hartaing | residence |
| Méréville | Etampes, Fr. | 1784–94 | Bélanger | transformed |
| Monceau | Paris | 1778 | Carmontelle | transformed |
| Mon Refuge | Vienna | 1795? | Ligne | destr. |
| Moulin Joli | Paris | 1754–72 | Boucher, Robert, Watelet | destr. |
| | | | | |
| Nana | Ligovo, USSR | 1770? | ? | destr. |
| Neuwaldegg | Vienna | 1765 | ? | transformed |
| Nymphenburg | Munich, W.Ger. | 1719 | Carbonet, Girard, Cuvillés | manufactory-museum |
| | | | | |
| Oranienbaum | Lomonosov, USSR | 1713–63 | Schädel, Rinaldi | transformed |
| Over-Holland | Utrecht, Neth. | 1676 | ? | residence |
| Palazzo Colonna | Parma, It. | 1762 | Petitot | museum |
| Park Place | Henley-on-Thames, U.K. | 1760 | ? | school |
| Pavlovsk Palace | Pavlovsk, USSR | 1777 | Cameron, Brenna | museum |
| Peterhof Palace | Peterhof (Petrodvorets), USSR | 1716 | Leblond | museum |
| Petersham Lodge | Greater London | 1720? | Robert Morris? | residence |
| Petit Belœil | Vienna | 1790? | Ligne | destr. |
| Petit Trianon | Versailles, Fr. | 1775–89 | Robert, Mique, Ligne? | museum |
| Pillnitz | Dresden, E.Ger. | 1723 | Longelune, Pöppleman | museum |
| Pope's villa | Greater London | 1720? | Alexander Pope, Kent | school |
| Powąski | Warsaw | 1775 | Princess Czartoriska | war memorial |
| Prado | Marseille, Fr. | 1767–75 | Clérisseau, Embry | museum |
| Prince Max Palace | Dresden, E.Ger. | 1730? | Pöppleman | destr. 1894 |
| | | | | |
| Razumowsky Palace | Vienna | ? | ? | burned 1814 |
| Rheinsberg | Neuruppin, E.Ger. | 1734–78 | Knobelstorff | being restored |
| Rhoon | Rotterdam, Neth. | ? | ? | museum |
| Reisenberg | Vienna | ? | Ligne? | transformed 1809 |
| | | | | |
| Saint-James's folly | Paris | 1784 | Bélanger | residence |
| Sanssouci | Potsdam, E.Ger. | 1744–86 | Frederick II, Knobelstorff | public garden |
| Schönau | Toeplitz (Teplice), Czech. | ? | ? | ? |
| Schönbrunn Palace | Vienna | 1695 | Fischer von Erlach | museum |
| Schönhof | Krásný Dvůr, Czech. | 1785? | ? | school |
| Schwetzingen | Mannheim, W.Ger. | 1743–82 | Pigage, Petrini, Sckell | museum |

| Garden or Site | Nearest Town | Date of Creation | Architect(s) | Present Condition |
|---|---|---|---|---|
| La Solitude | Stuttgart, W.Ger. | 1764 | La Guépière | museum |
| Sofiówka (Sophievka) | Uman, USSR | 1798–1805 | Sophie de Witte, Stanislas Potocki | public garden |
| Stowe House | Stowe, U.K. | 1713–51 | Bridgeman, Kent, Brown | school |
| Strawberry Hill | Greater London | 1759 | Horace Walpole | school |
| Syon House | Greater London | 1762 | Brown | residence |
| Ter Meer (Zuilenberg) | Utrecht, Neth. | 1725? | Mawt | museum |
| Thalwitz | Leipzig, E.Ger. | ? | ? | ? |
| Tivoli | Brussels, Belg. | ? | Seckendorff? | destr. 19th cent. |
| Tivoli | Paris | 1773 | Boutin? | destr. 19th cent. |
| Toeplitz Palace | Toeplitz (Teplice), Czech. | 1780? | A. Legler, Ligne? | archives |
| Tournhout | Brussels | ? | ? | destr. 19th cent. |
| Tsarskoye Selo | Tsarskoye Selo (Pushkin), USSR | 1765–96 | Rastrelli, Neyelov, Cameron | public garden |
| Vallon Chéri (Terezia's Valley) | Nové Hrady, Czech. | 1780? | Countess Bucquoy | park |
| Vanbrugh Castle | Greater London | 1718 | Vanbrugh | school |
| Verkhiai | Vilna (Vilnius), USSR | 1780 | Gucewicz, Ligne? | school |
| Versailles Gardens | Versailles, Fr. | 1661–1775 | Le Nôtre, Robert | public garden |
| Villa Vigier (see Waldegg) | | | | |
| Waldegg | Solothurn, Switz. | 1777 | ? | residence |
| Wanstead House | Greater London | 1762 | ? | destr. 1823 |
| Weimar Castle | Weimar, E.Ger. | 1776 | Goethe, Duke of Weimar | govt. property |
| White Lodge, Richmond | Greater London | 1731–71 | Kent, Brown | school |
| Wilton House | Wilton, U.K. | 1737 | 9th Earl Pembroke, R. Morris, Chambers | residence |
| Wimbledon House | Greater London | 1641–1755 | Mollet, Brown | destr. 19th cent. |
| Windsor Castle | Windsor, U.K. | 1708–29 | Wise, Bridgeman | residence |
| Wörlitz (including Oranienbaum, the Luisium, and Sieglitzerberg) | Dessau, E.Ger. | 1764–96 | Eyserbeck, Erdmannsdorf, F. von Anhalt | park and school |
| Zijdebalen | Utrecht, Neth. | 1681 | ? | destr. 19th cent. |
| Zuilenberg (see Ter Meer) | | | | |

# Bibliography

For greater convenience, the bibliography is divided into three parts: (1) works by Charles-Joseph de Ligne; (2) primary sources; (3) modern works, where a section on exhibition catalogs precedes the main entries. The bibliographical information is as correct and complete as possible, covering all references in the notes, with the addition of some select titles that, although not cited, have been most helpful in preparing this edition/translation. Occasionally the entries are annotated.

## Works by Charles-Joseph de Ligne

### Anthologies

Among the following entries, arranged in chronological order, those marked with an asterisk feature selections from the *Coup-d'Œil* (various editions):

*Staël-Holstein, Germaine de. *Lettres et réflexions du Maréchal-Prince de Ligne.* Geneva: Paschoud, 1809. Reprint Paris: Taillandier, 1989.

C[hevalier] de B[oufflers]. *Œuvres choisies, littéraires, historiques, et militaires,* 2 vols. Geneva: Paschoud; Paris: Buisson, 1809.

*Propiac, Chevalier de. *Œuvres choisies du Maréchal-Prince de Ligne.* Paris: Chaumerot, 1809.

*Dupont, Ambroise. *Mémoires et mélanges historiques et littéraires par le Prince de Ligne* (5 vols.) Vol. 1. Paris: Dupont, 1827.

*Lacroix, Albert. *Œuvres du Prince de Ligne* (4 vols.) Vol. 4. Brussels: van Meenen; Turin: Bocca, 1860.

*Wormeley, Katharine Prescott. *The Prince de Ligne: His Memoirs, Letters, and Miscellaneous Papers.* (2 vols.) London: Heinemann; Boston: Hardy-Pratt, 1897. Vol. 1.

Klarwill, Viktor. *Erinnerungen und Briefe des Fürsten von Ligne.* Vienna: Mainz Verlag, 1920. Partial translation into French published Paris: Crès, 1923.

*Ashton, Leigh. *Letters and Memoirs of the Prince de Ligne.* London: Routledge; New York: Brentano's, 1927.

*Recouly, Raymond. *La Douceur de vivre.* Paris: Editions de France, 1927.

Cantacuzène, Charles-Adolphe. *Œuvres diverses du Prince de Ligne.* Paris: Mercure de France, 1934.

Schalk, Fritz. *Die französischen Moralisten.* Wiesbaden: Dietrich, 1940.

*Charlier, Gustave. *Œuvres choisies du Prince de Ligne.* Brussels: Office de Publicité, 1941.

Duchesne, Alfred. *Souvenirs et réflexions du Prince de Ligne.* Brussels: Office de Publicité, 1941.

Dumay, Raymond. *Pages intimes du Prince de Ligne.* Paris: La Trière, 1952.

*Morand, Paul. *Les Plus Belles Pages du Prince de Ligne.* Paris: Mercure de France, 1963.

*Judrin, Roger. *De fleur en fleur: Dans l'intime du Prince de Ligne.* Lausanne: La Guilde du Livre, 1964.

Juin, Hubert. *Anecdotes et portraits du Prince de Ligne.* Paris: Livre-Club du Libraire, 1964.

von der Burg, Hans. *Gestalten und Ideen.* Graz, Austria: Verlag Styria, 1965.

Guy, Basil. *Œuvres choisies: Nouvelle Anthologie critique.* Stanford French and Italian Studies 13. Stanford, Calif.: Anma Libri, 1978.

### Individual Works

*Colette et Lucas.* Edited by Félicien Leuridant. Brussels: Société des Iconophiles et Bibliophiles Belges, 1914.

## Primary Sources

*Coup d'Œil sur Bel-Œil.* Bel-Œil: Imprimerie du Prince Charles de ———, 1781.

*Coup d'Œil sur Belœil.* Text of 1786 edition, edited by Félicien Leuridant. Ath, Belgium: Coppin-Goisse, 1908. Reprint. Brussels: Hayez; Paris: Champion, 1930.

*Coup d'Œil sur Belœil et sur une grande partie des jardins de l'Europe* (Les Chefs-d'Œuvre méconnus). Text of 1786 edition, edited by Ernest de Ganay. Paris: Bossard, 1922. Reprint 1932.

*Coup d'Œil sur Belœil et sur une grande partie des jardins de l'Europe.* Vols. 8–9 of Ligne's *Mélanges militaires, littéraires, et sentimentaires.* Vienna and Dresden: Walther, 1795.

*Ecarts posthumes.* Edited by Félicien Leuridant. Brussels and Paris: Champion, 1922.

*Fantaisies militaires.* Edited by Waldemar de Heusch. Paris: Champion, 1914.

*Fragments de l'histoire de ma vie.* 2 vols. Edited by Félicien Leuridant. Paris: Plon, 1928.

*Der Garten zu Belœil* [*Coup d'Œil sur Belœil*]. Translated by W.-C. Becker. 2 vols. Dresden: Walther, 1799.

*Lettres à la Marquise de Coigny.* Edited by Jean-Pierre Guicciardi. Paris: Desjonquères, 1986.

*Mélanges militaires, littéraires, et sentimentaires.* 34 vols. Vienna and Dresden: Walther, 1795–1811.

*Mes Adieux à Belœil.* Edited by Ernest de Ganay and Charles Cantacuzène. Brussels, Paris, and London: Association des Ecrivains Belges, 1914.

*Mon Refuge; ou, satire sur l'abus des jardins modernes.* London: Spilsbury, Dulau and Didier, 1801. Contains a dedication to Count L. de S[égur]; Mon Refuge; Critique de ma critique; and a Supplément à tout ce que j'ai déjà dit en vers et en prose.

*Nouveau Recueil de lettres* [*Recueil de Weimar*]. 2 vols. Weimar: Au Bureau de l'Industrie, 1812. Critical edition by Henri Lebasteur, Paris: Champion, 1928.

*Préjugés militaires.* Edited by Waldemar de Heusch. Paris: Champion, 1914.

*Überblick von Belœil* [*Coup d'Œil sur Belœil*]. Anonymous translation. Dresden: Walther, 1797.

*Aedes Pembrochianae.* London, 1788. A guide to Wilton House, Wiltshire.

Austen, Jane. *Northanger Abbey* [1811]. Edited by Anne Ehrenpreis. Baltimore: Penguin Books, 1979.

Beaumarchais, P.-A. Caron de. *Le Mariage de Figaro* [1784]. Edited by E. J. Arnould. Oxford: Blackwell, 1952.

Berquin, Arnaud. *L'Ami des enfants* [1784]. Paris: Genets jeune, 1919.

*Beschreibung des hochfürstlichen Schlosses Esterház.* Pressburg [Bratislava], 1784.

Blaikie, Thomas. *The Diary of a Scotch Gardener at the French Court.* Edited by Francis Birrell. London: Routledge and Kegan Paul, 1931.

Boufflers, Stanislas-Jean de. [*Aline*] *La Reine de Golconde* [1761]. Paris: La Société des amis des livres, 1897.

Bruzen de la Martinière, A. *Le Grand Dictionnaire historique, géographique, et critique.* 10 vols. The Hague: Gosse Junior, 1726–39.

Burke, Edmund. *An Enquiry into Our Ideas of the Sublime and the Beautiful* [1756]. London: Routledge; New York: Columbia, 1958.

Butler, Samuel. *Hudibras* [1663]. Oxford: Clarendon, 1967.

Caesar [Gaius Julius Caesar]. *De Bello Gallico.* Edited by Harper and Tolman. New York: The American Book Company, [1891].

Cardon-Landerer. *Plan perspectif de la campagne de Scoonenberg.* Brussels, 1781.

Carmontelle [Louis Carrogis]. "Le Jardin anglais, proverbe." Edited by C. D. Brenner. In *Le Développement du proverbe dramatique en France,* 45–52. University of California Publications in Modern Philology 20. Berkeley: University of California Press, 1937.

———. *Le Jardin de Monceau, près de Paris.* Paris: Delafosse, 1779.

Casanova de Seingalt, Jacques. *Mémoires.* 3 vols. Edited by Robert Abirached. Paris: Gallimard-Pléiade, 1960.

———. *Quelques Remarques au sujet du Coup d'Œil sur Belœil.* Edited by Frans Hellens. Liège: Dynamo, 1962.

Castiglione, Giuseppe, C.M. *Palaces, Pavilions, and Gardens.* Paris: Jardin de Flore, 1978.

Cerutti, Joseph-Antoine, S.J. *Les Jardins de Betz, poème accompagné de notes instructives sur les travaux champêtres . . . fait en 1785.* Paris: Desenne, 1792.

Chabanon, P-M-G. de. *Lettre sur la manie des jardins anglais.* Paris: Moutard, 1775.

Chambers, Sir William. *Designs of Chinese Buildings, Furniture, Dresses, Machines, and Utensils.* London, 1757. Written in English and French.

———. *Dissertation sur le jardinage de l'Orient.* London: Griffin, 1772. Written in French and English.

———. *An Explanatory Discourse by Tan Chet-Qua* [1773]. Edited by Richard Quaintance. Los Angeles: Augustan Reprint Society, 1978.

———. *Plans, Elevations, Sections, and Perspective Views of the Gardens and Buildings at Kew.* London: Haberkorn, 1763.

Coleridge, Samuel Taylor. *Biographia Litteraria, or Biographical Sketches.* 1817. Reprint, London: Dent; New York: Dutton, 1962.

Colonna, Francesco. *The Dream of Poliphilo (Hypnerotomachia Poliphili)* [1499]. Related and interpreted by Linda Fierz-David. Translated by Mary Hottinger. New York: Pantheon, [1950].

Coronelli, Vincenzo. *Ville del Brenta.* Edited by Gustavo Costa. Milan: Il Polifilo, 1960.

Cournand, Antoine de, Abbé. *Les Quatre Ages de l'homme.* Paris: Buisson, 1782.

Craven, Elizabeth Berkeley, Lady. *A Journey through the Crimea . . . in the Year 1786.* Dublin: Chamberlain, 1789. French translation, 1793.

Czartoriska, Isabella, Princess. *Myśli różne o sposobie zakładania ogorodów.* Wrocław, 1805.

Delille, Jacques, Abbé. *Les Géorgiques de Virgile.* Paris: Bleuet, 1770. See E. Guitton, *Jacques Delille,* 595–615.

———. *L'Homme des champs; ou, les géorgiques françaises.* Strasbourg: Levrault, 1800. Latin translation, 1808.

———. *Les Jardins; ou, l'art d'embellir les paysages, poème.* Paris: Didot, 1782.

*Description des principaux parcs et jardins de l'Europe, avec des remarques sur le jardinage et les plantations.* 3 vols. Allemagne [Vienna], 1812. A pastiche of the *Coup d'Œil;* dedicated to the Prince de Ligne; attributed to Karl Robert Schindelmayer.

*A Description of Holland.* London: Knapton, 1743.

Dézallier d'Argenville, Antoine-Joseph. *Theory and Practice of Gardening.* Translated by John James. London: Lintot, 1728. First edition in French, 1709.

———. *Voyage pittoresque des environs de Paris.* Paris: de Bure, 1755.

Duchesne, Antoine-Nicolas. "Relation du voyage à Reims" [ca. 1780]. Edited by Ernest de Ganay. *Revue de Versailles* 23 (1921): 29–48, 81–99.

*Encyclopédie; ou, dictionnaire raisonné des arts et métiers, par une société de gens de lettres.* 35 vols. Edited by Denis Diderot et al. Paris: Briasson, David, Le Breton and Durand; Neuchâtel: Fauche, 1751–80.

Favart, Charles-Simon. *La Rosière de Salency.* Paris: Ballard, 1769. With music by André Grétry, 1779.

Fontanes, Louis de. "Fragment d'une lettre sur la nature et sur l'homme" [1777]. In *Œuvres de M. de Fontanes,* 2:26–29. Paris: Hachette, 1839.

Fougeret de Monbron, L-C. *Le Cosmopolite.* "Londres," 1753.

Fourier, Charles. *Théorie des quatre mouvements et des destinées générales.* Leipzig [Lyon]: Pelzin, 1808.

Gessner, Salomon. *Idylles et poèmes champêtres* [1757]. Translated by Abbé Huber. Lyon: Bruyset, 1762.

Girardin, René de. *De la composition des paysages sur le terrain; ou, des moyens d'embellir la Nature autour des habitations en y joignant l'utile à l'agréable.* Geneva and Paris: Deloguette, 1777. Reprint. Paris: Editions du champ urbain, 1979.

Girardin, Stanislas de. *Promenade; ou, itinéraire des jardins d'Ermenonville.* Paris: Mérigot, Gattey et Guyot, 1788. Reprint. Paris: Editions du champ urbain, 1979.

Goethe, Johann Wolfgang von. *Die Leiden des jungen Werthers.* [1774]. Basel: Amerbach, 1947.

———. "Requiem dem frohesten Manne des Jahrhunderts." In C-J. de Ligne, *Œuvres choisies,* edited by Basil Guy, 245–49.

Grohmann, Johann Gottfried. *Recueil de dessins d'une exécution peu dispendieuse.* Venice: Remondini, 1805.

Gros de Besplas, J-M. *De l'utilité des voyages.* Paris: Berthier, 1763.

d'Harcourt, François. *Traité de la décoration des dehors, des jardins, et des parcs* [ca. 1775]. Edited by Ernest de Ganay. Paris: Emile-Paul, 1919. See D. Wiebenson, *The Picturesque Garden in France,* 124.

Hegel, Georg Wilhelm. *Hegel's Philosophy of the State and History.* Edited by G. S. Morris. German Philosophical Classics 6. Chicago: S. C. Griggs, 1882. Originally composed as *Philosophie der Geschichte* in 1808.

Heidelhoff, Viktor. *Ansichten der herzoglichen Württembergischen Landsitze Hohenheim.* Stuttgart, 1797.

Héré de Corny, Emmanuel. *Recueil des plans, élévations, et coupes tant générales qu'en perspectives des châteaux, jardins, et dépendances que le Roi de*

*Pologne occupe en Lorraine.* 2 vols. Paris: François, 1753–56.

Hirschfeld, Christian. *Théorie de l'art des jardins.* 5 vols. Leipzig and Amsterdam: Weidmann, 1779–85.

Homer. *The Odyssey.* Translated by E. V. Rieu. Baltimore: Penguin Books, 1948.

Horace [Quintus Horatius Flaccus]. *Opera Omnia.* Edited by A. J. Macleane. London: Whittaker-Bell, 1853.

Hume, David. "On the Standard of Taste" [1741]. In *Essays Moral, Political, and Literary,* 231–55. London: Oxford University Press, 1963.

Hurtaut, Pierre, and Jean-Baptiste Magny. *Dictionnaire historique de la ville de Paris et de ses environs.* 4 vols. Paris: Moutard, 1779.

"Le Journal de Baudour." *Annales Prince de Ligne* 10 (1929): 19–188.

Knight, Richard Payne. *The Landscape: A Didactic Poem in Three Books.* London, 1794.

Krafft, Johann Carl. *Plans des plus beaux jardins pittoresques de France, d'Angleterre, et d'Allemagne.* 2 vols. Paris: Levrault-Pougens, 1809–10.

Krafft, Johann Carl, and Nicolas Ransonnette. *Recueil d'architecture civile aux environs de Paris et dans les départements voisins.* Paris: Crapelet-Bance aîné, 1812.

Laborde, Alexandre de. *Description des nouveaux jardins pittoresques de la France et de ses anciens châteaux.* Paris: Delance, 1808 [1815?]. Grand infolio; dedicated to the Prince de Ligne.

Laborde, Jean-Benjamin de. *Description générale et particulière de la France.* 4 vols. Paris: Pierres, 1781–84. See the catalog *Le Gothique* "retrouvé," 105–9, for details of this complicated publication.

Laclos, Pierre-Ambroise Choderlos de. *Les Liaisons dangereuses* [1782]. Paris: Folio, 1979.

Lagarde[-Chambonas], Auguste de. *Fêtes et souvenirs du Congrès de Vienne.* 2 vols. Paris: Appert, 1843.

Latapie, François. See Thomas Whatley.

Lavergne, ———. *Les Eléments, poème.* Paris: Costard, 1770.

Le Camus de Mézières, Nicolas. *Description des eaux de Chantilly et du Hameau.* Paris: l'Auteur, 1783.

Lerouge, Georges-Louis. *Détail des nouveaux jardins à la mode; ou, jardins anglo-chinois.* 20 cahiers. Paris: l'Auteur, 1776–89. Includes ten plates on Baudour, 7:15–18 and 8:16–21. Complete bibliographical information in D. Wiebenson, *The Picturesque Garden in France,* 125.

Lezay-Marnésia, C-F-A. de. *Essai sur la Nature champêtre en vers.* Paris: Prault, 1787.

L.L.G.D.M. "Lettre sur les jardins anglais." *Journal encyclopédique* (1775): 132–42.

Louis XIV, King of France. "Manière de montrer les jardins de Versailles." Edited by Christopher Thacker. *Garden History* 1 (1972): 49–69; 6 (1978): 31–38.

Luce de Lancival, Jean-Charles. *Poème sur le Globe.* Paris: Aux Marchands de Nouveautés, 1784.

Lysons, Daniel. *The Environs of London: Being an Historical Account of the Towns, Villages, and Hamlets within Twelve Miles of That Capital.* 4 vols. London: Caddell and Davis, 1792–96.

Martial [Marcus Valerius Martialis]. *Epigrammaton liber.* Edited by J. Borovskij. Leiden: Brill, 1982.

Mavor, William F. *A New Description of Blenheim. 6th Edition, Much Improv'd, with a Preliminary Essay on Landscape Gardening.* Oxford: Slatter and Munday, 1803.

Molière [Jean-Baptiste Poquelin]. *L'Amour médecin* [1665]. In *Œuvres,* 2:291–322. Paris: Flammarion, 1944.

Morel, Jean. *Théorie des jardins; ou, l'art des jardins de la Nature.* Paris: Pissot, 1776.

Nerval [Gérard Labrunie]. *Les Filles du feu* [1853]. In *Œuvres complètes,* edited by Albert Béguin and Jean Richer, 1:167–465. Paris: Gallimard-Pléiade, 1952.

Ovid [Publius Ovidius Naso]. *Metamorphoses.* Edited by F. J. Miller. 2 vols. Cambridge: Harvard University Press; London: William Heinemann, 1916.

*Parallèle raisonné entre les deux poèmes des jardins* [par Rapin et Delille]. The Hague and Paris: Belin, 1782.

Parini, Giuseppe, *Il Giorno* [1765]. Edited by Attilio Colombo. Florence: La Nuova Italia, 1956.

Petrarch, Francesco. *The Sonnets and Love Poems* [Canzoniere]. Translated and edited by Thomas H. Bergin. New York: Heritage Press, [1966]. In Italian and English.

Pope, Alexander. *Essay on Man* [1734]. Oxford: Roxburghe Club, 1962.

Price, Uvedale. *An Essay on the Picturesque.* 2 vols. London: J. Robson, 1794–98.

Racine, Jean. *Andromaque, tragédie* [1667]. In *Théâtre de Racine,* edited by H. Bouillane de Lacoste, 207–83. Paris: Hazan, 1947.

———. *Phèdre* [1670]. In *Théâtre de Racine,* edited by H. Bouillane de Lacoste, 783–859. Paris: Hazan, 1947.

Rademaker, Abraham. *Hollands Arkadia.* Amsterdam: Schenk, 1730.

Repton, Humphry. *Sketches and Hints on Landscape-Gardening* [1794]. Edited by John Nolen. London: Constable, 1907.

Richardson, Jonathan. *An Essay on the Theory of Painting.* London, 1715.

Rousseau, Jean-Jacques. *Julie; ou, la nouvelle Héloïse* [1761]. Edited by Daniel Mornet. 4 vols. Collection des Grands Ecrivains de la France. Paris: Hachette, 1928.

————. *Œuvres.* Edited by Bernard Gagnebin and Marcel Raymond. 4 vols. to date. Paris: Gallimard-Pléiade, 1965–.

Saint-Lambert, Jean-François de. *Les Saisons, poème.* Amsterdam, 1769.

Saugrain, C-M. *Curiosités de Paris, Versailles, Marly, etc.* 2 vols. Paris: Saugrain aîné, 1716. Several editions of this work were published in the eighteenth century.

Schindelmayer, Karl Robert. See *Description des principaux parcs et jardins.*

Searle, John. *Plan of Mr Pope's Garden As It Was Left at His Death.* London: R. Dodsley, 1745.

Seeley, Benton. *A Description of the House and Gardens . . . at Stow.* 1774. Reprint. Buckingham: Seeley, 1777; 12th edition, London: Rivington, 1788.

Staël-Holstein, Germaine Necker de. *Dix Années d'exil* [1821]. Edited by Simone Balayé. Paris: Bibliothèque 10/18, 1966.

————. *Lettres de Madame de Staël . . . conservées en Bohême.* Edited by Maria Ullrichová. Prague: Akademia, 1958.

Thiéry, Luc-Vincent. *Guide des amateurs et des étrangers voyageurs à Paris.* 2 vols. Paris: Hardouin et Gattey, 1787.

————. *Guide . . . aux environs de Paris.* 2 vols. Paris: Hardouin et Gattey, 1788.

Thomson, James. *The Seasons, etc.* 1726. Reprint. London: J. Millan, 1730.

Vigée-Lebrun, Elisabeth. *Souvenirs.* 3 vols. Paris, 1835–37.

Virgil [Publius Virgilius Maro]. *The Works of Virgil.* Edited by John Conington. 3 vols. London: Bell, 1898.

Voltaire [François-Marie Arouet]. *The Complete Works.* Edited by Theodore Besterman et al. 135 vols. Geneva, Banbury, and Oxford: The Voltaire Foundation, 1968–. Vol. 2, *La Henriade,* edited by O. R. Taylor; vol. 7, *La Pucelle,* edited by Jeroom Vercruysse; vol. 49, *Candide,* edited by René Pomeau; vol. 59 *La Philosophie de l'histoire,* edited by John Brumfitt; vols. 83–84, *Notebooks,* edited by Theodore Besterman; vols. 85–135, *Correspondence and Related Documents,* edited by Theodore Besterman.

————. *Lettres philosophiques* [1734]. Edited by Gustave Lanson and André-M. Rousseau. 2 vols.

Société de Textes Français Modernes. Paris: Didier, 1964.

————. *Œuvres.* Edited by Louis Moland. 52 vols. Paris: Garnier Frères, 1877–85. *Tancrède,* 5:489–562; *Epître à Mme Denis,* 10:378–82; *Le Voyage de Berlin,* 10:397–402; *Relation du bannissement des jésuites,* 27:1–16.

————. *Le Siècle de Louis XIV* [1751]. Edited by A. Adam. 2 vols. Paris: Garnier/Flammarion, [1967].

Walpole, Horace. *A Description of the Villa . . . at Strawberry Hill.* Strawberry Hill: T. Kirgate, 1774.

————. *Essay on Modern Gardening.* Strawberry Hill, 1771. See Isabel Chase, *Horace Walpole, Gardenist.*

————. *The Yale Edition of Horace Walpole's Correspondence.* Edited by Wilmarth Sheldon Lewis et al. 42 vols. New Haven, Conn.: Yale University Press, 1933–81.

Watelet, Claude-Henri. *Dictionnaire des arts.* 5 vols. Paris: Prault, 1792.

————. *Essai sur les jardins.* Paris: Prault, 1774. Echoes Whatley (or Latapie), but is briefer.

[Whatley, Thomas]. *L'Art de former les jardins modernes.* Paris: Jombert, 1771. First edition in English, 1770, but written around 1756, according to Isabel Chase in *Horace Walpole, Gardenist,* 155. The French edition contains a "Discours préliminaire" by François Latapie that was important for the development of French theories about English gardens.

# Modern Works

## Catalogs

*Alexander Pope's Villa.* Edited by Morris R. Brownell. London: Greater London Council, 1980.

*L'Art des jardins classiques.* Lunéville: Musée de Lunéville, 1967. An exhibition at Lunéville Castle.

*De Bagatelle à Monceau, 1778–1978: Les Folies du 18ᵉ siècle à Paris.* Paris: Musée Carnavalet, 1978. An exhibition at the museum.

*The Garden: A Celebration of One Thousand Years of British Gardening.* Edited by John Harris. London: Mitchell Beazley and New Publishing Perspectives, 1979. An exhibition at the Victoria and Albert Museum, Kensington.

*Le Gothique "retrouvé" avant Viollet-le-Duc.* Paris: Caisse Nationale, 1979. An exhibition at the Hôtel de Sully.

*Grandes et petites heures du Parc Monceau.* Paris: Ville de Paris and Musée Chernuschi, 1981.

*Jardins en France, 1760–1820: Pays d'illusion, terre d'expériences.* Paris: Caisse Nationale, 1977. An exhibition at the Hôtel de Sully.

*Les Joies de la Nature au 18ᵉ siècle.* Paris: Bibliothèque Nationale, 1971. An exhibition at the Bibliothèque Nationale.

*Le Prince de Ligne et son Temps.* Belœil: Château de Belœil, 1982. An exhibition in Vienna and Belœil.

*Versailles: Collection Grossœuvre.* Paris: Meynial, 1934. An auction catalog with an important section on guidebooks, 22–34.

## Secondary Sources

Acke, Daniel. "Le Prince de Ligne, moraliste." *Nouvelles Annales Prince de Ligne* 2 (1987): 77–161.

Adams, William. *The French Garden, 1500–1800.* New York: Braziller, 1979.

Allen, B[everly] Sprague. *Tides in English Taste, 1619–1800.* 1937. Reprint, 2 vols. New York: Pageant Books, 1958.

Andrews, Malcolm. *The Search for the Picturesque.* Aldershot: The Scolar Press, 1987.

*Annales Prince de Ligne.* Edited by Félicien Leuridant. 20 vols. Brussels: Bureau des Annales, 1920–38.

*Architektura Leningrada.* Leningrad and Moscow: USSR Academy of Architecture, 1953.

Aubin, Robert A. "Grottoes, Geology, and the Gothic Revival." *Studies in Philology* 31 (1934): 408–16.

———. *Topographical Poetry in Eighteenth-Century England.* New York: Modern Language Association, 1936.

Ayscough, Florence. *A Chinese Mirror.* Boston: Houghton Mifflin; London: Jonathan Cape, 1925.

Baltrusaitis, Jurgis. "Jardins et pays d'illusion." *Traverses* 5/6 (1976): 94–110.

Barrell, John. *The Idea of Landscape and the Sense of Place.* Cambridge: Cambridge University Press, 1972.

Batten, Charles. *Pleasurable Instruction: Form and Convention in Eighteenth-Century Travel Literature.* Berkeley: University of California Press, 1978.

Bauër, Roger. "Remarques sur l'histoire du ou des joséphismes." In *Utopie et institutions,* edited by Pierre Francastel, 107–12. The Hague: Mouton, 1963.

Bean, W. J. *The Royal Botanic Gardens, Kew.* London: Cassell, 1908.

Beecher, Jonathan F. *Charles Fourier: The Visionary and His World.* Berkeley: University of California Press, 1986.

Benhamou, Reed. "From *Curiosité* to *Utilité:* The Automaton in Eighteenth-Century France." *Studies in Eighteenth-Century Culture* 17 (1987): 91–105.

Berenson, Bernard. *The Sense of Quality.* New York: Schocken Books, 1962.

Blanc, André. "Le Jardin de Julie." *Dix-Huitième Siècle* 14 (1982): 357–76.

*Blenheim Palace, a Guide.* London: David Green, 1971.

Blunt, Anthony. "The *Hypnerotomachia Poliphili* in France." *Journal of the Warburg and Courtauld Institute* 1 (1937): 117–37.

Bourde, André. *Agronomie et agronomes en France au 18ᵉ siècle.* 3 vols. Paris: SVPEN, 1967. Paginated consecutively.

Braham, Allan. *The Architecture of the French Enlightenment.* Berkeley: University of California Press, 1980.

Brenner, Clarence D. "A Neglected Pre-Romantic: Billardon de Sauvigny." *Romanic Review* 28 (1938): 52–54.

Brion, Marcel. *Romantic Art.* New York: McGraw-Hill, 1960.

Brissenden, R. F. *Virtue in Distress.* New York: Oxford University Press, 1974.

"British and American Gardens." *Eighteenth-Century Life* 8, n.s. 2 (January 1983). Several important contributions under the British rubric.

Brogden, William. "Stephen Switzer: La Grand Manier." In *Furor Hortensis: Essays on the History of the English Landscape Garden in Memory of H. F. Clark,* edited by Peter Willis, 21–30. Edinburgh: Elysium, 1974.

Bronne, Carlo. *Belœil et la maison de Ligne.* Belœil: Fondation Ligne, 1979.

Brownell, Morris R. *Alexander Pope and the Arts of Georgian England.* Oxford: Clarendon Press, 1978.

Burda, Hubert. *Die Ruine in den Bildern Hubert Roberts.* Munich: Fink, 1967.

Butor, Michel. "L'Isle au bout du monde." *Répertoire,* 3:59–101. Paris: Editions de Minuit, 1968.

Carrott, Richard G. *The Egyptian Revival: Its Sources, Monuments, and Meanings.* Berkeley: University of California Press, 1978.

Cartwright, Michael. *Diderot, critique d'art.* Diderot Studies 13. Geneva: Droz, 1969.

Champagne, Paul. "Le Prince de Ligne, moraliste." *Annales Prince de Ligne* 16 (1935): 288–305.

Charageat, Marguérite. *L'Art des jardins.* Paris: Presses Universitaires de France, 1962.

Chase, Isabel. *Horace Walpole, Gardenist*. Princeton, N.J.: Princeton University Press, 1943. Contains the text of Walpole's *Essay on Modern Gardening*, first edition, 1771.

Ciołek, Gerard. *Gärten in Polen*. Warsaw: Budownictvo i Architektura, 1957.

Clark, H. F. "Eighteenth-Century Elysiums. The Role of 'Association' in the Landscape Movement." *Journal of the Warburg and Courtauld Institute* 6 (1943): 165–89.

Clark, Kenneth. *The Gothic Revival*. Oxford: Oxford University Press, 1928.

Coats, Alice. *Garden Shrubs*. London: Batsford, 1963.

Coats, Peter. *Great Gardens of Britain*. London: Artus, 1977.

———. *Great Gardens of the Western World*. New York: Putnam, 1963.

Connolly, Cyril, and Jerome Zerbe. *Les Pavillons: French Pavilions of the Eighteenth Century*. New York: Macmillan, 1962.

Connor, Patrick. "China and the Landscape Garden: Reports, Engravings, and Misconceptions." *Art History* 2 (1979): 429–40.

———. *Oriental Architecture in the West*. London: Thames and Hudson, 1979.

Conroy, Peter V., Jr. "Dramatic Theory and Eighteenth-Century Gardens." *University of Toronto Quarterly* 49 (1980): 252–65.

———. "French Classical Theater and Formal Garden Design." *Dalhousie Review* 61 (1981): 666–82.

———. "Le Jardin polémique chez Rousseau." In *Cahiers de l'Association Internationale des Etudes Francaises*, 91–107. Paris: Les Belles Lettres, 1982.

Cordier, Henri. "Les Correspondants de Bertin." *T'oung Pao*, 2d. ser., 15 (1913); 16 (1914); 17 (1915); 18 (1917); 21 (1922).

Cowell, Frank Richard. *The Garden as a Fine Art, from Antiquity to Modern Times*. Boston: Houghton Mifflin, 1978.

Curtil, Jean-Claude. *Entre la glaise et la gloire*. Paris: Editions du champ urbain, 1979. On Ermenonville.

Dauvergne, René. *Les Résidences du Maréchal de Croÿ (1718–84)*. Paris: Hachette, 1951.

Davis, Terence. *The Gothick Taste*. Rutherford, N.J.: Fairleigh Dickinson University Press, 1975.

De Backer, Hector. *Bibliographie du Prince de Ligne*. Brussels: Société des Iconophiles et Bibliophiles Belges, 1916.

Dion, Marie-Pierre. *Emmanuel de Croÿ (1718–84)*. Brussels: Editions de l'Université de Bruxelles, 1987.

Dokoupil, Zdeněk. *Historické zahrady v Čechách a na Moravé*. Prague: Nakl. československých výtrarných umělců, 1957.

Domchowski, Zbigniew. *The Architecture of Poland*. London: Polish Research Architectural Review Centre, 1956.

Duchet, Michèle. "La Littérature de voyages." *Cahiers du Sud* 62 (1966): 1–14.

Du Colombier, Pierre. *L'Architecture française en Allemagne*. 2 vols. Paris: Presses Universitaires de France, 1956.

Dumolin, Marcel. *Notes sur les vieux guides de Paris*. Paris: Alcan, 1924.

Dumont-Wilden, Louis. *La Vie de Charles-Joseph de Ligne, prince de l'Europe française*. Le Roman des Grandes Existences. Paris: Plon, 1927.

Dupront, Alphonse. *Les Lettres, les sciences, la religion, et les arts dans le société française de la deuxième moitié du 18ᵉ siècle*. 4 fascicles. Les Cours de la Sorbonne. Paris: Centre de Documentation Universitaire, 1963.

Duval, Marguérite. *The King's Garden*. Charlottesville, Va.: University of Virginia Press, 1982.

Duvignaud, Jean. *Sociologie du théâtre*. Paris: Presses Universitaires de France, 1965.

Erdberg, Eleanor von. *Chinese Influence on European Garden Structure*. Cambridge: Harvard University Press, 1937. Useful catalog at end that frequently mentions Ligne.

Etlin, Richard A. *The Architecture of Death*. Cambridge: MIT Press, 1984.

Everdell, William. "The Rosières Movement, 1766–1789: A Clerical Precursor of Revolutionary Cults." *French Historical Studies* 9 (1975): 23–36.

Fabre, Jean. "Stanislas Leszczynski et le mouvement philosophique." In *Utopie et Institutions*, edited by Pierre Francastel, 25–42. The Hague: Mouton, 1963.

Fargher, Richard. *Life and Letters in France. The Eighteenth Century*. New York: Scribner, 1970.

Fauchier-Magnin, G. *Les Petites Cours de l'Allemagne au 18ᵉ siècle*. Paris: Hachette, 1947.

Fleming, Laurence, and Alan Gore. *The English Garden*. London: Michael Joseph, 1980.

Frankl, Paul. *The Gothic: Literary Sources and Interpretations through Eight Centuries*. Princeton, N.J.: Princeton University Press, 1960.

*The French Formal Garden*. Edited by Elizabeth Macdougall. Washington: Dumbarton Oaks, 1974.

Frye, Northrop. *The Anatomy of Criticism*. Princeton, N.J.: Princeton University Press, 1957.

*Furor Hortensis: Essays on the History of the English Landscape Garden in Memory of H. F. Clark*. Edited by Peter Willis. Edinburgh: Elysium Press, 1974.

Fussell, Paul. *Abroad.* New York: Oxford University Press, 1980.

Gajek, B., and F. Götting. *Goethes Leben in Daten und Bildern.* Frankfurt am Main: Inselverlag, 1966.

Ganay, Ernest de. "Fabriques aux jardins." *Gazette des Beaux-Arts* 45 (1955): 287–98.

———. "Le Prince de Ligne, amateur et écrivain des jardins." *Annales Prince de Ligne* 16 (1935): 134–44.

Gay, Peter. *The Age of Enlightenment.* New York: Time-Life Books, 1966.

*The Genius of the Place: The English Landscape Garden, 1620–1820.* Edited by John Dixon Hunt and Peter Willis. New York: Harper and Row, 1975.

Germann, Georg. *The Gothic Revival in Europe and Britain: Sources, Influences, and Ideas.* Cambridge: MIT Press, 1973.

Gerndt, Siegmar. *Idealisierte Natur: Die literarische Kontroverse um den Landschaften des 18. und frühen 19. Jahrhunderts.* Stuttgart: Metzler, 1981.

Ginsberg, R. "The Aesthetics of Ruins." *Bucknell Review* 18 (1970): 89–102.

Girouard, Mark. *Life in the English Country House: A Social and Architectural History.* New Haven, Conn.: Yale University Press, 1978.

Godwin-Jones, Robert. "The Rural Socrates Revisited." *Eighteenth-Century Life* 7 (1981): 86–104.

Goldstein, L. *Ruins and Empire.* Pittsburgh, Pa.: University of Pittsburgh Press, 1977.

Gossman, Lionel. *Mediaeval Philosophies of the Enlightenment: The World and Work of Lacurne de Sainte-Palaye.* Baltimore: Johns Hopkins University Press, 1968.

Grieve, Anne. "Fabriques et folies." In *Jardins et paysages,* edited by André Parreaux and Michèle Plaisant, 1:157–69. Villeneuve-d'Ascq: Presses de l'Université de Lille, 1977.

Guitton, Edouard. *Jacques Delille et le poème de la nature en France, de 1750 à 1820.* Paris: Klincksieck, 1974.

Gusdorf, Georges. *Naissance de la conscience romantique au siècle des lumières.* Paris: Payot, 1976. See especially chap. 6, "Ville, campagne, jardin."

Guy, Basil. "Contribution à la bibliographie du Prince de Ligne." *Le Livre et l'estampe* 61–62 (1970): 3–32.

———. "Les Deux Infinis: Two French Formats from ca. 1765–1815." *Nouvelles de la République des Lettres* 2 (1984): 33–45.

———. *The French Image of China.* Studies on Voltaire 21. Geneva: Institut et Musée Voltaire, 1963.

———. "The Prince de Ligne and the Exemplification of Heroic Virtue." In *Eighteenth-Century Studies Presented to Robert Niklaus,* edited by John Fox et al., 73–86. Exeter: University of Exeter Press, 1975.

———. "Le Prince de Ligne et les Turcs." In *Le Gai Saber: Gedenkschrift Manfred Sandmann,* edited by M. Cranston, 13–43. Potomac, Md.: Studia Humanitatis, 1983.

———. "The Prince de Ligne, Laclos, and the *Liaisons dangereuses.*" *Romanic Review* 55 (1964): 260–67.

Hadfield, Miles. *A History of British Gardening.* London: Murray, 1979.

Hajos, G. *Romantische Gärten der Aufklärung. Englische Landschaft-Kultur des 18. Jahrhunderts in und um Wien.* Vienna/Cologne: Böhlau, 1989. Neuwaldegg, pp. 143–54.

Hall, Colette, et al. "Paradox in Paradise." In *Man, God, and Nature in the Enlightenment,* edited by Donald C. Mell, Jr., Theodore E. D. Braun, and Lucia M. Palmer, 107–19. East Lansing, Mich.: Colleagues Press, 1988.

Harris, John. "English Country-House Guides." In *Concerning Architecture: Essays on Architectural Writers and Writing Presented to Nikolaus Pevsner,* edited by John Summerson, 58–74. London: Allan Lane, 1968.

———. *Sir William Chambers, Knight of the Polar Star.* Studies in Architecture 9. London: Zwemmer, 1970.

Hartmann, Geoffrey. *Beyond Formalism.* New Haven, Conn.: Yale University Press, 1970. See especially 311–36 on the *genius loci.*

———. "Wordsworth, Inscriptions, and Nature Poetry." In *From Sensibility to Romanticism: Essays Presented to Frederick A. Pottle,* edited by Frederick Hilles and Harold Bloom, 389–413. New York: Oxford University Press, 1970.

Hautecoeur, Louis. *Histoire de l'architecture classique en France.* 5 vols. Paris: Picard, 1943–57.

———. *Les Jardins des dieux et des hommes.* Paris: Hachette, 1959. Frequent mention of Ligne, pp. 167–90.

Hayez, Frédéric, and Jeroom Vercruysse. "L'Imprimerie privée des Princes de Ligne au 18ᵉ siècle." *Nouvelles Annales Prince de Ligne* 2 (1987): 7–75.

Hazard, Paul. *La Crise de la conscience européenne.* Paris: Boivin, n.d. The 1935 edition in 3 vols. (same publisher) is to be preferred because of the notes.

Hazelhurst, F. Hamilton. *Gardens of Illusion: The Genius of André Le Nostre.* Nashville, Tenn.: Vanderbilt University Press, 1981.

Henne, Alexandre, and Alphonse Wauters. *Histoire de la ville de Bruxelles.* 3 vols. Brussels: Librairie encyclopédique, 1845.

Hennebo, Dieter, and Alfred Hoffmann. *Geschichte der deutschen Gartenkunst.* 3 vols. Hamburg: Broschek, 1962–65.

Henrey, Blanche. *British Botanical and Horticultural Literature before 1800.* 3 vols. London: Oxford University Press, 1975.

Hentschel, Wilhelm. *Die sächsische Baukunst des 18. Jahrhunderts in Polen.* Berlin: Deutsche Bauakademie, 1967.

Herget, E. *Die Sala Terrena im deutschen Barock.* Frankfurt am Main: Klostermann, 1954.

Hermant, Abel. "Le 18ᵉ siècle vivant." In *La Vie parisienne au 18ᵉ siècle,* 7–27. Conférences du Musée Carnavalet. Paris: Payot, 1928.

Herrmann, Wolfgang. *Laugier and Eighteenth-Century French Theory.* London: Zwemmer, 1962.

Hibbert, Christopher. *The Grand Tour.* London: Weidenfield and Nicolson, 1969.

Hillairet, Jacques. *Dictionnaire historique des rues de Paris.* 2 vols. Paris: Editions de Minuit, 1963.

*Historische Landhuizen.* Edited by H. Schellart. Deventer, Holland: Ankh-Hermes, 1975.

Honour, Hugh. *Chinoiserie: The Vision of Cathay.* New York: Harper and Row, 1961.

———. *The European Vision of America.* Cleveland: The Cleveland Museum of Art, 1975.

Huisman, Philippe, and Marie Jallut. *Marie-Antoinette.* New York: Viking, 1971.

Hunt, John Dixon. "Emblem and Expression in the Eighteenth-Century Landscape Garden." *Eighteenth-Century Studies* 4 (1971): 294–317.

———. *The Figure in the Landscape: Poetry, Painting, and Gardening in the Eighteenth Century.* Baltimore: Johns Hopkins University Press, 1976.

———. *Garden and Grove: The Italian Garden in the English Imagination.* London and Melbourne: Dent, 1986.

Huschke, Wilhelm. *Park um Weimar.* Weimer: Bölhaus, 1956.

Hussey, Christopher. *The Picturesque: Studies in a Point of View.* London and New York: Putnam, 1927.

Hyams, Edward. *Capability Brown and Humphry Repton.* New York: Scribner, 1971.

———. *A History of Gardens and Gardening.* New York: Praeger, 1971.

Ilyin, M. "Russian Parks of the Eighteenth Century." *Architectural Review* (Feb. 1964), 100–111.

Jacoubet, Henri. *Le Comte de Tressan et le genre troubadour.* Paris: Presses Universitaires de France, 1923.

*Jardins et paysages: Le Style anglais.* Edited by André Parreaux and Michèle Plaisant. 2 vols. Villeneuve-d'Ascq: Publications de l'Université de Lille, 1977.

Jarry, Madeleine. *Chinoiserie: Chinese Influence on European Decorative Art.* New York: Vendome, 1981.

Jellicoe, Geoffrey, and Susan Jellicoe. *The Landscape of Man.* New York: Van Nostrand Reinhold, 1975, esp. pp. 207–50.

Jones, Barbara. *Follies and Grottoes.* London: Constable, 1953.

Kamuff, Peggy. *Fictions of Feminine Desire: Disclosures of Heloise.* Lincoln: University of Nebraska Press, 1982. See especially pp. 97–122 on the Elysée de Julie.

Kaufmann, Emil. *Architecture in the Age of Reason.* 1955. Reprint. New York: Dover, 1968.

Kennett, Audrey. *The Palaces of Leningrad.* New York: Putnam, 1973.

King, R. *The Quest for Paradise.* London: Whittet-Windward, 1979.

Kirbatov, Vassily. *Sadi i Parki.* Petrograd: M. O. Wolff, 1916.

Kislink, I. "Le Symbolisme du jardin et l'imagination créatrice chez Rousseau, Bernardin, et Chateaubriand." *Studies on Voltaire* 185 (1980): 297–418.

Klemperer, Viktor. *Delilles Gärten: Ein Mosaikbild des 18. Jahrhunderts.* Berlin: Akademie-Verlag, 1954.

Knox, Brian. "The English Garden in Poland and Bohemia." In *The Picturesque Garden and Its Influence outside the British Isles,* edited by Nikolaus Pevsner, 101–16. Washington, D.C.: Dumbarton Oaks, 1974.

Koch, Heinrich. *Sächsische Gartenkunst.* Dresden: Deutsche Bauzeitung, 1910.

Kordt, Walther. *Die Gärten von Brühl.* Cologne: DuMont-Schauberg, 1965.

Kubiček, Aloys. "L'Obélisque du Prince Charles de Ligne à Josefov en Tchécoslovaquie." *Annales Prince de Ligne* 19 (1938): 12–14.

Kurth, Willy. *Sanssouci: Ein Beitrag zur Kunst des deutschen Rokoko.* Berlin: Henschelverlag, 1962.

Kusch, Manfred. "Landscape and Literary Form." *L'Esprit créateur* 17 (1977): 349–60.

———. "The River and the Garden." *Eighteenth-Century Studies* 12 (1978): 1–15.

Landon, H.C. Robbins. *Beethoven: A Documentary Study.* New York: Macmillan, 1970.

*Landscape in the Gardens and the Literature of*

*Eighteenth-Century England*. Edited by David C. Streatfield and Alistair M. Duckworth. Los Angeles: W. A. Clark Memorial Library, 1981.

Larson, James. *Reason and Experience: The Representation of Natural Order in the Work of Carl von Linné*. Berkeley: University of California Press, 1971.

Laubriet, Pierre. "Les Guides de voyage au début du 18ᵉ siècle." *Studies on Voltaire and the Eighteenth Century* 32 (1965): 296–325.

Lee, Rensselaer W. "*Ut pictura poesis:* The Humanistic Theory of Painting." *The Art Bulletin* 21 (1940): 197–269.

Leuridant, Félicien. *Une Education de prince au 18ᵉ siècle*. Brussels: Lamertin, 1923.

———. *Guide du château, des jardins, et du parc de Belœil*. Brussels: Bureau des Annales, 1935.

———. "Refugiés français à Belœil, 1790–1794." *Terre Wallonne* 3 (1913): 283–96.

———. *Le Vieux Château et la cense du parc à Belœil*. Brussels: Falk, n.d.

Lewis, Wilmarth Sheldon. *Horace Walpole*. The A. W. Mellon Lectures in the Fine Arts 9. New York: Pantheon, 1961.

Likhachev, D. S. *Poeziia Sadov*. Leningrad: Akademia Nauk, 1982.

Lobsien, Eckhard. *Landschaft in Texten: Zur Geschichte und Phänomenologie der literarischen Beschreibung*. Stuttgart: Metzler, 1981.

Loehr, George. "L'Artiste Jean-Denis Attiret et l'influence exercée par sa description des jardins impériaux." In *Actes du Colloque international de Sinologie*, edited by Joseph Dehergne, 69–84. Paris: Les Belles Lettres, 1976.

Löffler, Friedrich. *Das alte Dresden*. Dresden: Sachsenverlag, 1955.

Łojek, Jerzy. *Dzieje pięknej Bitynki*. Warsaw: Institut Widawniczy-Pax, 1972.

Lope, Hans Joachim. "Coup-d'Œil sur Belœil: Gartenarchitektur beim Prince de Ligne." In *Gedächtnisschrift für Fritz Schalk*, edited by Wido Hempel, 208–23. Frankfurt am Main: Klostermann, 1983.

———. "Sur les Traces d'Ovide: Présences de l'antiquité dans les *Lettres de Crimée*." *Nouvelles Annales Prince de Ligne* 2 (1987): 175–94.

McCannell, Dean. *The Tourist: A New Theory of the Leisure Class*. New York: Schocken Books, 1976.

McCannell, Juliet F. "A Re-Interpretation of Rousseau's *Passion Primitive*." *PMLA* 92 (1977): 890–902.

McCarthy, Michael. *The Origins of the Gothic Revival*. New Haven, Conn.: Yale University Press, 1987.

Mack, Maynard. *The Garden and the City: Retirement and Politics in the Later Poetry of Pope, 1731–1743*. Toronto: University of Toronto Press, 1969.

McKillop, Alan. "Local Attachment and Cosmopolitanism." In *From Sensibility to Romanticism: Essays Presented to Frederick A. Pottle*, edited by Frederick Hilles and Harold Bloom, 191–218. New York: Oxford University Press, 1970.

Mahler, Gérard. "Le Kahlenberg au cours des âges." *Annales Prince de Ligne* 15 (1934): 5–11.

Malins, Edward. *English Landscaping and Literature, 1660–1840*. London: Oxford University Press, 1966.

Manwaring, Elizabeth. *Italian Landscape in Eighteenth-Century England*. New York: Russell and Russell, 1925.

Marin, Louis. "L'Effet sharawadgi ou le jardin de Julie." *Traverses* 5/6 (1976): 114–31.

Martin, Peter. *Pursuing Innocent Pleasures: The Gardening World of Alexander Pope*. Hamden, Conn.: Shoe String Press, 1983.

Mauzi, Robert. "Delille, peintre, philosophe, et poète dans *les Jardins*." In *Delille est-il mort?* edited by Paul Viallaneix, 169–200. Clermont-Ferrand: Bussac, 1967.

———. *L'Idée du bonheur dans la littérature et la pensée francaises du 18ᵉ siècle*. Paris: Armand Colin, 1960.

Miller, Naomi. *Heavenly Caves: Reflections on the Garden Grotto*. New York: George Braziller, 1982.

Milward, R. J. *Tudor Wimbledon*. Wimbledon, 1972.

Moir, Esther. *The Discovery of Britain: The English Tourists, 1540–1840*. London: Routledge and Kegan Paul, 1964.

Monglond, André. *Le Préromantisme français*. [1935]. Reprint. 2 vols. Paris: Corti, 1965.

Monk, Samuel E. *The Sublime: A Study of Critical Theories in Eighteenth-Century England*. New York: Modern Language Association, 1935.

Moore, Charles, W. Mitchell, and W. Turnbull, Jr. *The Poetics of Gardens*. Cambridge, Mass.: MIT Press, 1989.

Mor, Antonio. "Le Prince de Ligne, prosateur." *Lettres romanes* 9 (1955): 15–37.

Mornet, Daniel. *Le Sentiment de la nature en France, de Jean-Jacques Rousseau à Bernardin de Saint-Pierre*. Paris: Hachette, 1907.

Mortier, Roland. *La Poétique des ruines en France*. Geneva: Droz, 1974.

———. "Le Prince de Ligne." In *La Belgique autrichienne, 1714–94*, 285–300. Brussels: Crédit communal, 1987.

———. "Le Prince de Ligne." In *Histoire illustrée des lettres françaises de Belgique*, edited by Gustave Charlier and Joseph Hanse, 221–32. Brussels: La Renaissance du Livre, 1958.

Mosser, Monique. "Le Rocher et la colonne: Un Thème d'iconographie architecturale au 18ᵉ siècle." *Revue de l'Art* 58/59 (1983): 53–74.

Muraro, Mario. *Venetian Villas*. New York: Rizzoli, 1986.

Murray, Peter. "L'Architecture de Burlington et Kent." In *Utopie et institutions*, edited by Pierre Francastel, 49–54. The Hague: Mouton, 1963.

Nemoianu, Virgil. *Micro-Harmony: The Growth and Uses of the Idyllic Mode in Literature*. Bern, Frankfurt, and Las Vegas: Peter Lang, 1977.

Neumeyer, Eva. "The Landscape Garden as Symbol: Rousseau, Goethe, and Flaubert." *Journal of the History of Ideas* 8, no. 2 (1947): 187–217.

Nicolson, Nigel. *Great Houses of the Western World*. New York: Spring Books, 1968.

Niklaus, Robert. "*Tableaux mouvants* as a Technical Innovation." In *Eighteenth-Century French Studies: Literature and the Arts*, edited by E. Dubois et al., 71–82. London: Oriel, 1969.

Nola, Jean-Pierre de. "Goût français et mode anglais dans le *Coup-d'Œ:1 sur Belœil* du Prince de Ligne," *Revue de littérature comparée* 57 (1983): 173–84.

Nolhac, Pierre de. *Hubert Robert*. Paris: Manzi-Joyant, 1910.

———. "Le Prince de Ligne à Trianon." *Annales Prince de Ligne* 1 (1920): 115–19.

Olausson, Magnus. "Freemasonry, Occultism, and the Picturesque Garden towards the End of the Eighteenth Century." *Art History* 4 (1985): 415–17.

O'Neal, John C. "Morality in Rousseau's Private and Public Society at Clarens." *Revue de métaphysique et de morale* 89, no. 1 (1984): 58–67.

Ostrowski, J. "Tschifflik, la maison de plaisance du roi Stanislas à Deux-Ponts." *Dix-Huitième Siècle* 4 (1972): 315–22.

Oulié, Marthe. *Le Prince de Ligne; ou, un Grand Seigneur cosmopolite au 18ᵉ siècle*. Paris: Hachette, 1927.

*The Oxford Companion to Gardens*. Edited by G. Jellicoe, S. Jellicoe, and others. New York: Oxford University Press, 1986.

Pageaux, Denis. "Voyages romanesques au siècle des lumières." *Etudes littéraires* 1 (1968): 205–14.

Paley, Morton. *The Apocalyptic Sublime*. New Haven, Conn.: Yale University Press, 1986.

Pasteur, Claude. *Le Prince de Ligne: L'Enchanteur de l'Europe*. Paris: Perrin, 1980.

Patterson, Annabel. *Pastoral and Ideology: Virgil to Valéry*. Berkeley: University of California Press, 1988.

Paulson, Ronald. *Emblem and Expression*. Cambridge: Harvard University Press, 1976.

Perey, Lucien [pseud.]. *Histoire d'une grande dame au 18 siècle*. 2 vols. Paris: Calmann-Lévy, 1892.

Pevsner, Nikolaus. *Leipziger Barock*. Dresden: Jess, 1928.

———. *Studies in Art, Architecture, and Design*. 2 vols. New York: Walker, 1968.

*The Picturesque Garden and Its Influence outside the British Isles*. Edited by Nikolaus Pevsner. Washington, D.C.: Dumbarton Oaks, 1974.

Poggioli, Renato. "Work in Progress: The Pastoral of the Self." *Daedalus* 88 (1959): 686–99.

Pomeau, René. "Voyage et lumières." *Studies on Voltaire and the Eighteenth Century* 57 (1967): 1269–89.

Pötschner, Peter. *Wien und die wiener Landschaft*. Salzburg: Galerie Welz, 1978.

Prest, John. *The Garden of Eden: The Botanic Garden and the Re-Creation of Paradise*. New Haven, Conn.: Yale University Press, 1982.

Queneau, Raymond. *Exercices de Style*. Paris: NRF-Gallimard, 1947.

Rae, Isobel. *Charles Cameron, Architect to the Court of Russia*. London: Elek, 1971.

Reil, Franz. *Vater Franz, sein Leben und sein Lebenswerk*. Edited by Bernhard Heese. Berlin: Schwalbe, 1936.

Rex, Walter E. *The Attraction of the Contrary: Essays on the Literature of the French Enlightenment*. Cambridge: Cambridge University Press, 1987.

Rice, Howard, Jr. *Thomas Jefferson's Paris*. Princeton, N.J.: Princeton University Press, 1976.

Ridehalgh, Anna. "Preromantic Attitudes and the Birth of a Legend: French Pilgrimages to Ermenonville, 1778–1789." *Studies on Voltaire and the Eighteenth Century* 215 (1983): 231–52.

*"Romantic" and Its Cognates: The European History of a Word*. Edited by H. Eichner. Manchester: Manchester University Press, 1972.

Rosenblum, Robert. *Transformations in Late Eighteenth-Century Art*. Princeton, N.J.: Princeton University Press, 1974.

Røstvig, Maren-Sofie. *The Happy Man: Studies in the Metamorphosis of a Classical Ideal*. 2 vols. Oslo: Universitietsforlag; New York: Modern Language Association, 1962–71.

Rostworowski, Emmanuel. "Stanislas Leszczynski et les lumières à la polonaise." In *Utopie et institutions*, edited by Pierre Francastel, 15–24. The Hague: Mouton, 1963.

Designer: Wolfgang Lederer
Editor: Stephanie Fay
Production Coordinators: Ellen Herman and David Peattie
Compositor: Huron Valley Graphics
Text: 11/14 Bulmer
Display: Bulmer
Printer: Thomson-Shore, Inc.
Binder: Thomson-Shore, Inc.